Tired of Weeping

WOMEN IN AFRICA
AND THE DIASPORA

Series Editors

STANLIE JAMES
AILI MARIE TRIPP

Tired of Weeping

Mother Love, Child Death, and Poverty in Guinea-Bissau

Jónína Einarsdóttir

The University of Wisconsin Press

The University of Wisconsin Press
1930 Monroe Street
Madison, Wisconsin 53711

www.wisc.edu/wisconsinpress/

3 Henrietta Street
London WC2E 8LU, England

1   3   5   4   2

Printed in the United States of America

Library of Congress Cataloging-in-Publication Data
Einarsdóttir, Jónína.
Tired of weeping : mother love, child death, and poverty
in Guinea-Bissau / Jónína Einarsdóttir.
p.   cm.—(Women in Africa and the diaspora)
Includes bibliographical references and index.
ISBN 0-299-20130-9 (cloth : alk. paper)
ISBN 0-299-20134-1 (pbk. : alk. paper)
1. Papel (African people)—Psychology.
2. Papel (African people)—Kinship.
3. Papel (African people)—Mortality.
4. Children—Guinea-Bissau—Biombo—Mortality.
5. Mothers—Guinea-Bissau—Biombo—Psychology.
6. Biombo (Guinea-Bissau)—Social life and customs.
I. Title.   II. Series.
DT613.45.P36E56   2004
305.235´086´942096657—dc22   2004005379

Illustrations on pages 3, 27, 60, 88, 106, 138, and 164 by Manuel Júlio

In memory of
Santa, Kodé, Idair, Ocante, Rufino, Jonina

and
the many children who died during my fieldwork

and
my mother Sigríður Skúladóttir

Contents

Illustrations

Preface and Acknowledgments

In this book I examine mother love in a setting characterized by poverty and high child mortality. The work is based on anthropological fieldwork conducted from 1993 to 1998 in the Biombo region in Guinea-Bissau, West Africa. Sadly, child death is a common event in Biombo, and about one-third of all children born alive are likely to die before they reach the age of five. Most of these deaths are preventable. I have written this book to illuminate the added burden these unnecessary deaths are on the life of their mothers. Through narratives of individual women, general ethnographic descriptions, and theoretical considerations I want to shed light on mothers' struggles to save the lives of their children. By this approach I intend to inspire scholars, professionals, students, activists, and others who are concerned with the plight of disadvantaged populations in a world of plenty.

In the Biombo region I am deeply indebted to the mothers who participated in my work. I hope the book rightly reflects their common concern to give birth to many children, girls and boys, who all survive. Odete Felix, my friend, assistant, and translator, was crucial for my work. I am grateful for her seriousness and skilful translation. My youngest son, Ólafur Páll, when he was two years of age, rejected all collaboration with nannies, but Walter, Odete's son, caught his confidence, rapidly taught him to speak Kriol, and introduced him to life in Quinhamel village.

Quinhamel is a small village where I felt at home from the first day; I found myself surrounded with good neighbors and friends. In particular, my thoughts go to Dulce and Alberto Passa and their children Bruno, Sanqueia, and Alaquedna (Roquita) who became best of friends with my sons. Alberto tragically passed away on April 29, 2001, at the age of forty-four. I will remember his dedication to the people he served as a regional head nurse for fifteen years, as well as his happy mood and endless, amusing stories. The regional medical officer, Dr. Paulo Djatá, his wife Zinha, and their children, as well as Bacar Demba Embalo and family all made this a pleasant neighborhood to live in.

I thank Rosa, Sábado, Aduladja, Teresinha, Braima, and Edok for all help and enjoyable companionship. I am also grateful to the health workers in the Biombo region for all their help while sharing common interests, friendship, and joyful times. I think of Samba and his daughter Bailo, who both died in the rainy season in midsummer 2002, as sharing their lives in *gloria*.

I am indebted to Hólmfríður and Björk for making the Icelandic School in Quinhamel a reality using my sons' bedroom as a classroom, and Salvör for being a pupil in the school and a good "sister." Christina de Carvalho was also a welcome addition to my extended family during her two research periods on measles. During the last three years in Quinhamel my sons attended the Swedish School in Bissau under the skillful leadership of Nina Michelgård and staff. Anna and Bengt Sandkull were kind to open up their house for me in Bissau to give me time to rethink my field notes, and Bill Turpin was always close at hand as *djumbaidur* and fixer of any problem. The DCA staff that worked in Guinea-Bissau was important to me during my entire stay. In particular, my gratitude goes to Ing–Marie, Aase, Lorenz, Removille, Mariama, and João for their warm friendship and fruitful collaboration.

This book is a revision of my doctoral dissertation, defended in June 2000 at the Department of Social Anthropology at Stockholm University. I want to express my gratitude to my supervisor, Don Kulick, currently Professor of Anthropology at New York University. I greatly benefited from Don's ability to focus on the main arguments while remaining interested in the details. Don created a productive and stimulating environment for his group of doctoral students, which allowed us to share experiences and thoughts about each others' work. I was privileged to be part of that group with Sigrun Helmfrid, Anna Gavanas, Ann Elsburg-Frisell, Fanny Ambjörnsson, Thais Borges Machado, Lena Gemsöe, Åse Ottosson, and Örjan Bartholdsson. I am also grateful to Britt–Marie Thurén, my supervisor during part of my fieldwork. Collectively, I owe thanks to all the colleagues and other staff at the department headed by Professor Ulf Hannerz and Professor Gudrun Dahl.

I am indebted to many people who have read and commented on earlier versions or parts of this book, and to those who inspired me during fieldwork and during the writing process. In particular, I want to thank Eva Poluha, Almaz Terrefe, Britta Nordström, Karin Norman, Alberto Zamberletti, Mamadu Jao, Fransisco Días, Gilberto Landim, Augusto Paulo, Lars Rudebeck, Inger Lundgren, Tove Holmqvist, Judith Narrow, Marianne Bull,

Clara Saravia, Sylvi Furnes, Ilda Lourenço-Lindell, Lars Smedman, and Ann-Charlotte Olstedt. I also thank Terry G. Lacy for thoughtful correction of the English.

Last but not least I want to thank my husband, Geir, for always enjoying life wherever he happens to be staying. Geir has read endless versions of this book and he has always been willing to debate its form and content. Our sons Gunnlaugur, Einar, and Ólafur Páll, are to be credited for the ease with which they have switched between worlds in response to their parents' capricious wishes. Most recently they are discovering Iceland, where I grew up with my parents Sigríður Skúladóttir, who died on July 24, 1999, and Einar V. Ólafsson, four sisters, and three brothers in Laxárdalur, the valley of sheep, salmon, and Sagas.

I am indebted to Steve Salemson, associate director at the University of Wisconsin Press, for facilitating the publishing process and for friendly and prompt correspondence. I am also grateful to the anonymous reviewers who, through insightful and appropriate comments have helped me to refine the ethnographic descriptions and theoretical argument. I have also been helped by the guidance of the copyeditor in the final stages of the publication process.

Despite all the insightful comments, wise recommendations, helpful corrections, and encouragement I have received from my supervisors, colleagues, friends, family members, and others, I take the responsibility for all errors and shortcomings that persist.

DCA (DanChurchAid) in Denmark, represented by Lisbeth Overgaard, made this study possible. I could not have conducted this work without the support of Lisbeth and other DCA staff in Copenhagen.

Tired of Weeping

Introduction

This book is about Papel mothers' struggle to keep their children alive and their desperation when they fail. As a resident in the Biombo region in Guinea-Bissau for nearly five years, I could not escape the experience of child death. On the second day of my stay in the village of Quinhamel, Braima's daughter died. She was one year old and I never got to meet her. The little girl had spent a good part of her short life on the veranda that surrounded my new home. Later, Kodé and Santa, who also played on the same veranda, left this world. Idair, Ocante, Rufino, Jonina, and many more children in my neighborhood died as well. Friends and collaborators lost their children. While writing my field notes, through the window of my working room I heard—all too often—crying mothers, grandmothers, and other close female relatives when they left the mission hospital with a little lifeless body. I quickly learned that mothers' weeping was an unmistakable sign of how vulnerable the life of a child is in Biombo.

Mother Love and Child Death

There are two popular theses about mother love that circulate within Western academia and popular wisdom. The first takes mother love to be always present, self-sacrificing, and unconditional, while the second holds that mother love inevitably erodes in societies with extreme poverty and high expectancy of child death. The aim of this book is to challenge the latter position, which I refer to as the neglect thesis. The neglect thesis holds that impoverished mothers who experience high child mortality will neglect their children and fail to mourn their deaths. I do not deny that there may be mothers for whom both of these assumptions might be true. Yet, I argue that poverty and high child mortality do not necessarily produce negligent and unremorseful mothers.

The nature of emotions, including mother love, is a debated issue. Within biomedicine, maternal affection is frequently seen as an evolutionary adaptive emotion dependent on hormones released through biological processes related to childbearing (Klaus et al. 1972, Klaus and Kennell 1976, Klaus et al. 1995). Among essentialist feminists, mother love is commonly assumed to be innate and instinctively constituted (Kristeva 1980).[1] Social scientists often take humans to have an emotional "core" or universal potential for an emotional repertoire; there is, however, disagreement about to what extent these common human characteristics are shaped by culture and social context (Brison and Leavitt 1995; Oatley and Jenkins 1996; Reddy 1997, 1999; Rosaldo 1989; Rosenblatt 1993).[2] Others treat emotions as culturally constructed and only comprehensible within the framework of culture (Abu-Lughod 1993; Lutz 1986, 1988; Lutz and Abu-Lughod 1990). The anthropologist Nancy Scheper-Hughes takes that position when she argues that "mother love is anything *other* than natural and instead represents a matrix of images, meanings, sentiments, and practices that are everywhere socially and culturally produced" (1992:341).[3]

In the monumental work *Death without Weeping* (1992) Scheper-Hughes presents her study of "maternal thinking" among Brazilian mothers in the shantytown of Alto do Cruzeiro.[4] She argues that through delayed attachment mothers selectively neglect some of their weakest children to death, thus allocating scarce resources for the survival of stronger ones. According to Scheper-Hughes, the Alto mothers conceive of their infants as not fully human, and without individual personalities (412–16), as beings who sometimes "want to die" (315–16). The mothers take comfort in Catholic preaching about the afterlife and the idea that "God's will" will be done, which allows them to hold back their grief whenever a child's death takes place during the first year of life (401–2). As a general conclusion Scheper-Hughes writes: "I have no doubt . . . that the local culture is organized to defend women against the psychological ravaging of grief, I assume that the culture is quite successful in doing so" (430). Scheper-Hughes affirms that this process of delayed maternal attachment applies only to the poor women; for the better-off middle-class women in the area "child death is as shocking and aberrant as for affluent women anywhere else in the world" (328).

Scheper-Hughes is ambivalent about the universality of her findings. She repeatedly emphasizes the importance of the local political, social, and historical context in the cultural construction of maternal thinking; she makes "no claims to universality" (1992:342). Nor does she argue for a "culture of poverty" to describe the particular situation of Alto mothers and their children. Nevertheless, Scheper-Hughes takes "the fragility and 'dangerousness' of the mother-infant relationship to be the most immediate and visible index of scarcity and unmet needs" (25). Further, she would not be surprised "to discover some resonances and resemblances with mothering practices at other times and places" (342). Scheper-Hughes suggests that in societies where impoverished mothers must give birth under hostile conditions passive infanticide and selective neglect may be seen as survival strategies. She maintains that "modern notions of mother love derive, in the first instance, from a 'new' reproductive 'strategy': to give birth to few infants and to 'invest' heavily (emotionally as well as materially) in each one from birth onward" (401–2). However, where child mortality and fertility are high, Scheper-Hughes argues, the reproductive strategy is to have many children but "to invest selectively in those considered the 'best bets' for survival in terms of preferred sex, birth order, appearance, health or perceived viability" (402). This "pre-demographic transition, reproductive strategy" requires cultural construction of maternal thinking that allows fatal neglect of weak infants and thus spares mothers the grief following "the death of each and every fragile child" (402).[5]

The primatologist Sarah Blaffer Hrdy maintains that "a mother's commitment to her infant—and in the case of humans, this is what we mean by 'mother love'—is neither a myth nor a cultural construct" (1999:315). Instead, Hrdy believes that there is a bioevolutionary adaptation for maternal attachment. She writes, "mothers evolved not to produce as many children as they could but to trade off quantity for quality, or to achieve a secure status, and in that way increase the chance that at least a few offspring will survive and prosper" (10). In contrast to Scheper-Hughes, Hrdy argues selective neglect and outright infanticide are adaptive reproductive strategies not only for the poor but also for the economically better off. Hrdy emphasizes the importance of innate maternal responses to infant appearances, but points out that there are exceptions that these innate responses cannot explain, such as "the many modern mothers who throw themselves utterly and wholeheartedly into care of babies unlikely to survive" (459–60). Such "ethical behavior" must be examined in terms of "the mother's social and economic circumstances, religious beliefs, as well as learned attitudes about children and about how families 'should be'" (460).

Within evolutionary approaches, cultural and ethical aspects are often interpreted as evolving to enforce adaptive behavior, if these aspects are considered at all. According to Hrdy, once infanticide "is developed, customs encouraging psychological distancing between mother and neonate become institutionalized" (1994:34). Further, Hrdy argues that infanticide is often facilitated by beliefs that delay the attribution of human identity to newborns or by customs that allocate the responsibility of survival from parents to the infant. Helen L. Ball and Catherin M. Hill argue that killing of deformed infants, the weaker twin and other "lowered-viability infants" is an adaptive strategy that aims to increase reproductive success, while "emic explanations for the killing of infants (e.g., fear, inhumanity, etc.) operate at a proximate level (i.e., are the immediate triggers of a practice)" (1996:857).

Historians who have studied childhood history in Europe and North America have focused on infanticide and neglectful and abusive care of children. Lionel Rose, who examined infanticide in Britain in the period 1800–1939, explains the phenomenon as an inborn human response to pressure or a biological necessity when birth control was poorly understood. He concludes that when times become difficult, "the young and helpless become ready victims and we must not delude ourselves that our instincts are anything but elementally animal whatever religious and ethical ideals we aspire to" (1986:187). Some historians explain the high child mortality in Europe in terms of mothers' negligent care and indifference to their children's survival, as evidenced by the recruitment of wet-nurses, maternal abandonment, or infanticide (Ariès 1962, Badinter 1980, Shorter 1975, Stone 1977). These historians do not wholly agree on which came first: maternal indifference or child mortality. Nor do they agree on the nature of the relationship between maternal neglect and child mortality.[6]

Philippe Ariès (1962) argues that a high infant mortality was the main cause of maternal indifference, which he sees as a strategy applied to avoid inevitable grief. Similar to Scheper-Hughes, Lawrence Stone (1977) asserts that maternal indifference was produced by the high child mortality and that it contributed to additional deaths. On the other hand, Edward Shorter (1975) and Elisabeth Badinter (1980) emphasize maternal indifference and poor care as important factors in high child mortality, but they do not identify a causal relation. Badinter, in contrast to Rose, argues that the cruel and discriminatory maternal care of children in eighteenth-century France demonstrates that no such thing as maternal instinct exists and that mother love is a cultural construct, produced in a specific cultural context, in a particular place and historical time.[7]

The neglect thesis, as advocated by evolutionary approaches and applied by some of the historians cited above, holds that impoverished mothers neglect or kill their unviable or unwanted infants to enhance human survival. Scheper-Hughes's (1992) argument appears to bolster this position.[8] However, there is a fundamental difference in theoretical framework. Hrdy (1999) maintains that human mothers have biologically evolved to neglect or eliminate "low quality" or unwanted infants, whereas Scheper-Hughes argues that mothers' selective neglect is made possible through the cultural construction of historically entrenched maternal thinking, political economy, and religion. According to Scheper-Hughes, the cultural production of maternal indifference spares poor mothers the destructive consequences of grief, but at the same time it contributes to selective neglect and deaths of unviable infants and survival of the strongest.[9]

Scheper-Hughes's work differs significantly from much of sociobiological research in that she draws upon the use of firsthand information from mothers who were involved in passive infanticide. Scheper-Hughes was "there." She actually witnessed what she interprets as maternal neglect and lack of grief. Scheper-Hughes gives voice to mothers who expressed that they were "pleased to have a little *coração santa* [blessed heart] in heaven looking after them." She declares she is inclined to believe mothers who tell her "the death came as a blessing or a great relief" (1992:423). Alto mothers say they will only begin to love their babies when the babies start to "show us who they are and what kind of being we now have here" (438). They maintain that "little babies are interchangeable and easily replaced" (355), babies "are not so connected . . . alive or dead, it makes no real difference to them" (364). Why should mothers weep?

I find Scheper-Hughes's ethnographic description of Alto mothers' interaction with their infants and young children, their conceptions of infants and young children, as well as their ideas about the nature of diseases, death and the afterlife convincing and compelling. On the other hand, I do not endorse entirely her interpretations, and I argue against the universality of the neglect thesis, which holds that mothers in societies with high fertility and high child mortality will respond to that situation with selective neglect of young children, in particular weak or disabled ones, and a lack of mourning when they die. Nor do I maintain that mother love is universal "womanly script." I argue that cultural values and ethical considerations related to religion and kinship ideologies, as well as gender relations and subsistence are all important factors in shaping reproductive practices and, in turn, maternal affection and dedication. I base my argument on fieldwork conducted among the Papel people of Guinea-Bissau.

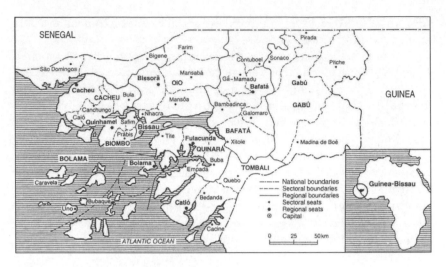

Map 1. The Republic of Guinea-Bissau

Fieldwork Setting

The Republic of Guinea-Bissau, a small, coastal West African state extending over 36,120 square kilometers, is one of the poorest countries in the world (see map 1 and table 1). According to the Human Development Index (HDI), Guinea-Bissau ranks 166th of 175 countries included (UNDP 2003).[10] Fertility is high and child mortality at all ages is among the highest in the world. Malnutrition among Guinean children is prevalent (20–40 percent of children under five years of age) and malaria, acute respiratory infections, and diarrhea are important causes of child mortality (Gunnlaugsson, Silva, and Smedman 1993). Tuberculosis (Koivula 1998) and HIV infection (HIV-1 and HIV-2) are serious public health problems with rates of HIV-1 increasing (Andersson 1999, Holmgren 2002, Norrgren 1998, Poulsen et al. 1989).

The Papel make up about 7 percent of Guinea-Bissau's multiethnic population of approximately 1.2 million inhabitants. There is no consensus on the exact number of ethnic groups that live in the country; depending on references there are about twenty to twenty-five groups, each with its own language or dialect (Galli 1990, Galli and Jones 1987). The four largest ethnic groups make up more than 75 percent of the total population: Balanta (30 percent), Fulani (20 percent), Manjaco (14 percent), and Mandinga (13 percent).[11] Although each ethnic group has its own language or dialect, Kriol (Creole), spoken by more than 50 percent of the population, is Guinea-Bissau's most widely used language (Diallo 1987, Nassum 1994, Santos 1987). The use of Kriol, which has its origin in early contacts of the Portuguese and the inhabitants in West Africa, is rapidly expanding (Bull

Table 1. Socioeconomic and health indicators for the Republic of Guinea-Bissau and, where available, for the Biombo region.

Indicator	National	Biombo
Population in 1998	1,161,000	62,423
Population annual growth rate (%), 1990–98	2.2	—
Surface area (km2)	36,125	837
People per km2	30	75
Urban population (%), 1998	22	—
Per capita GNP (US$), 1997	230	—
Population (%) earning under US$1 a day, 1990–96	88	—
Enrollment (% male/female) in school, 1990–97		
• primary	81/47	—
• secondary	9/4	
Literacy (% male/female) of persons at least 15 years of age 1995	48/16	—
Access to health care (%)		
• <8 km	92	—
• <5 km		59
Number of births per 1000 population	42	—
Total fertility rate (children per woman), 1998	5.7	—
Contraceptive prevalence rate (%), 1990–98	1	—
Maternal mortality (deaths per 100 000 live births), 1985-2001	910	—
Life expectancy at birth, 1999	45	—
Child mortality (deaths per 1000 live births), 1990-95		
• perinatal	47	40
• neonatal	56	48
• 1–11 months of age	92	115
• under-five years of age	277	335
Breastfeeding prevalence (%), 1990-95		
• 12–17 months	98.7	98.5
• 18–23 months	85.8	87.8
• 24–29 months	41.6	41.1
• 30–35 months	11.8	10.5
HIV/AIDS prevalence rate (%), 15-49 years, 2001	2.8	—
Human Development Index rank, 2003	166 of 175	—

Sources: Aaby (1997), Djatá (1998), UNDP (1998, 2003); UNICEF (1999).

1988, Cabral 1984, Rougé 1986, 1995). Roughly 10 percent of the population speak the official language of Portuguese, however it is rarely used for daily communication.

Distinctions between ethnic groups are frequently made along religious lines, though religious adherence does not entirely follow ethnic group allegiance (Jao 1995a). Muslims, mainly Fulani and Mandinga, make up 45 percent of the total population while those adhering to African religions, primarily Balanta, Manjaco, and Papel, compose half of the population. About 5 percent of the population is Christian, including Roman Catholics and various Protestant denominations.[12]

Another important distinction used in daily language, which cuts across ethnic belonging and religious adherence, is that between *djintis di tabanka*, a Kriol term for "village people" and *djintis di prassa*, those who live in semirural or more urbanized areas.[13] However, the use of these terms is relative. For the village people, those who live in Bissau are all *djintis di prassa* while those who live in the real *prassa*, that is, the urban center of Bissau, call everyone else *djintis di tabanka*. The *tabanka-prassa* distinction also refers to social status: *djintis di prassa* dress and behave in a "modern" manner and they are described as "civilized." The *djintis di tabanka*, many of whom are illiterate, are considered uncivilized or *atrasadu* (backward) by others, though they also sometimes portray themselves as such. There is also a difference in the use of language: the village people use African languages for daily communication while the language of the *prassa* is Kriol.

Increasingly Kriol is becoming the first language of children, particularly in urbanized, ethnically mixed areas. Kriol is widely spoken among the Papel, a minority of whom do not speak the vernacular language. The Papel language belongs to the Niger-Congo family, and is part of the northern branch of the Western Atlantic group, together with the languages of the Manjaco and the Mancanha (Cissoko 1987, Murdock 1959). Not only the languages but also the social, political, and economic structures of these groups have similarities, but they see themselves as "kinsmen" rather than "brothers."

Papel Land

My setting for fieldwork, the Biombo region, is commonly called Papel land or *tchon di Papel* in Kriol.[14] It is a flat swampy marshland also referred to as Biombo Island, because formerly the region was an island separated by sea from the mainland (map 2). Geographically the capital Bissau is situated on Biombo Island, and the Biombo region received status as a separate administrative unit from Bissau in the late 1980s. The Biombo region has about 62,000 inhabitants, of whom 53 percent are women. Almost three-quarters of Biombo's inhabitants are Papel and a little less than one-fifth are Balanta (Djatá 1998). Considering the ethnic composition of the population and its predominantly rural character, I estimate that at least 90 percent adhere to local religions, mainly Papel and Balanta.[15] Christian converts, among them some partially or temporary converted, hardly exceed 5 percent. A still smaller Muslim minority lives in the region.

Biombo is a disadvantaged region in terms of subsistence and infrastructure. Even though they are primarily agriculturists, the Papel are not able, and probably have not been able, to sustain themselves for centuries. Their neighbors, the Balanta, are Guinea-Bissau's chief agriculturists, and according to historical sources dating back to the sixteenth century, the

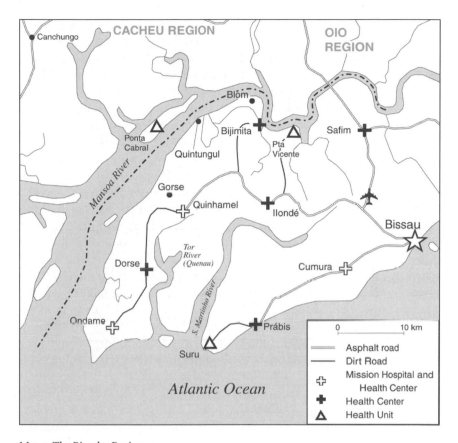

Map 2. The Biombo Region

Papel were dependent on them for food (Rodney 1970:32).[16] Malnutrition among children is common and child mortality rates are higher in the Biombo region than national statistics indicate (see table 1). A well-controlled study conducted in 1990–95 in Guinea-Bissau shows that the Biombo region had the highest mortality rate among children less than five years of age (Aaby et al.). Of the ethnic groups, the Papel had the highest child mortality: 337 out of 1,000 children died before they had reached five years of age.

Biombo is the most densely populated of Guinea-Bissau's nine regions outside Bissau, with an estimated 73 inhabitants per square kilometer. There are approximately 136 villages in Biombo, with a median population of 316 inhabitants. While the Balanta tend to settle in more isolated villages by the sea and close to the rice fields, the Papel are more likely to build their houses along the roads. Boundaries between Papel villages are sometimes blurred, and contact between villages is extensive. Biombo's inhabitants travel frequently to Bissau to visit family members and friends, or for business.

The Papel divide themselves in seven matrilineal lineages with each lineage represented by a totem.[17] Children belong to the lineage of their mother and have the totem of her group but they are given the surname of their father. Residence is ideally patrilocal and polygyny is frequent. Inheritance is matrilineal. This means that the eldest sister's son of the deceased is the inheritor of his land, goods, and compound. The heir also acquires certain rights and responsibilities in relation to the wives and the children of the deceased.[18] A man will replace his paternal surname with that of his mother's lineage when he inherits the compound from his maternal uncle.

A local myth says the Papel descend from the first residents of Biombo Island. According to the myth, a Biafada hunter came from the town of Sacala, in the region of Quinara to the uninhabited island of Biombo. He passed the river at its narrowest point at Bijimita. For a while the Biafada man came to Biombo only for hunting, until he finally settled there with his family. A Mancanha man from the village Có came later and stayed with the Biafada hunter, but when he wanted to leave, the old Biafada man asked him to stay and gave him responsibility for the land.[19] The descendants of these two men are the Papel. Little by little the Papel concentrated in Bissau, which became their center, but they also expanded with time to other parts of the Biombo Island.[20]

The origin of the name Papel, preferred by some to be spelled Pepel, is a mystery. Moreira (1993:16) notes that already in 1594 the name Papel was being used as an alternative to the name Brame.[21] In colonial literature the name Brame was interchangeably used with the name Papel as a term for all the groups Papel, Manjaco, and Mancanha (Crowley 1990:282–89, Moreira 1993:17–18, Pélissier 1989a:34–35). Almeida (1963), citing earlier colonial writings, suggests that the designation Papel, or Pepel, has origin in the words Çapeos, Çapés, Çapijs, Sapes, Sapés (or Safés, Safis). At the same time, Almeida acknowledges some disagreement on this point.[22]

At the time of the arrival of the Portuguese to Papel land in the sixteenth century, the Papel population was already organized in kingdoms, with the Bissau king as supreme ruler and the chiefs of Biombo,[23] Tor, Cacete, Bijimita, Safim, and Antula as vassals (Mendy 1994, Rema 1982). Today the Papel territory is divided into thirteen distinct kingdoms (Carreira 1962, Cissoko 1987). The kings govern each of their kingdoms independently, and they function as moderators and religious leaders. Since independence, the Papel kings have had no political mandate within the structure of the Guinean state, but some of the kings allied themselves with the new regime and entered its official administration (Carvalho 1998, Landim 1987).[24] Throughout the centuries relations between the Papel kings and the Portuguese colonial power were quite extensive, though not always friendly.

Colonial History

According to historical sources, the Papel together with other small ethnic groups such as the Manjaco, Mancanha, and Balanta were pushed by Mandinga warriors of the Mali Empire to the coastal area, which is today Guinea-Bissau (Pélissier 1989b, Rodney 1970). These peoples never became integrated into the Mali Empire in the thirteenth century nor did they convert to Islam. The Papel were more affected by Portuguese private traders who began to settle in communities called *prassa* (fortress, marketplace, square) to facilitate trade in the sixteenth century (Rodney 1970:74–93). These settlers were named *lançados* (literally, one who throws himself on somebody) by the Portuguese administration because they settled among the African population against prohibitions of the crown. The *lançados* had local assistants, mostly Papel and Manjaco, who were either employed or enslaved. The assistants were called *grumetes* (cabin boys) because trade was dependent on boats for transport of goods along the rivers. The *grumetes* adopted some of the Portuguese customs, names, and clothing as well as the Christian religion. The Portuguese settlers and their assistants communicated in Kriol, a Portuguese-based pidgin. The children the white settlers had with local wives or women slaves often became successful intermediaries between the Europeans and African traders in the interior of the continent. The *lançados,* their families, and *grumetes* are the founders of the Kriol community.

Beginning in the sixteenth century, slaves became the most lucrative export for the Portuguese (Galli and Jones 1987; Mendy 1994; Pélissier 1989a, 1989b; Rodney 1970). The *lançados* initiated slave raids in the coastal area, but more often they collected slaves from local raiders. The local raiders attacked neighboring ethnic groups, but some captured slaves even within their own group.[25] The Muslim Mandinga were the most active slave raiders at the beginning of the slave trade but later they lost out to the Fulani, Muslim nomads who had begun to enter the area in the fifteenth century. The interests of the Kriol community did not always coincide with the local rulers in the coastal areas, mainly Papel and Manjaco, to whom they had to pay tribute. They also had conflicting relations with the Portuguese crown, which tried to maintain a monopoly of trade.

Cacheu, situated in Manjaco land in the northern part of Guinea-Bissau, was the major collection point for slaves, particularly in the beginning of the slave trade (Crowley 1990; Gable 1992; Lopes 1987; Mendy 1994; Pélissier 1989a, 1989b; Rodney 1970). In the latter half of the seventeenth century the Portuguese crown began to establish Bissau as its trade center, where some *lançados* had already settled in the sixteenth century. The Portuguese had great difficulties in keeping control over Cacheu, and at first sight Bissau appeared to be easier, as relations with the Papel kings of Bissau were friendly (Rodney 1970:141–42). In 1696, with the help of Franciscan missionaries, the Portuguese crown finally got an authorization from the Papel king, Becompolo Có, to construct a fortress in Bissau (Mendy 1994, Rema 1982, Rodney 1970:142–51). The king, who was himself involved in trade of slaves, ivory, and wax, converted to Catholicism the very same year, but he died shortly afterwards.[26] Becompolo Có's successor was not as friendly to the Portuguese, although he nominally accepted Christianity. The successor resisted fiercely all attempts against free trade, and the Portuguese had also great difficulties in fortifying Bissau against the French and the British. The Papel population refused to provide construction material, water, or labor for the building.[27]

The resistance against a trade monopoly was strong among the inhabitants in Bissau, the Kriol and Papel populations, which obliged the crown to abandon Bissau in 1707. In 1753, however, despite resistance, the population in Bissau could not prevent the return of the representatives of the Portuguese crown. Hostilities continued with several outbreaks of war. The Papel had a well-equipped army with European rifles they had acquired through trade (Galli 1987, Pélissier 1989a, Mendy 1994). Their guerrilla style war strategy was difficult for the Portuguese to defeat. In addition, the Papel, who often allied themselves with the Kriol-speaking population, had spies within the Portuguese fortress. They managed to partially resist the trade monopoly of the Portuguese crown.

In 1879 the Portuguese crown decided to administer the areas under their influence on the West African coast of Portuguese Guinea as a separate administrative province from Cape Verde (Galli and Jones 1987, Mendy 1994, Pélissier 1989a). Enormous resources were used to acquire military and administrative control over the province. Resistance among the African population was considerable and wars broke out throughout the country with heavy losses for the Portuguese. A turning point came with the military campaigns in 1912–15 directed by the Portuguese Captain João Teixeira Pinto (Lopez 1987, Crowley 1990, Mendy 1994). Teixeira collaborated with the Senegalese Abdul Njai, who was notorious for vandalism and banditry. The joint army of Njai, who had recruited some 400 soldiers in Senegal, and Taxeira Pinto was brutal: local people were massacred, houses burnt, and animals and other valuables stolen. The army rapidly gained control over the interior of the country in 1913, and thereafter over Bissau. In 1915 they marched to the interior of Biombo Island and finally they killed the king of the Biombo kingdom. According to contemporary sources, "his eyes were extracted, and he was buried alive" and his pregnant wife was shot in the womb (Mendy 1994:249).

A new administrative era began in the Portuguese colonies in 1926 when António de Oliveira Salazar became finance minister in Portugal after a military coup (Galli 1987, Lopes 1987). Salazar gave high priority to legislation and administration in the colonies. In Portuguese Guinea, the Fulani were recruited to collect taxes and administer the occupied areas where there was a lack of cooperative locals. The Kriol population and people from Cape Verde were assigned to intermediate and higher levels of the colonial administration. Only the Portuguese and a few Cape Verdians assumed the highest posts in the administration. The population was divided into two groups, the indigenous and the civilized or so-called assimilated *(assimilados);* the latter group was reserved for those few who were sufficiently accustomed to Portuguese manners, education, and religion.[28]

Enforced cultivation, which had already begun in the late nineteenth century, was continued for deliveries of agricultural produce (Crowley 1990, Galli 1987). In the 1940s, cashew plantations were introduced in an effort to diversify exports. The traditional labor-intensive production of rice, which had been cultivated in the area for at least a millennium,[29] declined in most parts of the country as young men, mainly Manjaco, but also Papel, immigrated to Senegal for work. In addition, many of the local chiefs who were appointed by the Portuguese did not have authority to mobilize available labor to maintain the dikes and prevent the sea from flooding the rice fields.[30] Furthermore, prices of agricultural products were low and peasants were unwilling to trade with the Portuguese. Instead, they smuggled their products to neighboring countries where prices were more favorable.

Only during the last years of the colonial epoch were improvements in trade, education, and living conditions initiated by General Spinola, who later led the military coup against the fascist regime of Salazar in Portugal in 1974 (Galli 1987).

Independence

The charismatic Amilcar Cabral founded PAIGC (Partido Africano de Independência de Guiné e Cabo Verde) in 1956 (Crowley 1990, Galli and Jones 1987, Lopes 1987, Rudebeck 1974). After the colonial authorities had responded to a strike among harbor workers with a massacre in Bissau in August 3, 1959, PAIGC began its preparations for an armed struggle for independence. Military action against the Portuguese began in 1961 and the war lasted for thirteen years. PAIGC, which was originally a Kriol-based organization, received its strongest support among the forest and savannah-woodland populations in the northern and southern parts of the country, as well as from the island population, the Bijagos. Some Muslim populations allied with the Portuguese, as they had done earlier. The Papel in Biombo retained a somewhat isolated position, but some fought on the Portuguese side while others allied with PAIGC. In Biombo, as elsewhere, many of the local chiefs, who had gained power with the support of the

Portuguese, had a hard time balancing between the fighting sides (Crowley 1990, Gable 1992).

The war of independence brought major changes to all of Guinea-Bissau's population of roughly half a million inhabitants in 1960 (Crowley 1990, Lopes 1987). PAIGC, with support from Cuba and the Soviet Union, rapidly expanded the liberated areas within the interior of the country. The Portuguese, with support from their Western allies in NATO, concentrated troops in Guinea-Bissau. Rural people were evacuated from the most isolated villages to deter collaboration with the rebels. Many fled their homes, and some 150,000 Guineans sought refuge in Senegal. Cultivation of rice, the main dietary staple, declined because of forced resettlement, abandonment of villages, and bombing of dikes by the Portuguese.[31] During this period of displacement and social rupture interethnic contacts increased and the spread of Kriol was extensive. At its peak the Portuguese army numbered about 40,000 soldiers. Though the war was fought in the countryside, the army was mainly based in Bissau, which had about 50,000 inhabitants in 1960. The city expanded rapidly as people escaped the fighting in the countryside. By 1974 the population of Bissau had doubled.

On September 24, 1973, a young Guinean battlefield commander, Bernando João Vieira, popularly known as Nino, declared the Republic of Guinea-Bissau and Cape Verde a unilaterally independent state (Galli 1987). Amilcar Cabral, the leader of the victorious PAIGC, had been murdered in January the very same year by a naval commander who had been expelled from duties within PAIGC for misbehavior and abuse of power. Cabral's half brother Luís Cabral was appointed as the first president of the Republic of Guinea-Bissau and Cape Verde. Following the military coup in Lisbon in April 1974, General Spinola announced Portugal's recognition of the new republic.

The postindependence period is frequently divided into two distinct economic periods (SIDA 1989, 1994). The first, from 1974–82, was a period of a centralized dogmatically socialist planned economy, which resulted in a serious economic crisis and a severe shortage of products for sale at official marketplaces. The Kriol-speaking population and Cape Verdians occupied the most rewarding administrative functions within the centralized state bureaucracy. On November 14, 1980, Nino, the prime minister, seized power through a military coup. This coup was partly directed against the Cape Verdians and it ended the union between Guinea-Bissau and Cape Verde, which thereafter became two independent republics.

The second period after independence was characterized by economic liberalization in accordance with the structural adjustment programs dictated by the World Bank. In 1982 preparations began for a reform program that was implemented in 1983 with financial help of the International

Monetary Fund (IMF). After a period of "structural adjustment" and "readjustment" of the economy, goods became available on the market, but the prices of basic consumer goods were high.[32] The salaries of the civil servants rapidly deteriorated, and unemployment and social unrest grew. Dependence on external aid increased, as did foreign debt. Inflation was rampant and the Guinean peso was continually depreciated.[33] The year 1996 was characterized by a particularly high inflation rate partly due to speculations related to the integration of Guinea-Bissau to the West African Monetary Union (WAMU) and the CFA zone in May 1997 (Aguilar 1998:9–10).

The 1990s were characterized by political liberalization with a multiparty system (Rudebeck 2000). In July and August 1994 there were parliamentary and presidential elections, the first democratic elections in Guinea-Bissau's history.[34] The former governing party, PAIGC, won the parliamentary elections while Nino, the former president and general secretary of PAIGC, won the presidency. On June 7, 1998 war broke out in Guinea-Bissau. The chief of the army, Ansumane Mané, supported by the majority of the military, revolted the day after he had been sacked by president Nino for allegedly having smuggled weapons to separatist guerrillas in the southern Senegal province of Casamance. Mané denied the allegations and accused the president of corruption and dictatorship (Andrén 2000, Rudebeck 1998). Eleven months later, on May 7, 1999, Nino lost the war despite military support from the neighboring countries of Senegal and Guinea. Portugal, his former wartime enemy, granted him political asylum. However, Nino is still feared by his opponents for his famous fighting spirit. He belongs to the Papel lineage Bajoukumum who are known as fighters and said to attack like their totem the hyena.

The victorious military junta handed over power to an interim government headed by the president of the parliament (Andrén 2000, Rudebeck 2000, 2001). Elections were held on November 28, 1999, and January 19, 2000. The candidate for the Party for Social Renewal, Kumba Yala, professor of philosophy and lawyer, won the presidential election and together with other opposition parties his party won a majority in the parliament. Nevertheless, the relationship between civil and military power was restrained. In November 2000, Mané appointed himself first commander in chief and some days later supreme commander, a position constitutionally reserved for the president (Rudebeck 2001:96–98). Troops loyal to the government responded to Mané's provocation by capturing the military base. Mané managed to flee with a few men to Biombo region, where he was later killed in the village of Blom.

The military uprising in 1998 resulted in political instability and cuts in international aid.[35] President Yala was accused of unlawful arrests of political opponents and journalists, restrictions in the freedom of the press, abuse of power, and mismanagement. He dissolved the parliament and postponed parliamentary elections repeatedly. After countless government reshuffles, strikes by civil servants requesting their wages and children out of school for almost two years Yala's rule came to an end by a bloodless military coup in September 2003. The coup was greeted by ordinary people and most politicians. Henrique Rosa, a businessman, was appointed as interim president by the army. Parliamentary elections, held on March 28, 2004, brought the former governing party, PAIGC, back to power; presidential elections are secheduled in 2005. It is evident that the war and its aftermath have further contributed to the precarious situation of the Guinean population, not least for children, whose fate is the focus of this book.

Fieldwork

The background to my choice of setting for fieldwork in Guinea-Bissau has a history. My husband Geir and I went to live in Bissau in 1982. For three years I worked as a volunteer for the Swedish nongovernmental organization Groups of Africa (ARO). I was assigned as a coordinator of studies and teacher to train laboratory technicians at the National Public Health Laboratory (LNSP) in Bissau. Geir, a medical practitioner, worked within the maternal and child health services in Bissau. After three exciting years in Bissau we moved to Stockholm, Sweden. Geir finished his pediatric specialization and defended his dissertation on child health and breastfeeding, which was based on data from Guinea-Bissau. I began my studies in social anthropology and prepared for anthropological fieldwork with a focus on breastfeeding.

In 1993 we returned to Guinea-Bissau together with our three sons, born in 1986, 1987, and 1991, respectively. Geir and I had signed a two-year work contract with the Danish nongovernmental organization DanChurchAid (DCA), which was extended to nearly five years. Geir was assigned as a medical advisor to the regional health board of Biombo. I had a volunteer contract. According to my job description I would use my anthropological competence to study relevant issues for the health work in the region. The theme I had originally planned for my dissertation, the ethnography of breastfeeding women in the region, was to be a priority. We lived in the village of Quinhamel, the administrative center of the Biombo region, situated some forty kilometers from the capital Bissau. Quinhamel has about 2,500 inhabitants, most of whom are Papel, but the village center, the *prassa*, is home to a mixture of different ethnic groups, many of whom are health workers, teachers, police, public servants, and merchants, among others.

On arrival in Quinhamel village our house was already arranged for us by DCA; it was made of adobe bricks, cemented and with a roof of corrugated iron. Most importantly there was a cemented veranda and an attached *djamberem* (a hut with open walls and straw roof) where one could breathe the somewhat fresher outdoor air protected from sunlight. A major issue for Geir and me was to organize schooling for our sons. The public school in Quinhamel had to deal with all the problems that characterize such institutions in countries ridden by poverty. When we arrived, communication with Bissau was difficult as the road was very hard to travel. For the first two years in Quinhamel we ran a school in our home, but during the last three years of our stay, with a new and better road, our sons attended the Swedish School in Bissau. My sister-in-law was the first teacher of the so-called Icelandic School in Quinhamel and her daughter, born in 1985, brought the group to three students. Thus, in Quinhamel village I was part of an extended family of seven members.

Once the practical side of having a family in the field was resolved, I immersed myself in fieldwork. More than ever my private life and professional concerns became intensely intertwined. My first task before beginning formal fieldwork was to find a translator and assistant. As a volunteer working in the health services of Biombo, I asked for proposals from the regional health board. After I indicated some fundamental criteria for my assistant, Odete Felix, a woman of my age and mother of six children, was appointed by the board and paid by DCA. She is Catholic and has a few years of schooling. Odete assisted me with all my more formal collection of data such as the various surveys I conducted. She was also crucial in identifying key informants. In addition, Odete functioned as a translator when we talked with people who either did not speak Kriol or preferred to speak Papel. Through my earlier experience during three years in Bissau as a teacher I had acquired fluent Portuguese, but my competence in Kriol was rudimentary. However, from the very beginning of our collaboration Odete and I spoke Kriol together. In the beginning of my fieldwork I was determined to learn the Papel language but I changed my mind when I realized how easily I could communicate with Kriol. My confidence in Odete as a translator further supported that decision.[36]

A common problem for many anthropologists while beginning fieldwork is to legitimate one's presence. Odete's friendly comportment, and her wide network of family members and friends likely contributed to the ease I felt in that respect. My situation was also facilitated by the fact that my husband, *dotor* Geir as he came to be called, replaced *dotora* Hanne, a Danish physician whose contract was over. Foreign aid workers and missionaries are well-recognized categories of people within Guinean society.[37] While we were the only foreign aid workers in Quinhamel besides a British volunteer who stayed there during our first year, foreign missionaries had a long history in the region. The Catholic mission, with a varied number of foreign nuns, monks, and missionaries, has had a center in Quinhamel since the early 1950s (Rema 1982).[38] During the first weeks of my fieldwork I was sometimes mistaken for a nun. I understood that the nuns' involvement in curative care of children was considered by many mothers to be a mixed blessing; their "strong" medicines were appreciated, but mothers sometimes felt intimidated by the nuns. Fortunately, I quickly became situated as the wife of the white *dotor* in Quinhamel, and in that capacity, it was considered natural that I be interested in children's health.

Anthropological fieldwork is always bound up with ethical concerns. Those issues I found most difficult to handle were child diseases and death. How much should I become involved in finding care for sick children? Should I urge mothers to take their sick children to the National Hospital in Bissau even though I knew care given there was not the best and economically beyond the reach of most people? Should I contribute with my own economic resources and time? I have no answers to these questions and others like them. In any case, regardless of my own thoughts on the matter, I too often entered situations in which I found myself to have become, against my intention, a "professional rescuer" (see Gottlieb and Graham, 1993:147). Becoming a professional rescuer may not be the ideal position for an anthropologist striving to establish a respectful and sharing relationship with those studied, but a lack of concern for others in the community is no better. I tried to reduce my involvement in cases of disease to those where I thought my intervention might make a real difference, or perhaps even save a life.[39] Even so, it was not an easy strategy to follow.

In her book *Death without Weeping* Scheper-Hughes's discusses her own reactions to the death of children. She writes: "I eventually learned to 'distance' myself from the deaths and to pick up and continue, as they [the mothers] did, with the strands of my life and work in the shantytown. I learned, as they did, to 'conform' and to tell myself that, after all, perhaps it was 'meant' to be so" (1992:16). Children continuously died in my surroundings from the very first days in Quinhamel, but I never got used to child deaths. Whenever a child died I always found it difficult, indeed, more so the longer I stayed. I wonder whether Scheper-Hughes takes it as an act of solidarity to inform readers that she learned to distance herself from child deaths, as did Alto mothers. Or is my response to child deaths just a simple reflection of the reactions of those mothers I worked with, as Scheper-Hughes claims in her case?

Methodological Approach

The fieldwork in Biombo consisted of periods of a systematically planned collection of data, on the one hand, and a continuous private participation in daily life, on the other. Informal encounters, ad hoc activities, and the daily dilemmas of practical life left me with knowledge and understanding of the complexity of life in Biombo.

My family members contributed to a multitude of connections and situations I took advantage of. Geir was involved in health work throughout the entire region and in Bissau. I exploited his network of friends and contacts. I benefited, for instance, from the personal experiences and insights of health care workers in the region, who also helped me contact individuals with experiences relevant to my work. My sons' play with other children, whether they ran after a football, made slingshots, hunted birds, collected cashew nuts, *asa koku* (burned the cashew nuts to open up the shell), *suta* mango (threw whatever they could find up in the mango trees in the hope that fruit would fall down), or played with Lego building bricks, all contributed to new insights. As my youngest son systematically refused to collaborate with nannies I often took him with me while on visits within and outside Quinhamel. This happened particularly during the first year of fieldwork when I was still breastfeeding. In my discussions with mothers it definitely contributed to a sense of mutual understanding.[40]

Each of the five years in Quinhamel had its distinctive characteristics, both in terms of private experience and professional work. The DCA classified Guinea-Bissau as a hardship country for their employees, so we traveled to our home country for recreation once a year. Thus, for my family each year began in August/September and ended when we went for vacation to Iceland and Sweden less than a year later.

The first year (1993–94) was characterized by arrival, installation, and intensive fieldwork. I began formal fieldwork with a regional survey on care-seeking behavior for children. Through this survey I got to know the whole of Biombo. I also practiced my Kriol before I began to investigate breastfeeding, the main theme of study. For two to three months Odete and I visited households in twenty-four villages distributed throughout the region. We arranged informal discussions with those found at home. Mothers were always involved in the discussion, as were elderly men and women, and often (but not always) fathers. Our conversations focused on children's diseases, alternatives for cure, and the costs of health care.

This was my first period of fieldwork. Every day I learned about new things. My head was full of words without meaning, and questions piled up. Sorcery was everywhere. I learned about the useful concept *uso*, which means custom or tradition. I heard many times that "when the cat has caught the child only *uso* helps." I learned that this "cat" that "caught the child" caused an illness that belonged to the "animal diseases," which is an important category of childhood diseases (chapter 4). Odete and I interviewed a number of women who cure these diseases. I also used every opportunity to discuss general aspects of the Papel culture, such as their history, lineage system, kings, and commoners. Due to the scarcity of literature on the Papel I spent much time during my entire fieldwork learning about the fundamentals of their society.[41]

Breastfeeding, my original theme for the dissertation, was my next focus for formal fieldwork. I began with a broad approach: everything that concerned breastfeeding was of interest. First I discussed the topic with Odete's family members, her neighbors and friends. In turn, they directed us to other women who had interesting breastfeeding histories, for instance those who had "bad milk," which I had come to know about through my own and Geir's earlier work on breastfeeding (Einarsdóttir 1988, Gunnlaugsson and Einarsdóttir 1993). I spent much time on women's general life situation during this period of fieldwork (chapter 1), and conducted a follow-up study of questions that arose during the care-seeking behavior study. After three or four months I decided to narrow my approach and quantify some of the phenomena and behaviors I had learned about. I began to wonder whether I was only looking for the rare and exotic aspects of child health and breastfeeding. How many children were really victims of sorcery and the animal diseases? How many mothers had bad milk? How was the breast milk quality determined? Are there any mothers without milk? For how long were children breastfed? How many children had been fed with a bottle? Next I did a survey through which I registered all children under five years of age in a nearby village and interviewed their mothers or other responsible caregivers about these and other questions (chapters 2 and 4).

While working on this survey I came to know about a child who was suspected of being a spirit child. Shortly afterwards, the child died during a diagnostic ceremony, which, I was told, was a definite proof of its non-human nature. I had heard the concept spirit child before, but I had not grasped the real meaning, and sometimes I wonder if I ever will. From then on, I started to collect histories about these children, and throughout my years in Biombo I came to know several more such children (chapter 5).

The second year (1994–95) was different from the first one. I had just finished with the survey of children under five when a cholera epidemic broke out in Guinea-Bissau in late October 1994.[42] The Biombo region became heavily affected. A couple of weeks before the outbreak of the epidemic I had assumed half-time work for a few months as a gender officer at the Swedish embassy,[43] and suddenly I was involved in cholera studies during the other half of my time. Both the work at the embassy and the epidemic were new experiences for me. It was at times abrupt to divide time between the air-conditioned, orderly, and clean environment at the embassy and the harsh consequences of a cholera epidemic in the villages. Through the work at the embassy I got to know, although superficially, the world of the international organizations, with their many meetings and seminars. At the same time Geir, his colleagues, and I, with Odete's help, worked in collaboration with the Centers for Disease Control and Prevention (CDC) in Atlanta to conduct a number of studies on cholera. These addressed the question of how funerals might contribute to the transmission of cholera (Gunnlaugsson and Einarsdóttir 1999, Gunnlaugsson et al. 1998), risk factors for mortality in cholera (Gunnlaugsson et al. 2000), and how health education aimed at prevention of cholera was understood and accepted in a Papel village (Einarsdóttir, Passa, and Gunnlaugsson 2001). Cholera was not considered to be a childhood disease among the population but during these epidemics children under five and adults had a similar incidence of clinical infection in cholera. The findings of the cholera studies, or cholera in general, are not the subject of this book. Nonetheless, participation in these studies contributed to my insights into the Papel way of thinking about diseases, death, and afterlife, as well as their ways of acting when a disaster endangers their life (chapter 4).

The third year (1995–96) was a year of reflections but also additional fieldwork for my thesis. In the autumn I drove my children to the Swedish school in Bissau, where for a time I also spent the day at the house of Swedish friends. For the first time since I had started my fieldwork, I had the possibility of working undisturbed by visitors, and with almost continuous access to both electricity and water. I summarized and sorted my field notes, and identified information that was missing. Breastfeeding was still the focus but my interests were increasingly directed toward other themes as well. I prepared an additional survey to learn more about marriage, women's reproductive experiences, child deaths, spirit children, and fosterage. I began with a census of a village with approximately 700 inhabitants. This village was more remote than the first one I had studied. Together with Odete and two sons of the village chief we registered all the inhabitants living in the village, including all those who were away for education or occasional work. First we registered the chief of the compound and his wives and all the children they were responsible for; then all married sons, their wives, and their children. Finally, we registered other men who had come to the compound to inherit from their mother's brother and their families. Care had to be taken to include not yet remarried widows and their dependents. After the census I had detailed interviews with all eighty-seven mothers and caregivers of children under five. I took reproductive histories for all these women (chapter 2 and 4). This survey was extended over a period of seven months and it gave me insights into still more aspects of the Papel culture, in particular when it concerns foster practices (chapter 3) and mothers' interpretations of child diseases and deaths (chapters 4 and 5).

While I had enjoyed my life throughout the years in Biombo I admit that the fourth year (1996–97) was the most difficult one right from the start. When I came back from vacation I was told that Santa, the two-year old daughter of our maid, had died two weeks earlier. Oddly enough I had come back with Scheper-Hughes's book *Death without Weeping* in my bag. I read that book quickly and decided to revise my fieldwork strategy. However, the absence of DCA's administrator in Bissau due to illness kept me occupied with work at the DCA office for a while. A new cholera epidemic broke out, and this time even our close neighbors came to the health center in Quinhamel for treatment. As before, I used every opportunity to learn more about those themes that occupied my mind. This year I was particularly interested in issues such as the afterlife of children, conceptualization of infants and young children, and reasons why mothers wept at child deaths (chapters 3, 4, and 5).

Our fifth and last year (1997–98) in Biombo was pleasant but busy. Cholera was still raging when I returned from my annual vacation, and I inevitably became involved in cholera work for several weeks. It was time to conduct follow-up research for our study on cholera. Had people's ideas about the nature, transmission, and prevention of cholera changed since our study in December 1994? This study gave me opportunity to discuss, once more, causes of diseases and death, and their consequences for the afterlife. Then I spent some time on a study on the functioning of so-called village health units in the Oio region. It was a unique opportunity to get to know better other parts of Guinea-Bissau. Finally, in the last phase of my fieldwork, I narrowed my focus to child death and mothers' mourning.

A follow-up of child survival in the second study village was a sad experience: 23 of the 120 children who had entered my survey during the period from December 12, 1995 to July 1, 1996 were dead by the time I returned in February 1998. Yet, it was a positive experience to come back to the village on a regular basis. I noticed that new houses had been built. Three new water pumps were provided by a Japanese development project and in use. Women valued these pumps as now they had access to fresh water closer to home. New children were born. Virgina, whose twin boys had both died the year before, gave birth to a girl, and the third and youngest wife of the village chief gave birth to her first-born.

In April 1998 it was time to leave. Nobody suspected that war was looming. The war, which broke out six weeks after my departure, continued for eleven months and left the Guinean population in a disastrous situation. The war and its aftermath were with me every day during the writing of this book. In the morning before I started my writing I first checked all websites that might have some information about the latest events. It was not always encouraging reading. The first news reported that "Fighting flares in Guinea-Bissau," then that "Fighting racks Bissau, neighboring

Senegal launches attack" and still "Fighting intensifies in Guinea-Bissau, several embassies reported hit." No more encouraging were the headlines: "Post-colonial Guinea-Bissau plunges into darkness," "Impoverished and neglected, Guinea-Bissau suffers anew," or "Guiné sangrenta" ("Bloody Guinea"). Then the news began to focus on human suffering: "Huge exodus from Guinea-Bissau capital," "200 feared drowned," "Guinea-Bissau evacuees tell of fighting, water shortage," and "UN warns of famine in Guinea-Bissau." One morning I read "Portugueses refugiados em Quinhamel" ("Portuguese refugees in Quinhamel") and the news of about twenty foreigners who had fled to Quinhamel. There was nothing about the fate of the local population. A report with the headline "Viver o inferno com medo da Guerra" ("To live in hell with the fear of war") was more informative. It reported that the Biombo region had received about 120,000 refugees from Bissau who were in need of accommodation and food. The population in the region had tripled, an area that in normal years is unable to feed its people.

The Outline of the Chapters

The long-term fieldwork I conducted in the Biombo region is based on a multitude of entry points into the society and resulted in both qualitative and quantitative information. For the purpose of this book I have chosen to concentrate mainly on the qualitative data.

I have done my best to disguise the identity of those individuals who appear in the following pages. Sometimes I have altered details in individual biographies. All personal names, except mine, are pseudonyms. To further reduce risk of identification, I minimize accounts of my own or my family's involvement in some of the stories told in this book.[44] I have also chosen to reduce the use of names for places, and thus I refer to anonymous villages or more urbanized centers by using the Kriol designation *prassa*. All Kriol terms are printed in italic and Papel concepts are italic and boldface. To ease the burden to the reader I have translated most concepts and sayings to English; however, a few terms I will use in Kriol throughout the book. These and other important Kriol concepts are listed in the glossary.

In this book I will examine Papel mothers' experiences of bearing children, their child care practices, as well as their interpretations of and practical and emotional reactions to their children's diseases and deaths. Chapter 1, "Marriage Relations," gives crucial background information about the lives of Papel mothers. It situates women as wives and co-wives within the matrilineal kinship system. Through personal stories and descriptions of social conditions the chapter illuminates various aspects of a Papel marriage.

Chapter 2, "Burdens of Birth," describes women's motives for having children as well as their experiences of menstruation, pregnancy, birth, and breastfeeding. The birth and early motherhood practices of the Papel are compared to Western ideal birth practices that emphasize emotional support for mothers during birth, immediate infant-mother communication after delivery, and early initiation of breastfeeding as crucial for maternal bonding.

Chapter 3, "Conceptualization of Children" describes and explores how the Papel mothers conceptualize their infants and young children. Do they attribute humanity and personality to newborns? How are these conceptions reflected in care practices, name-giving procedures, and general upbringing? Foster practices and mothers' concerns about leaving their children to grow up with others are also discussed.

Chapter 4, "Diseases and Death," examines concepts of diseases, death, and the afterlife. What are the Papel ideas about the afterlife of children and the causes of their deaths? Various categories of childhood diseases and the characteristics of care seeking behavior for children are examined, as well as mothers' reactions to death and mourning. Do these findings support the thesis that relates neglectful care and lack of grief to high mortality?

Chapter 5, "Nonhuman Children," begins with a summary and discussion of infanticide in a cross-cultural perspective. I examine how spirit children, most of whom are born disabled or deviant in some way, are identified, how health care is sought out for them, and how they are mourned by their mothers. Are these children selectively neglected in terms of health care? Do mothers grieve when they die?

The concluding chapter summarizes my findings and argues that it is essential to consider how kinship, gender relations, religion, and the economy form cultural values attributed to reproduction and motherhood, and how these, in turn, shape maternal sentiments. Thus, I agree with Scheper-Hughes's presentation of maternal thinking as shaped by the social and cultural context. However, I argue against the suggestion that poor mothers in settings with high child mortality, as a psychological survival strategy, will adapt to the situation with delayed attachment, selective neglect of some of their infants, and lack of grief when young children die.

1

Marriage Relations

During my fieldwork I was often confronted with contrasts. Sometimes I experienced the hopelessness and desperation of the mothers. Despite heavy and incessant work they could hardly feed themselves and their children. Their husbands, and men in general, were frequently commented on as *ka bali nada* (totally worthless). The world of mothers was full of constraints, and adversity marked their lives. I could see it with my own eyes: these women were unhappy, exploited, oppressed, and powerless. At other times, I admired the pride and self-confidence of these very same women, their initiative, and their ingenious solutions to diverse obstacles. Social gatherings were often easy-going, and relaxed and women shared humorous stories, *brinkadeira* (fun, jokes), and danced. I listened to people of all ages who talked about their mothers and grandmothers with love and respect. I concluded that these women knew how to enjoy life, and they were certainly respected, bright, and enterprising.

How can I explain these varied views? Are my interpretations of the women's situation in Biombo somehow inconsistent? Am I oscillating between the two extremes of either attributing them no agency, or too much: one day perceiving them as oppressed and passive victims in an unfair and harsh world, the next day glorifying their daily struggle for survival?

The question of women's subordination was a central issue in feminist anthropological studies in the 1970s (MacCormack and Strathern 1980, Ortner and Whitehead 1981, Reiter 1975, Rosaldo and Lamphere 1974). Women's relative status or power was estimated through cross-cultural comparisons and their subordination was mainly taken for granted.[1] The implications of symbolic interpretations and varied cultural logic of gender was examined and important factors for female domination, such as mode of production, division of labor, and structures of power, were studied. While in 1977 a review of studies on women's status called for further research (Quinn 1977), another review in 1988 concluded that "the old and simple determinants, along with the concept of 'status,' have been found to be multidimensional; they have given way to complex embedded processes" (Mukhopadhyay and Higgins 1988:486).

One of the questions raised in the 1970s concerned the relationship between rules of tracing descent and women's status. Alice Schlegel (1972) argued that there was a general tendency to allocate more power to women in matrilineal societies than in patrilineal ones, in particular when residence was also matrilocal. Schlegel found a great deal of variation in female status within matrilineal societies, depending on the interplay of authority between a woman's husband and her brother; she concludes that matrilineal groups in Africa are husband dominant. Schlegel was concerned with "the matrilineal puzzle," a term first used by Audrey Richards in 1950. According to Richards (1950:246–51), the term refers to the conflicting interests of a husband and her brother in the same woman and her children. Victor Turner, who studied the opposing character of matrilineal kinship ties, emphasized "how they resist disruptive forces put into action by conflicts of interest which arise within the institutional complex of matriliny itself" (1996 [1957]:129). As such, the matrilineal descent contributed to both equilibrium and disorder. Anthropologists have since emphasized the fragile, contradictory nature of matrilineal societies and the frequent tensions between males and conflicting marriage relations (Douglas 1969, Holy 1996:102–15, James 1993:124–30, Stone 1997:109–50). These societies are commonly documented as having high rates of divorce, individual mobility, and strong bonds between mothers and their children.

Recently, older studies on matrilineal societies have been revisited and new findings presented (Brantley 1997, Crehan 1997, Lovett 1997, Peters 1997a). Pauline E. Peters (1997b) points out that since the 1970s authors concerned with matrilineal societies find women to have more authority than formerly recognized. Still, according to Peters, recent studies highlight "the degree to which matriliny was misperceived, misrepresented and derogated by travelers, missionaries, the colonial state and non-matrilineal African groups" (134). She emphasizes the importance of thinking of matrilineal societies as a cluster of features rather than a totality. For Peters matrilineal societies do not contain more "puzzles" than others, "but more contradictions are produced" for these societies as they are minorities within the larger society as well as globally (141). Further, she argues, "the matrilineal puzzle is worth revisiting, but with a more explicit gendered and historical approach" (142).

Focus on gender has contributed to a resurgence in kinship studies.[2] After a crisis in kinship studies, mainly due to controversy around the definition of kinship, Sylvia Junko Yanagisako and Jane Fishburne Collier declared in 1987 that their "goal is at once to revitalize the study of kinship and to situate the study of gender at the theoretical core of anthropology by calling into question the boundary between these two fields" (1987:1). They note that both gender and kinship "have foundered on the unquestioned assumption that the biological given difference in the roles of men and women in sexual procreation lies in the core of the cultural organization of gender, even as it constitutes the genealogical grid at the core of kinship studies" (49). Like Schneider (1984), Yanagisako and Fishburne argue that anthropological theory of kinship has always been based on Western folk theory of sexual reproduction, and only by calling the biological 'facts' into question can we begin to ask how other cultures might understand gender, kinship, and procreation.[3] As an alternative to the study of kinship, a domain "already marked out" and with an arbitrary distinction between biology and culture, Janet Carsten proposes study of relatedness described "in terms of indigenous statements and practices" (2000b:3). Carsten argues this would allow for a cross-cultural comparison of "ways of being related," and contribute to new understandings about "how relatedness may be composed of various components—substance, feeding, living together, procreation, emotion—elements which are themselves not necessarily bounded entities but may overflow or contain parts of each other or take new forms" (34).[4]

Anthropologists have long wrestled with the relation between structure and agency. The concepts "limited good" (Foster 1965) and "culture of poverty" (Lewis 1966) echo a tradition that tends to strip disadvantaged people of agency and at times blame the victims by identifying the cause of the misery as inside their own heads. Paul Farmer (1999:6–12, 82–88) warns against "an exaggeration of personal agency" frequently found in commentaries on those at high risk of contracting HIV. Instead of taking into account structural violence, which emerges from the unequal distribution of power and resources, victims may be blamed for not protecting themselves.[5] According to Farmer (1996:274), the world's poor, particularly women, are those who suffer most from structural violence.[6] Concerned with the experiences of mothers facing extreme poverty and violence in Brazil, Scheper-Hughes opts for "a middle ground," and she warns against either reducing "the subjectivity and agency of subjects to a discourse on victimization" or "romanticizing human suffering or trivializing its effects on the human spirit, consciousness, and will" (1992:533). On the other hand, Sherry Ortner (1996) emphasizes the importance of practice theory for gender studies and proposes the term "serious game" as a model of practice. In all "serious games," which have more or less outspoken rules, she argues, there are numerous players who participate. By thinking in terms of players, Ortner proposes that subjects are not simply passive, but active and intentional. Thus she refocuses attention on subjects' struggles and power (20).

Throughout this book I am concerned with Biombo mothers' dedication to their children, in other words, their struggle to keep them alive. How can I avoid presenting that struggle as either hopeless or a heroic act? While I take the structures that curtail the actions of individual mothers into account I take seriously Ortner's proposal (1996) to think of their fight for the lives of their children as a "serious game." One of the most important arenas in which this game is played in Biombo is the Papel marriage, which is the focus of this chapter. In the following pages I will present a general description of Papel marriage practices, as well as the stories of individual women. Views presented of men are inevitably influenced by the women's somewhat unfavorable portrayals of them. I examine marriage with a particular attention to the division of labor, decision making, and emotional relationships in line with Connell (1987).[7] I have chosen to present the fundamentals of the Papel matrilineal kinship system following Ladislav Holy's description of today's anthropological interest in kinship: "Instead of starting from the description of the kinship system of any particular society, anthropologists now pay attention to kinship relations inasmuch as these are of relevance in the processes on which their study focuses" (1996:5). How are the lives of Papel women affected by the custom of tracing a person's descent through a mother's lineage *(djorson)*, which is expressed in daily language as "coming from breast milk" *(sai na liti)* or gestation from "a shared womb" *(junta barriga)*? Are there any other important relationships?

I begin this chapter with an introduction to two contradictory characteristics of daily life in Biombo: continuity and change. Continuity is emphasized with reference to the matrilineal kinship structure and *lei di prumedu* (the original law), which includes the sphere of religion. At the same time, the changing times *(mundu i abri* or "the opening of the world")* are

also noted. Marriage practices are highly marked by these two contradictory trends.

Times Are Changing

Apili is an old woman in the neighborhood. She lives with several grandchildren in her own house on the outskirts of the village. Apili's house is
newly constructed, made of adobe bricks and corrugated iron. There is a
lovely cemented veranda around the house that always provides shade.
Apili's children are grown up and they take good care of her. She is also on
reasonably good terms with her husband, who lives in another house, some
300 meters away, with Apili's younger co-wife and their children.

Apili likes to have fun, and in the cashew season she serves fermented
cashew wine to visitors.[8] One day I join her and Maria, Apili's friend who
often passes by for a bit of gossip. It is about noon and Apili is busy clean-
ing fish and cutting mango for lunch; the rice is already boiling on the
stove. Apili is stripped to the waist and I note the elaborate scarification she
has on her chest. I ask her why so many old women have scarification on
their body. "Oh oho, you mean this . . . this was only done to be able to
boast," Apili says, and explains that in the old days a girl whose marriage
was already planned would go with some girlfriends to an old man who
would use a little knife to cut into the skin on her back and chest. Apili
laughs:

> There were girls who could not tolerate the pain and they gave up, you
> understand. So they had scarification only on one side of their chest or their
> back. Others endured the pain or did not feel any discomfort at all. Or so
> they said. You know girls were proud of their ornamental cuts, and those
> who did not complain were considered courageous. But those who gave up
> or did not dare felt ashamed.

Apili stands up to look after her stove and get us more wine. "Times are
changing. Today no young girl has cuts made on her body. Adult women
who have scars often feel ashamed and try to hide them with clothes," she
tells me. "It is like that, Maria, isn't it?" Maria nods. She is in her forties and
has no cuts on her body.

Apili gulps down a full cup of wine. "Jónína, times are changing. You
want to hear about the marriage arrangements of the old days? If you were
lucky your marriage was already planned when you were born." Apili explains to me that when a pregnant woman was close to giving birth, a man
who wanted to marry the woman's child (if it turned out to be a daughter)
brought the woman firewood as a declaration of his interests. Later the
suitor sent his father to the family of the girl to confirm his desires. If the

parents agreed he would fulfill the marriage transactions and later marry the girl when she was considered physically mature enough, twelve to sixteen years old. Nowadays it is rare that a marriage of a girl is arranged before her birth, Apili tells me.

Maria explains that parents still want to decide whom their daughters are to marry, since both have an interest in their children's marriages. Often a father is concerned that his children will marry within his own mother's lineage. "You know, because children belong to their mother's lineage the father wants his first son and his first daughter to marry within his own lineage. The mother's brother has the right to arrange the marriage of the second girl," she explains.

"So fathers still decide whom their children marry?" I ask.

"Yeah," Maria answers hesitantly. After a short silence, she adds: "But not always in that sense. Anyway, some fathers really want to decide. In case the mother of the girl, or the girl herself, does not agree with the proposed marriage, they will try to hinder the plans. If they are good at arguing they may succeed."

Later I learn that in the old days, men also decorated their body with cuts. Inácio, an old man, tells me: "Long time ago, men had cuts made on their arms. It was no longer done when I was young. We have stopped that. Today neither men nor women have cuts made on their bodies. The world is more clever today."

To endure pain to adorn one's body, once a source of virtue and pride, is today a reminder of backwardness and stupidity. Likewise, today a girl's marriage is rarely arranged before her birth, and it is no longer solely up to her father or her mother's brother to find her a husband. Nonetheless, a Papel girl is still born to marry, and a mother, no less than a father, has an interest in finding her daughter a good husband. It is essential for a woman to enter a ceremonial Papel marriage, not only for economic and reproductive reasons but for religious reasons as well.

Religion

Most of the Papel who reside in Biombo practice religion according to what they call the original law. They believe in reincarnation, which means that human souls *(defuntu)* circulate through deaths and births between "this world" *(es mundu)* and "the other world" *(utru mundu)*. The one and only God of the Papel, named **Ursi** in Papel, or *Deus* in Kriol, decides who is to enter the other world. Those who die old, when God calls on them, are welcome to settle in the world of the dead. Those who die untimely deaths are not welcome because God has not asked for them to come. They are victims of *mufunesa* (misfortune).

The Kriol word *mufunesa* is frequently used in Guinea-Bissau. It connotes a mishap or a tragedy caused by an intentional agent, either a human being, dead or alive, or a supernatural force. *Mufunesa* cannot be alleviated without an identification of the agent and a ritual action to eliminate it. The meaning of *mufunesa* is based on the assumption that a number of supernatural, invisible entities influence events and social relations in the human world. These supernatural beings tend to reside in items such as amulets, horns, wooden sticks, or a hut, but also in particular places, often close to a water source, by the sea, or at the base of a tree. These locations function as shrines where the spirits or supernatural beings can be consulted in case of problems, such as marital conflicts, bad harvest, theft, infertility, disease, or death. An individual or a group of supplicants ask it to grant a request through the mediation of a religious specialist, who collaborates with the respective entity. A kind of vow or contract is made, and when the request is completed an offering *(torna boka)* has to be given, otherwise the supplicant risks having her or his family suffer still more problems.[9] If a request is not fulfilled, the supplicant is free from fulfilling her or his part of the vow. Religious specialists, females and males, such as *balobeiru (**n'pene**)* and *djambakus (**nessai**)* mediate contracts of this type.[10] They also do divinations of various types, called *bota sorti* (casting lots), as do many other ritual specialists and healers (see chapter 4).[11]

Balobeiru can mediate the word of God, either through an ancestral spirit or a divine instrument named *kansaré (**bukau**)*. *Balobeiru* who mediate the word of God through an ancestral spirit are of particular interest to their lineage, and they exercise influential roles as advisers and helpers in both public and private matters.[12] The souls of persons who die untimely deaths or those whose funeral rites have not been properly performed will wander around in this world, and they may harm or even cause death to those who belong to the same lineage. Some of these souls will finally settle in a kapok tree *(Ceiba pentandra)* and indicate a person to become its collaborator.[13] Each *baloba* belongs to the lineage of the ancestral soul that has settled in it, as does its respective *balobeiru* or collaborator.

It is not only through the ancestral spirit that a *balobeiru* can mediate the word of God. The second kind of *balobeiru* can hear the word of God through *kansaré,* which is a powerful community-based divination instrument, materialized in a bier.[14] *Kansaré* is divine and works independently of lineage. It serves the whole community, particularly in combating disasters, such as war, drought, and epidemics like cholera and measles. *Kansaré*'s primary role is nonetheless to identify sorcerers *(fetiseru),* that is, persons who are engaged in "bad work" *(mal feitu).* Yet, it is not itself used for bad work, in contrast to ancestral spirits, who like humans have their weaknesses and might be tempted to become engaged in sorcery. In addition, a *kansaré* is consulted for individual and family matters.

Djambakus is a religious specialist, a woman or a man, who is a collaborator or an "owner" of *iran* or **ussai** (spirit). *Iran* is a term that refers to a wide range of spiritual beings and forces, but also to the ceremonial places dedicated to these spirits.[15] *Iran* often choose a new collaborator within the same family as the former *djambakus,* but not necessarily the same lineage. Most Papel compounds have their own *iran* whose collaborator or *djambakus* is one of their members. A *djambakus* combats sorcery by collaborating with *iran,* but at the same time a *djambakus* is capable of engaging in sorcery on his or her own. Many *djambakus* specialize in healing, using a wide range of herbal medicines and the spiritual powers of their respective *iran.* An *iran* is sometimes described as "a child who is sent to run errands" *(meninu mandadu),* which means that an *iran* obeys orders. However, sometimes an *iran* has a will of its own (see chapter 5).

Both *balobeiru* and *djambakus* are appointed to become religious specialists through *mufunesa.* A person who repeatedly suffers *mufunesa* such as child death, disease, infertility, loss of property, or failing health, will finally begin to suspect that some ancestral spirit, *kansaré* or an *iran,* is sending a sign that she or he should become a *balobeiru* or a *djambakus.*

Paula is one of the women with whom I often discuss child deaths. She frequently begins to talk about her own *mufunesa.* When I first meet Paula she had given birth to seven children, three of whom had died, and had one miscarriage. Besides, all her pigs get sick and die while the neighbors' pigs thrive. Her husband is a miserable human being, Paula complains. Her father, who was a prominent *djambakus,* is dead, as is her mother. Later, Paula gave birth to a girl who died at the age of two. Paula became very anxious. She interprets her daughter's death as an indication that she should become a *djambakus.* She tells me she has confirmed through a series of divinations that the *iran* who collaborated with her father is giving her a sign. The problem is that the inauguration ceremony requires economic resources beyond her means. Paula hopes she will be able to arrange for her inaugural ceremony *(ronia iran)* later in life.

Papel women are highly involved in religious life as ritual specialists. In particular, they are involved in a separate female-dominated religious sphere related to *kansaré.* In this context women control the leadership and membership of certain ritual activities.[16] They also frequently participate in religious services. Women's involvement in religious activities, both as providers and participants, is most commonly centralized around questions related to fertility, health (in particular survival of children), and marriage.[17] The reason most often mentioned for women's obligation to marry is religious.

Marriage

Without entering a Papel marriage a woman will not be properly buried, which has consequences for her afterlife. A husband, his heir, or whichever man has paid a bride price for a woman is responsible for performing "the beating-the-drum ceremony" *(toca tchur)* for her. Without the performance of this ceremony a woman's soul will not be allowed to settle in the other world. A woman should be buried at her husband's home and he should arrange for this costly ceremony. In turn the husband (or his heir if the husband is deceased) inherits her private belongings, such as clothes and ornaments, stored in her *mala* (box).

Within the village there are two categories of marriageable men. The first category includes men who have moved to the compound of their mother's brother to inherit from him. Men in this category are likely to be older men and they already have one or more wives they themselves have married, as well as the wives they have inherited from their maternal uncle. The second category of marriageable men are called "sons of the house" or *fidju di kasa.* These men have not yet inherited from their maternal uncle and they live in the compound of their fathers. They are often young men without a wife, but they can also be older men with one or more wives they have married. Upon marriage, a young woman comes to live in the compound *(moransa, **merz**)* of her husband.

Resources are required for a man to marry. The bride price must be paid to the bride's family and the wedding ceremonies must be arranged. Frequently young men migrate to Senegal or to the interior of Guinea-Bissau to earn the money needed to finance a bride price. In earlier times men used to marry late, or around thirty years old. Today men marry younger, sometimes as young as twenty. At times people are preoccupied with the increased value of the bride price and the prestige of a grandiose marriage party. The groom and his family pay all the costs, which vary greatly depending on the status of the families involved as well as the girl's estimated worth. The bride price for a disabled girl, for example, is reduced depending on her impairment.[18]

A husband should provide his wife with a house *(kasa, **ku**)* of her own, or at least a separate room, in his compound. It is also his duty to provide rice for his wife and her children. No parent wants her or his daughter to marry a man who is unable to sustain a family because of impairment. Pupra is in his late thirties and he is blind. Despite his handicap, Pupra repairs the fishing nets and maintains the fences around the gardens. He is unmarried and according to his mother he will most likely never marry. His mother feels pity for her son but is resigned to the fact that no girl wants to marry him. Some people say that a blind man, or a disabled one, can marry but only if his father is rich enough to pay the bride price and give his son rice from his fields.[19] Nonetheless, disabled men are at a disadvantage when it comes to marriage. At the same time, being unmarried does not have as serious religious consequences for men as for women. The family may be able to support an unmarried son and can arrange for his funeral upon his death. Pupra's mother explains: "With disabled girls it is different, it is easier to find them a husband. A disabled girl can always become an additional wife to an already married man. She can contribute to the household in some way, and of course the bride price will be reduced. You understand, all women have to marry, if not they can't be buried properly."

It is considered to be shameful for parents to have to bury an adult unmarried daughter. A Papel woman who never marries according to the ritual custom of her people will be treated as an unmarried girl, so-called *badjuda*, for her whole life, even if she has children. Further, the daughters of an unmarried woman are not allowed to marry according to Papel custom. Mothers are, however, not only concerned about the marriages of their daughters but also of their sons.

No mother wants her son to suffer because of a lazy or badly behaved wife. A woman's daughter-in-law will move into her compound and assist with the work and hopefully take good care of her when age becomes a burden. Ideally, the relations between a mother-in-law, called *dona* (a term also used for grandmother, and a range of other related elderly women), and her daughter-in-law (*neto*, a term also used for a grandchild) are ideally characterized by affection and mutual respect. "These two women love the same man, a son and a husband, and thus they will like each other. Or at least it used to be like that," Juana explains. "A daughter-in-law should treat her *dona* with respect and give her food, and the *dona* should carry her infant on her back, and take care of other children when her daughter-in-law goes for a journey." Nevertheless, I am told, some daughters-in-law do not take adequate care of their *dona*. A widow who is unlucky with her daughter-in-law may have no other alternative than to return to her natal household, to one of her daughters' homes, to the home of some close relative, or to manage by herself.

Arranged Marriage

The arrangement of marriages is obviously an important issue for women, both as future wives and mothers. A group of women who are discussing marriage do not agree as to whether or not parents should arrange marriage for their daughters.

"You should never force your daughter to marry a man she does not like," Segunda maintains. "Thank God that forced marriage is not so common today."

"Is this really true?" I ask. "Aren't there many young girls married to old men in the villages?"

"That's true, but these girls are village girls, they don't attend school. They are backward," she responds. She is right in that few village girls go to school.[20]

"School is a problem," explains Nintica, a village woman in her forties. "Look at those girls who go to school. They do not accept arranged marriages. Even in the villages some run away before or after marriage. It is good for girls to go school, but I am not sure what is better, that a girl goes to school and becomes pregnant, or stays at home and becomes properly married. We know that with time you will learn to love your husband. All parents want their daughters to marry a good husband. When the marriage is not arranged young people think too much about appearance. A good looking man is not always the best one."[21]

Ana, a village woman in her thirties has no doubts that a girl should never be married without her consent. If the girl discovers that her own choice of a husband was a bad one she can leave him, she argues. Ana's husband forced their daughter to marry a man from an influential family, but the man was violent and hit her daughter so badly while pregnant that she miscarried. "It is always best to decide yourself and then you have nobody to blame," Ana says.

Segunda and Ana start discussing girls who become pregnant with young men in the hope that their fathers will allow them to marry those men. These girls hope that their appointed suitor will not want to marry them if they are already pregnant by somebody else. However, fathers may forestall such a situation by giving their daughters away for marriage at an even younger age.

"That's right, fathers more often than mothers want to force their daughters to marry, but girls who choose their own husbands are not always so lucky," Nintinca argues. "You might find out that your husband is a sorcerer, or that you don't like his family. I was lucky, I was married against my will, and my marriage is a good one."

"Look at my bad luck . . . I chose my husband myself and he is hopeless," Helena proclaims. Not without exhaustion in her voice, she adds, "There does not seem to be any rule to what is the best way to find a good husband. Marriage is a question of good or bad luck."

With or without the support of their mothers, some girls do not accept their arranged marriages. As the women here indicate, this applies in particular to girls in more urban areas and girls who have attended school. The latter are seen as unwilling to marry elderly men or men without an education. Parents also fear that daughters will return from school with a "package" *(enkumenda),* which means they become pregnant, as commonly happens. Some girls run away to Bissau, or somewhere else, either before the arranged marriage is realized, directly after the marriage ceremony, or later. Escapes always require that the girls have a place to go, that is, someone who is willing to take them into their home despite their disobedience.

Suicide is a more desperate escape from an unwanted marriage. One girl killed herself because she was forced to marry a man she didn't want three months earlier. The girl never accepted her husband and refused food from his house; instead, food from her parents' house was taken to her every day. The women who comment on this event are quite shocked. "To kill oneself because of a marriage is too much. You never know how your life will be in the end," one of them argues, and the other women agree. Besides, the women are preoccupied about the afterlife of the girl. A person who "kills her head" *(mata si kabessa)* will not settle in the other world and might cause her own family many problems, they say.

Times are changing and many parents are worried about finding suitable husbands for their daughters. Geralda is one of them. She does not like arranged marriages and she says she will never allow her husband to arrange the marriage for their only daughter. She herself was forced to marry some fifteen years ago. She tried to protest but without success. Geralda maintains, however, that today's men are not honest when it comes to sexual behavior and marriage:

> It is not easy to have young daughters nowadays. Girls are better to have than boys because they help their mothers. The problem is that today it is difficult to find your daughter a good husband. You know, young men often stay away and so there are more girls than men. This situation makes men irresponsible. A young man pretends he will marry a girl but when she becomes pregnant he will not accept her anymore, nor does he take economic responsibility as the father of the child.

At least some young men accept the consequences of their actions. João's marriage is quite typical, and indeed, it is both a result of romantic love and a certain degree of parental enforcement. One day he gets to know a young girl from a neighboring village. They like each other and at some point she becomes pregnant. The girl's family demands that João marries her. He accepts but apparently he is not happy about it. João's mother is also disappointed. She feels her son is too young to marry (he's only twenty years old), and now he has to sustain a family. Of course, she admits, he was wrong; he should not have impregnated the girl. João, with the help of his mother and her family, has to buy several items such as rice, *panos* (textiles), a dog, wine, a pig, and hens to give to the family of the girl when he and several family members from his father's lineage go to the bride's compound to fetch her. I am not welcome to participate. "The old people will not like it," I am told. Instead, what happens when a suitor fetches his bride is explained to me:

> A bride will sit on her knees in front of the compound's *iran* (spirit) when a man comes to fetch her. He goes to her and stretches her waistband until it snaps.[22] Then, her family takes off all her clothes and she puts on a *pano* the man brings with him, you know, that's why we say that a man dresses his wife when he marries *(visti mindjer)*. The bride is taken away to his village, but a pig, a hen, and a dog are slaughtered and left with her family, together with wine.

I am invited to participate in the wedding party held at the home of João's father's brother. The bride's family does not participate, but had their own party in their village the night before, after the bride had left with the groom and his company. When I enter the house I see the bride sitting on a mattress in a dark room with two girlfriends. She is about sixteen years old, a nice-looking girl, dressed in a grayish, worn *pano;* she appears shy. An elderly woman enters the room, goes to the girl and smears red palm oil on her chest. Only when the festivities and all the ceremonies have finished will she wash off the red palm oil, I am told. The bride is embarrassed and tries to haul up the *pano* over her breasts. João enters the room and cuts a little lock from her hair, and then he goes outdoors where his friends are listening to African popular music. Gradually, the house is full of visitors and still more are outdoors. A little later an enormous amount of rice with sour milk and red palm oil is served. People push their way to the food. It is chaotic and noisy. Within a few minutes no more food is left; it is "famine time" *(tempu di fomi)*, the last month of the rain period and food is scarce in the community. Most of the visitors leave. Things become calmer. Some women clean up while others sit and chat.

A woman I recognize as João's paternal aunt looks tired and stretches her legs. She had been at the home of the bride the night before. "What a terrible crying. The poor girl never stopped crying, and I myself could not help crying also," she says. The women all agree that João made the best out of a difficult situation despite the fact that time was short for preparations: what counts is that he married the girl.

"What a big pig and beautiful hens João gave her family. And red wine in quantities," one of João's aunts says, then she adds: "Nonetheless, this marriage will not last long." Then she informs us that later in the evening one of the most holy wedding ceremonies will take place, where the family of the bride will participate. She wonders if I would be allowed to participate. "No," an elderly woman affirms. "The old people would not like it."

The next day, the so-called holy week (*semana sagradu*) of the wedding begins. For a week, the bride and other married women stay in a separate house. Only married Papel women are allowed to participate. Ana tells me that the holy week corresponds to the circumcision ceremony (*fanadu*) for boys, except that the girl will not be circumcised.[23] The groom and other men perform their ceremonies, she explains. When I ask Ana about more details she responds: "I will not tell you what happens during this week. It is sacred. I will not even tell my daughters. They will find out themselves when they marry. Nobody will tell you."

I become curious about the holy week. Later, I ask Juana about this week. She laughs and responds: "Nothing special, we eat good food and have fun." I also ask Segunda the same question. "We eat, drink, and dance," she answers. "That's all." None of these women is ready to give me any details. I decide to stop my inquiry, as it is unlikely to yield any clues. I seek solace in the fact that there are other outsiders who are not supposed to know. Why should I know? Indirectly I understand that there are various ceremonies performed and the other women will inform the bride about how she should behave as a respectable married woman. The importance of friendship and coming together of age groups (*mandjuandade*, **orana**) is repeatedly emphasized.[24] For sure, it is a great party.

Mixed Marriages

Today fathers are still said to be eager to marry their children within their own lineage but in practice their power is reduced. When a man and a woman decide they want to marry, the parents are not always happy with their choice.[25] This happens in particular when the partner is not Papel.

Mixed marriages are considered difficult; however, some are easier than others. Marriages with the Balanta or the Manjaco are seen as reasonably workable, and they are quite common. The marriages with the Islamic groups are, on the other hand, seen as particularly difficult. In practice, it isn't feasible for a non-Muslim Papel man to marry a Muslim girl. A Papel woman and a Muslim man will also have a hard time together, people say. Nevertheless, some Papel women consider Islamic men to be more polite to women and more concerned about their family than Papel men, which is appreciated. The problem is that Muslim men will most likely require their wives to convert to Islam.

Earlier the Catholic mission did not allow Papel people who married in the church to also marry according to the Papel tradition. Today the mission is not wholly insistent on this point, but it still expresses its disapproval.

Nonetheless, many Catholic couples have gone through both ceremonies. A Papel woman who marries a man of another ethnic group, or one who is Christian (Catholic or Protestant), will be under strong pressure from her family to go through the Papel marriage ceremony as well. Sábado and Mariama are both Papel, and like their husbands who are Manjaco and Balanta, respectively, they belong to Christian churches. Mariama is Catholic and Sábado is Protestant. To please their parents both have undergone the Papel marriage ceremonies. "You have to," Mariama says. "You understand, if not you will never be considered an adult woman. You will be *badjuda* (unmarried girl) for your whole life." Sábado, who lives in Bissau, finds the Papel customs somewhat tiresome and demanding. "The custom of the Papel is harsh *(duru)*. If you don't conform you always encounter a lot of problems," she complains. "There are so many ceremonies that have to be performed. A man who wants to marry a Papel woman has to find a Papel substitute for some of the ceremonies."

Mamadu, a young Muslim man, encounters many problems when he falls in love with a Papel girl, Linda. They decide to marry. Mamadu does everything to conform: he arranges what is necessary for the wedding such as a dog, a pig, wine, *panos,* and other items. He also contracts a married Papel man who is willing to be his substitute in those ceremonies in which he is not allowed to participate because he is not Papel. However, for some reason the wedding is repeatedly postponed. Augusta tells me that Linda's maternal grandmother does not want her granddaughter to marry a Muslim man, so she covertly obstructs the ceremony. Finally, the dog is dead, the pig is eaten up, and no wine is left. Mamadu realizes that he will never succeed in marrying Linda. They start to live together and with time their everyday life becomes somewhat complicated. Linda often drinks with her friends, but Mamadu, as a Muslim, is not happy about this. Linda is also outspoken and does not always behave respectfully in front of Mamadu and his friends. Still worse, she sometimes says his people are intolerant of non-Muslims. Finally, in a quarrel, Mamadu becomes furious and hits Linda, who takes all her belongings and leaves to live in her mother's house. Mamadu's neighbor, an elderly Muslim man, expresses his disapproval of Mamadu's loss of control; a man should not beat a woman like that. Of course Mamadu can blame himself; it is obvious that a Papel woman will never behave like a respectable Muslim wife, the neighbor argues. The neighboring Papel women agree that in fact Linda is lazy and has bad manners. They have advised her to take care; otherwise her relation with Mamadu would not last long. Linda regrets everything and wants to return to Mamadu, but he refuses to take her back. Later, Mamadu marries a Muslim girl who has given birth to their son. Linda remains unmarried. She is still a *badjuda.*

Subsistence

A husband and a wife have their separate spheres of action and responsibility with respect to the subsistence of the family.

A husband is expected to provide rice for his family. He is thus responsible for the rice fields, if he owns any. The sea has reclaimed a great proportion of the rice fields in Biombo. Outsiders, and indeed some Papel people, claim that the Papel men do not maintain their rice fields because of the matrilineal inheritance rules. These religiously sanctioned and rarely disputed rules indicate that the eldest sister's son of a deceased man is the heir of his land, goods, and compound. The relations between an adult man and his inheritor are not always said to be the best and he comes only to stay in his compound after his uncle has passed away. Cashew plantations and other fruit cultivations are often inherited in line with the law of the Republic, that is, children, males and females, will inherit from their parents.

According to the Papel tradition, the heir also inherits the wives of the deceased, but a widow can choose to leave her husband's compound for her father's house or someone else, possibly a lover.[26] The heir acts more like an administrator than the owner of the compound he inherits. He is likely to build a new house of his own while the widows and their children stay in the house(s) of the deceased. Papel men are said to be reluctant to maintain rice fields that they will not inherit, and some men are even unwilling to inherit from their mother's brothers. To inherit badly maintained or flooded rice fields as well as a number of aged wives who have to be fed and buried is considered a burden by many men. Besides, the heir may have to build new houses for the family. When a rich man dies, however, his sister's sons are all eager to get his property. Sometimes it is decided that more than one of the sister's sons will inherit from such a person.

Men who still have some rice fields prepare the fields and plant the rice while women take care of the transport of both plants and harvest.[27] Men make all major decisions about the rice fields, and they have authority over the harvest. A husband should provide enough rice for the daily consumption of wives, children, and other members of the compound. He should also give a part of the harvest to his wives who in turn give it to their own family members. Finally, he will reserve some rice for ceremonial use, for example, in case of a death or marriage.

Besides the traditional responsibility for rice, males, but mainly boys, tend cattle. Some men occasionally hunt animals such as forest goats, gazelles, porcupines, hares, and monkeys. Livestock is not slaughtered for daily consumption and large animals such as cows are only consumed during certain ceremonies. A few men fish from canoes with large nets in the rivers and ocean. The wives of these men are responsible for marketing the catch. Men are responsible for the construction of houses, but women and children assist in the construction work.[28] Some men specialize in iron-work, and Papel men are renowned for their weaving skills. Many men, in particular young men, take seasonal migratory work, such as extracting palm oil, or they migrate for longer periods, even years, as workers or weavers in Senegal or Gambia.

Women are responsible for taking care of children, as well as for the care of those who are sick and elderly. Women collect firewood, fetch water, prepare food, wash clothes, produce pots, and make palm oil, salt, and soap. As far as food is concerned women are responsible for the sauce (mafé) most often made of fish (rarely meat) and vegetables, which is eaten with boiled rice (bianda). Thus women make all major decisions about horticulture and fishing. Women do all the horticultural work and children help with tasks like watering. Women fish year-round with scope nets along the shore and in inland streams. With the help of children, they collect oysters, shrimp, various types of shellfish, and small fish. Certain women even fish from canoes with large nets, as do men.[29] Assisted by children, women tend pigs, goats, and poultry. They also sell fish, fruits, vegetables, kana,[30] palm oil, and palm wine all year around or seasonally, depending on the product. Women sell their products locally, in bigger towns or in the capital, Bissau, or they sell their products to intermediaries who are often female, so-called bida. Women play a crucial part in the cash economy of their family, and often they earn more money than their husbands do.

During the cashew season from April to June it is not considered worthwhile for women to engage in other economic activity than collection of cashew fruits and nuts. They collect the fruits, press them, and allow the juice to ferment to wine. The wine is sold for direct consumption or it is distilled to a strong alcoholic beverage (kana). Women sell the cashew nuts to traders for cash or rice and thereby they have become the de facto providers of rice for the family. Every year, the months August to November are recognized as the famine time in Biombo, because the rice acquired through exchange during the cashew season is finished and the rice in the fields, if there is any, is still not ripe. A couple of months before the cashew fruit is ripe again in April traders begin to offer rice on credit.

Today, the main challenge in everyday life is keeping up adequate supplies of rice. Providing rice has increasingly become the burden of women. Women complain a lot about men, in particular husbands, who do not fulfill their duty to provide the family with rice. Some women also argue their brothers are only concerned about their own wives and children, ignoring their sisters' need for help. Village men, however, have a better reputation than those living in urban areas. The village men work more, women say, in particular those who still cultivate rice fields. Nonetheless, the wives of rice cultivators still have complaints: their husbands only provide small quantities of rice to feed the family, while storing a lot of rice for ceremonial activities. As Maria puts it, "a rich man's family may eat very poorly, only because he wants to keep his rice to boast at ceremonial occasions."

Women are not perfect wives either. Some men complain their wives are lazy, steal resources from their compound and give them away to their own maternal families. Some men say that women sometimes refuse to cook food for them. Indeed, to cook food for a husband is said to be a sacred obligation. Juana explains:

> A Papel wife has to provide *mafé* and she has to cook food for her husband. If you do not cook food for your husband when he is working in the rice fields God will warn you. You will become sick. You will go and make a divination and find out that God is warning you. If you are found guilty you have to tell what you did wrong. You will explain that you prepared food for you and your children when your husband was working. You explain that you wanted to give your children something to eat because they are yours and belong to your lineage. You have to ask for mercy. God will also warn your husband if he treats you badly, and if he is found guilty he will have to explain what he did wrong. You understand, this is like a confession of sin in church, but then the priest is the only one to hear. This is an official confession.

A husband is culturally sanctioned to be the chief of his house. Nevertheless, people disagree about who makes the most important decisions within the household. Some say that men make all the important decisions within and outside the house; others say that women have the responsibility for the house and thus certainly make the most significant decisions. Still others claim that it depends on the personality and position of those involved. Whatever the case, people agree that the wife is the economic commander of her stove. Her money should be pooled together with the contribution of her husband and those of other eventual family members who may eat from her stove. She is then responsible for all purchases and expenditures, such as commercialized food items, but often also clothes, school fees, and health care services.

There is frequently mistrust between couples not only about their respective responsibilities but also the available resources. A woman is supposed to show her earnings to her husband before she spends them. She should also lend him money when he asks for it. In practice, however, a woman only informs her husband about her income if she is on good terms with him. She might refuse to lend him money, or she might claim that she does not have any to lend. Some men become suspicious when their wives earn too much. Segunda maintains that during the first years of her marriage she always informed her husband about all the money she earned. Once, Segunda had a lot of work and she showed her husband all the money she had earned. He accused her of adultery; there must be some rich lover who had given her all that money, he argued. Since then Segunda has never told her husband about her income. In any case, she asserts, she has to feed all their children, and him as well.

Polygynous Marriage

Papel men can have as many wives as they can afford to marry.[31] Thus, in daily life many married women not only have to manage with their husbands but also with a varied number of co-wives. Opinions on polygyny vary. Some people find it unacceptable under any circumstances; others say it depends on the situation. Still others say it is the only way, as it is men's nature to want many wives. Many women see polygyny as desirable because it alleviates their burden of domestic work, especially in the villages.[32] Many people acknowledge that polygyny causes problems in urban areas, but there men tend to have several houses called *kasa-um, kasa-dus, kasa-tres,* et cetera (first house, second house, third house). The "first house" is that of the official wife; the other houses are those of the man's mistresses. These arrangements may be more or less official, but often they are troublesome for those involved.

Ideally, co-wives treat each other as sisters or best friends and assist each other. In case of need, they should help each other and take care of each other's children. The first wife is the senior one and she should be *dona kasa* or the boss of the other women.[33] Ideally, the younger co-wives cook and the senior wife serves the food. However, relations between co-wives are not always good. Rivalry, jealousy, and hatred are well-recognized problems, frequently resulting in accusations of sorcery that lead to children being hurt. A mother would not boast of her luck with children in front of her less successful co-wife; that would be to tempt one's fate.

Imburquenha is an elderly village woman who is a senior wife with two younger co-wives. She argues: "You have to treat your husband well, you have to serve him food, you have to fetch water and firewood, and you have to sleep with your husband. You understand, so it is better to share a man with other women." Most women agree that it implies less work for women to have co-wives, particularly if they share a stove. But Papel co-wives do not always share a stove, especially in more urban areas. With expanded commercialization there is not only an increased tendency for a husband and a wife to have a separate economy but also for co-wives to have separate stoves. Maria summarizes:

> In those days when the husband furnished the rice his wives were more willing to share a stove, but now when women have to buy rice themselves they will not share a stove with a co-wife, particularly not during difficult times,

and when they have different numbers of mouths to feed. And when there is famine you will not share a stove with other people. You only think about feeding your own children and yourself. You would not risk spending your little rice or money on other people who may pretend they do not have any. In times of hunger you only take care of your own children, not those of your co-wives.

However, Maria points out that if co-wives are on good terms, and also in periods of hard work and when rice is abundant, such as during the cashew season, they often prefer to share a stove. "When I was a child my father always gave rice to each of his wives in accordance to the number of mouths they had to feed, but most of the time they did not share a stove." She emphasizes that her father used to treat all his wives equally and they had friendly relations. Maria and Imburquenha agree that a husband is most likely failing in his duties if his wives have bad relations.

A good husband respects the authority of his first wife in relation to the younger wives, he always contributes to each stove in accordance to the number of mouths it feeds, he gives all his wives similar gifts, and he never shows a preference for one of his wives. Only a few men seem to manage these duties, however. Impors, who is in his late sixties with three wives, is a successful husband. Adite, his senior wife is a striking woman. She likes to stroll around with the first child of her youngest co-wife on her back. Her own children are grown up, some are married and she already has a number of grandchildren. "Adite is still beautiful, despite her age," her neighbor points out to me with admiration in her voice. "Only when you have such a hardworking husband as Impors and younger co-wives who collaborate are you still beautiful when you become old."

One day I am invited to be present at a meeting on the women's situation and their rights. Both village and urban women are invited to participate, but a group of educated men from Bissau lead the discussion. Polygyny is one of the topics. The men refer to nature while discussing polygyny. "Men want many women. Men have a sexual need for women during their whole life while women become old earlier and their sexual desire for men will disappear," one of the men declares. The men talk about the custom of having mistresses (so-called "extra houses") and polygyny as the same phenomenon. "It is an adaptation to the Catholic tradition and life in urban areas," one of them argues.[34]

The women become upset. They do not accept this interpretation and argue that polygyny implies certain rules about responsibilities and rights for all involved: the man, his wives, and their children. The *kasa-um, kasa-dus* practice is anarchy without obligations and rights, they say. Some of the women are preoccupied with the lack of rights for the official wife, while others are more worried about the rights of those women belonging to the extra houses.

The men repeat their argument that polygyny is natural. Women cease to have sexual relations when they stop to give birth, they say. A young woman answers that women do not become old earlier than men do, it only appears so because women work too much.[35] She maintains that it is unacceptable when a man has more wives than he can sexually satisfy. "A young woman should not have to accept living with an impotent man [*omi mole* (soft man)]. Everybody knows that all men are not sexually potent for their whole life and it is a shame that a Papel woman is not allowed to divorce her husband if he is impotent," she argues. Another woman indicates that to stop having children and to stop having sexual relations are not the same thing. The discussion becomes a little chaotic, and finally a middle-aged man stands up and expresses his indignation: "It is shameful nowadays to observe elderly women flirt with young men. Of course women should have their rights, but some limitations are necessary to avoid risking the family, which is the most important institution of our society. Everybody should respect the family."

After a short silence a young woman comments ironically that people should respect each other. Then she tells us about an old neighbor woman:

> That old woman is the first wife of her husband. She and her husband have six children but three died in childhood. Now all her children have left home and live in Bissau. Some years ago her husband suddenly married a young wife. Now he only contributes to the stove of his young wife who has already given birth to two children. The old woman is alone with her stove, her health is bad and she has difficulties finding food. Still worse, she feels she has been humiliated. She should be the senior wife of her husband but instead she is more like an outcast.

Who is to blame? One of the men blames the young co-wife; she should show her senior co-wife more solidarity and at least give her food to eat. The women protest and argue that the husband is at fault. The old woman is not capable of being the chief wife because of her failing health, but regardless, he should show his first wife more respect. "It is natural for men to want new things, but they have to remember that what is new today is old tomorrow. You women, you have to fight for the older women, because you will be old yourselves one day," the man responds. A woman points out that the Balanta women bring up one of their nieces and later when the girl is old enough she becomes her caregiver's co-wife.[36] In that way the Balanta women secure loyalty within the group of co-wives. "A good idea," she murmurs thoughtfully, but then she adds: "But it is true. Women sometimes arrange for a co-wife when they have too much work, only because they want help. Sometimes they treat their younger co-wives badly. We women should treat each other with more solidarity."

When polygyny is discussed, the conclusion is frequently that it is natural for men to have many women, and that co-wives should have friendly and supportive relations. When co-wives argue women blame the husband, who should respect the rules of the game: he should recognize his senior wife's superior position within the group of co-wives and distribute all material and emotional favors equally. Often I hear women lament their situation and complain about their husbands or men in general. Juana sums up her view: "The Papel man of today is not worth anything, except to beget children. Men will not care for their children once they are born, they will not provide rice, nor will they pay for school, clothes, or medicines." The only merit some women attribute to the Papel man is his potential to impregnate his wife. However, not all women are equally lucky in that aspect either.

Young women frequently marry old men, and it is well recognized that such men may not always be virile enough to make them pregnant. A woman married to an impotent or infertile man is likely to leave him for another man or find a lover to have children with. Infertile husbands only rarely seem to hinder women from succeeding in their effort to have children of their own. Of course not all aged men are impotent. When I ask a village woman in her forties if her husband, recognized as one of the oldest men in his village, is the true father of her one-year old daughter she responds, laughing, "for sure he is; he never forgets to sleep with me, not even when he is dead drunk."

Juana maintains that it has always been, and still is, accepted that a young woman married to an old man will take lovers. In such cases, married women take young unmarried men as their lovers, but this should be kept secret within a group of close friends. When the lover marries, a woman should send her co-wife with a gift to be delivered to him through his mother. Juana maintains that married Papel men in the villages do not often have mistresses, or at least they usually did not in the old days. "If a man wants more women he can arrange a new wife," she argues.[37]

There are many opportunities for women to meet men. Women are quite free to travel and to avoid attracting sorcery on the road it is seen as reasonable not always to inform all family members about one's whereabouts. There are also opportunities for age mates to meet through the age groups, *mandjuandade*.[38] Both male and female youngsters who live in a certain area can form and name their own age group. These age groups are important for attendance at weddings and funerals as well as reciprocal assistance. Members also pool money and buy food and wine for parties.[39] Indeed, all the names of the groups I have been told indicate that the aim of these groups is to organize social gatherings and have fun. The name "With one shoe" refers to a person who is in such a hurry for a party that she or he forgets to put on both shoes. "Take my child" refers to a mother who needs a babysitter and "Knocking on the door" indicates a woman who comes home early in the morning and finds her furious husband unwilling to open the door. In such cases, a woman tells me, "You better take some of your share of wine home for your husband to calm him down."

Extramarital relations are common but not without problems, emotional and practical. Both women and men find it a humiliation to be deceived. Cuckolded men, or husbands who suspect they are, commonly react with violence.

Drinking and Violence

Violence is recognized to be a serious problem, particularly by women. Both women and men exercise violence. However, men are more often involved and they commit homicide more frequently than women do. Some people claim that rather than use violence women are more inclined to use sorcery to kill their enemies than men are; however, not everyone agrees about that. Violence can be both condemned and approved of depending on the context. Women beat children as a part of their upbringing, fight with each other, and defend themselves against their husbands. Men fight each other and beat women, their wives, and children. Use of force may be a demonstration of power, or seen as a feasible punishment or an instrument of education. Frequently violence is exercised when the perpetrator lacks arguments and tempers are high. Copious consumption of alcohol such as cashew wine, palm wine, or *kana* is a contributing factor.

Heavy drinking is a relatively new custom, some say.[40] In "the old days" there was no *kana*. Segunda remembers when she was a child and her father sent her to buy *kana* in the Portuguese shop. Money was limited so she would only buy half a liter. The shop assistant would wrap the bottle with a cloth and she would try to hide it in her *pano*. Only when inside the house where nobody could observe her would she hand it over to her father. "In those days we did not know how to boil *kana*," Segunda says. "But today with a lot of cashew, everybody drinks. Men drink, women drink, young people drink, and even children sometimes drink. Today everybody knows how to boil *kana*."

Drinking habits vary. Some people do not consume alcohol at all. Protestants, who are few in number, usually do not drink alcohol. A number of men and women do not drink simply because they just do not like it, or they have stopped for health reasons, for example, tuberculosis or stomach problems. In the old days, women normally did not drink and many elderly women in the villages do not drink alcohol, or they do so only at ceremonial occasions. Most women who are religious specialists use alcohol as part of their religious practice, and some of them drink a lot, as do many men involved in such practices. People drink very differently, I am told. Most people drink mainly at feasts or funerals; they may drink quite a bit on these occasions but not often otherwise. Others drink frequently, and among these some people always drink whenever alcohol is available. Still others go from house to house, village to village, in search of something to drink. When asked about drinking habits people respond openly. Drinking is not considered a shameful behavior. However, women lament their bad luck if their husbands are drunkards. Their situation is still worse in cases where their husbands are also violent.

In Biombo most violence appears to be committed between people who already know each other. I have not recorded any case of rape or physical assault committed by a complete stranger. There are always peers, friends, neighbors or family members involved. Nonetheless, fear of meeting strangers in a desolate place exists and precautions are taken.

"Some women would never dare to be alone in a lonely place or after dark. Other women are courageous. Some women do not fear anything. They walk alone in the dark, on the road, in the forest, and by the riverside. I am not like that. I am no hero," Ana explains to me.

"What should they be afraid of? Are women afraid that men they may meet will rape them?" I ask.

"You never know. Most men would not, but there are always some men who like to boast of their sexual vitality (ronka si maduresa)," she responds. "But some women are brave, they have a knife folded in their pano (clothes) to protect themselves."

Men are responsible for all the violence-related deaths I recorded during my fieldwork. In only a few cases the killing appears to have been planned, for instance when a group of young men in a distant village threw an old man into a hole they had dug and set him on fire. In other cases, the killing is accidental, as when a father and a son wrestled, just for fun. The son was young and strong and accidentally broke his father's neck. The next day he died. Often women are victims of abuse, and in some cases the violence is fatal. A man wanted a young girl and he tried to acquire her affection with sorcery. He was unsuccessful and the girl rejected him. The man became furious and beat her so badly that she died.

I recorded many incidents of violence that did not result in death. Often women fight with one other and frequently they argue about men. Violence within marriage is also common. While women say a husband has the right to physically punish a misbehaving wife, I have never heard women recognize such a legitimate specific beating. On the contrary, many times I heard about husbands illegitimately beating their wives. In cases of conflict between parents, children are said to support their mothers. A powerful man in a neighboring village regularly mistreats all his wives. He is clairvoyant and everybody fears him. One of his sons claims he beat his mother to death. The son has repeatedly tried to bring his father before the court, but for some reason the case never comes up.

Women beat their husbands, sometimes to defend themselves, sometimes not. Mariama is missing one of her front teeth because her husband hit her several years ago, but he has been to the health center to get treatment for wounds she has given him. "Now we are adults and we only fight each other occasionally," she says. In another case a man comes to the health center with a broken leg after his wife hit him when he was drunk. Another man has his face cut by his wife after she got fed up with his drinking habits. Still another man gets a fissure in his skull after his wife gave him a blow with a wooden pole. While a male villager maintains that the man can blame himself because he behaves badly when drunk, two women agree that his wife is a scoundrel who steals everything she can from her husband and gives it all to her own family. The list of casualties is still longer but every instance of violence has a story that the partners involved, neighbors, and family members interpret differently.

Segunda summarizes her opinion on violence within marriage: "Some husbands are difficult. They beat their wives too much. There is not so much to do about it. Some men are just malicious. That's life. Some women are good fighters. They give back. Other women are not so strong. They have a difficult time."

Divorce

Sometimes a woman finds it unbearable to stay with a violent husband and decides to leave him. A woman may also prefer to leave her husband for another man, perhaps in hope of a better economic life. In the daily language it is said that these women refuse their husbands *(nega si omi)*. Nonetheless, among the Papel divorce in a formal sense is difficult. Some of the commitments established in the marriage ceremonies can only be broken with repayment of the bride price to the husband. A husband's obligation to arrange the beating-the-drum ceremony for his wife upon her death, and a wife's obligation to wash her husband's body at his death, irrespective of whether they have been living together or not, cannot be removed without the repayment of the bride price.

A woman who has made up her mind to leave her husband is likely to pack her things and go. Often she will pretend she is going for a visit to her parents, a family member, or a friend for a short period of time. At first she may say that someone in her family is sick, her mother needs help, or that some problem impedes her from returning home to her husband. Little by little it will become obvious that she does not intend to return. When an adequate opportunity arises she will arrange for the transportation of her private belongings to her parents' home or wherever she wants to keep them. Whether or not the bride price will be paid back to the husband depends on the situation. When a young woman leaves her husband directly after the marriage he has a strong case for reimbursement from her father. However, if he has publicly maltreated her repayment of the bride price is unlikely. If a woman leaves her husband for another man, that man may decide, or be obliged, to repay the bride price to her husband. The bargaining position of a man whose wife leaves him will also depend on the relative strength of the families involved.

Children complicate divorce. The first husband, or the husband who has paid the bride price, has a right to all the children his wives have given birth to, regardless of their biological father. When a woman leaves her husband, the children are expected to stay in his household.[41] A breastfeeding child will always follow the mother but is returned to the father when weaned. Sometimes a child of divorce stays with neither parent and instead lives with a relative or the maternal grandmother (see chapter 3). A woman's decision about whether to leave her husband or not often depends on the possibility of taking her children with her, the relations she has with her co-wives, and the ages of her children. Women do not always accept leaving their children with the husband after divorce.

Borai's situation demonstrates the dilemma that mothers have when considering whether or not to leave an abusive husband. Her husband is disrespectful and sometimes he beats her. Borai never hits back because that is not her way. Her co-wife, however, has no problems with him. "She has a strong family behind her," Borai says. "Her family will never accept that he treats her badly and he knows that." One day Borai and her husband are quarrelling. He becomes angry and hits her so hard that she falls to the ground and loses consciousness. All the neighbors come and try to revive her. At last she wakes up with a terrible headache that lasts for two days. Borai decides not to go to the police. "It will not help," she argues. "The police will beat my husband and when he returns he will be in need of care. Besides that he will be very angry." However, she is tempted to leave him now, which would be considered legitimate because many people witness how he maltreats her. But she does not want to leave any of her children with their father. "The oldest son will not accept staying with him, and the youngest child is still breastfeeding, but the second boy will have to stay with him," she explains. "I don't want to leave him in his father's hands. His father will treat him badly because he will hate me if I leave him." Borai emphasizes that children normally take the side of their mothers in conflicts between parents, but her second boy, a six-year old, is still too young to have a say. Borai decides to see her mother's co-wife *(madrassa)* for advice, as both of her parents are dead. When she comes back she is somewhat depressed. "I have no strong family to help me," she says. Borai has been advised to stay with her husband. "You have to suffer still," she is told. Borai concludes that for the time being she has no other choice but to remain married.

Helena's situation is different—she wants to stay with her husband, but he wants to throw her out of his house. Two years earlier Helena had gone to the South to assist at the funeral of her best friend. There she met a man she liked and stayed with him for some months; eventually she tired of him and returned to her home village. When Helena came back she was pregnant. Her husband was not at all happy to hear about her situation and she decided to return to her father's compound to give birth. Helena is back with the child in her husband's compound. She says he has to accept her, she has no other place to stay, and she is still his wife. Helena's older co-wife laughs when I ask her opinion. She agrees with Helena: "It is obvious that he has to accept her, he has no other option."

Next time I meet Juana I tell her about Helena's situation. I argue that divorce appears more complicated for a man than a woman. Juana admits that men may have problems getting rid of unwanted wives, but there are ways, she says. A man who wants to divorce his wife can take all her belongings and place them outside the compound as an indication of his will. Of course the wife can refuse to leave, and if she has not committed any serious mistakes within the marriage her husband may have difficulty expelling her. A man can arrange for a car to take all her belongings away from his home. Or he can treat her so badly that she can't endure it anymore and leaves by herself. Still another alternative is to ignore the existence of an unwanted wife. In this case the husband does not contribute to his wife's stove anymore, does not sleep with her and, without warning, he may arrange for a new wife to take over cooking and all other wifely duties. Juana talks about such behavior as abandonment. She admits that an unhappy woman can leave her husband—just walk away—but only if she has somewhere to go and her children will not suffer.

One complication of divorce is men's reluctance to perform the beating-the-drum ceremony for a runaway wife. When I ask Juana whether some women may decide to stay with their husbands to secure their beating-the-drum ceremony she responds without hesitation: "No, never, you understand, most likely a husband dies before his wife. Besides, if a woman has good luck with her children they will arrange a respectable funeral for their mother and take care of her beating-the-drum ceremony."

Funerals

The funeral of a person is an important public event in which everybody participates. Ideally, the local community is informed about a person's death through the beating of the *bombolom* (a slit-gong drum used for communication) early the next morning. The very same drums are used to perform the beating-the-drum ceremony, which facilitates the entrance of the soul of the deceased into the other world. The performance of this essential ceremony requires the permission of the king and the spirits.[42] In addition, rice and alcoholic beverages are served and animals are offered. A drummer *(tokadur)* who is a specialist in beating the *bombolom* drum is recruited. However, if the necessary resources are not available and the spirits or the king does not accept the ceremony it will be postponed.

Another important ceremony, named *djongagu* (**odjedje**), also takes place after death, preferably as part of the funeral.[43] Before burial the corpse is put on a bier carried by men who do not belong to the family of the deceased. The corpse is asked about the cause of death. The men carrying the bier fall in a trance and their involuntary, forward and backward movements with the bier indicate the responses (yes and no) to the questions put to the body. *Djongagu* is also used to find out if the deceased was a sorcerer.[44]

The cause of death of the deceased comes to characterize the funeral. The funerals of those who die old, when God calls, are big parties with a lot of drinking and dancing, while the funerals of those who die untimely deaths are full of grieving and sadness. The beating-the-drum ceremony is considered to be particularly important if the person is an old man or a woman. Then a large number of cows, pigs, and hens are consumed to demonstrate the wealth and power of the dead person.

Maria does her best to help me understand the importance of having a respectable funeral or "weeping" *(tchuru)*. She talks about the funeral as a kind of a summary of a life: "Your value is in your *mala* [a box where women keep their private belongings], which will be demonstrated in the beating-the-drum ceremony. Your daughters wash your body, and your sons offer animals." Maria, and indeed other women I have met, find it unfair that the husband inherits the *mala*. They would prefer to give it to their daughters or sisters. Indeed, some women give away some of their possessions, such as garments, *panos* (textiles), and ornaments, when they feel death is close. It is nevertheless better not to give away too much, because before a husband or his substitute performs the beating-the-drum ceremony for his wife he will inspect her *mala*. If the *mala* has limited value he may resist performing a costly ceremony; this is even more likely if he and his wife were on bad terms or if she had left him. However, if his wife is rich and her *mala* is full of valuable things, he will perform her beating-the-drum ceremony regardless of the quality of their marital relations; otherwise he does not have the right to inherit her *mala*. Also, if his wife belongs to an influential family, her family may use whatever available means to force him to accept his responsibility.

Clara was a young woman from a nearby village who suddenly died. She had left her husband several years earlier but her body has been taken to his compound for burial. She had moved her *mala* to her father's home, but it had just been returned to the husband before I arrive at the funeral. Clara's brother, a young, tall man is almost crying when he explains to me his sister's situation. Clara had given birth to three children, all with different fathers. For the last few years she lived with a new husband in Bissau, but for the past few months he has been in Europe, "the white man's country" *(terra di branku)* and has not yet paid the bride price to Clara's husband. Clara's brother is worried because the first husband has still not asked the king for permission to perform the beating-the-drum ceremony. He wants to inspect the *mala* first. The brother's worries are justified. Clara is buried in the afternoon, without the beating-the-drum ceremony. The corpse is interrogated about the cause of death and it confirms that Clara's new mother-in-law killed her with sorcery: the mother-in-law was envious because her son had sent home more money to Clara than to her.

Some weeks later, a neighbor expresses to me her pity for Clara's family.

A person like Clara, who dies young, will not find peace in the other world. And when the beating-the-drum ceremony will finally be performed, her family members all begin remembering her again and they will cry still more. You understand, of course Clara's husband will not perform her beating-the-drum ceremony. Who is willing to spend money on a woman who has humiliated him? It's like that. A young woman like Clara does not have many valuables in her *mala*. Such is life. Maybe her brother will pay the costs for the beating-the-drum ceremony. He is still young. Her brother is no rich man, and her children are only kids yet.

Bó was wealthy and died in her late fifties; her situation was different Clara's. Bó had lived with her first husband for eight years without becoming pregnant. She left him and later she began to live with a Balanta man who finally paid the bride price to her former husband. With her second husband Bó gave birth to six children, sons and daughters, who all grew up to be successful. Her former husband was less fortunate—he married another girl but she never gave birth to a child and she finally left him. Later he married a widow with children.

Despite success with children in her second marriage Bó's life was not easy. Her new husband was violent. Once when he was drunk he hit her and she fell on her head. Gradually she lost the ability to move her right arm and leg. Despite actively seeking help from various healers and the official health care services, she died. Bó's sister commanded that she should be buried at the home of her first husband, even though her second husband had paid the bride price. Bó's first husband accepted at once all responsibility for a respectable funeral. Augusta, who attended the funeral, confirms that the body reached his home in the afternoon and the beating-the-drum ceremony began immediately. Bó was a rich and generous woman who had helped many people in difficult times. Although she was not young Bó died an untimely death, so her funeral was crowded and there was a lot of crying. The same day Bó was buried, her second husband came to the funeral with his two other wives. Augusta tells me that he offered a cow that "was of an ordinary size or a little smaller." On the way to the grave *djongagu* (the corpse divination ceremony) was performed. The four men who carried the bier had a difficult time. Bó was a heavy woman and her body was wrapped in so many shrouds that she was even heavier. The bier broke and those standing close had to give a hand quickly to prevent the body from falling to the ground. Finally, the questions were posed:

"Had the dead person made a contract with an *iran* [spirit] without fulfilling it?" The bier moved ahead indicating a negative response.

"Did an ancestor of her lineage kill her?" No.

"Did she ever steal from her chief [husband] and did that result in her death?" No.

"Did she ever make a contract with a spirit to kill a child of a co-wife?" No.

"Did a co-wife on bad terms with the dead woman kill her?" This time the bier moved backward to indicate "yes." The same question was asked again, and again the bier answered "yes."

"Did she kill herself?" No.

"Did she ever ask for help from a witch to kill somebody else?" No.

One of Bó's co-wives had killed her, Augusta tells me. She had noticed that Bó's second husband and her two co-wives had cried at the burial, but "no water came from their eyes."

Indeed, Bó's second husband had declared his intent to arrange for her funeral; he had paid the bride price, but Bó's sister did not accept his proposal. Bó's own children wanted to make a grandiose funeral for their mother, but not with their father. They wanted to take him before the court as the one responsible for their mother's death. The daughter of Bó's former co-wife and her husband also wanted to honor her. She could not stop crying. Bó was as dear to her as her own mother; she had taken such good care of her when her mother had left their common husband when she was a little girl. There was no lack of people and resources to give Bó an honorable funeral.

Women as Wives

What have we learnt about the Papel women as wives in marriage? What characterizes the division of labor, decision-making and women's most important emotional relationships? How are women's lives affected by the matrilineal kinship structure?

The division of labor between a husband and a wife has changed considerably due to a rapid agricultural shift from rice cultivation to cashew plantations in Biombo. The Papel themselves, as well as their neighbors, explain this shift in terms of the matrilineal inheritance. Furthermore, due to high export prices it is more economic to grow cashew nuts than rice. Women have an active role in the collection of cashew nuts, which are exchanged for rice or money. Thus, they are increasingly becoming the providers of rice for the family, something that was formerly recognized as a husband's marital obligation. Moreover, besides collection of cashew nuts, women are engaged in new income generating activities, mainly commercialization of vegetables, fruits, and fish. With an expansion of the market economy a wife tends to use her money more independently of her husband, in particular if they are on bad terms with each other, or if he is a bad provider. Many believe husbands do not contribute a fair share to the livelihood of the family. Today, many women not only provide food for the family but also pay for new costs related to child rearing, such as health care and school fees. At the same time husbands have not taken over any of women's work. Cooperation among co-wives is emphasized as important for reducing women's workload, but because co-wives often do not share a stove, this rarely happens. In general, women's workload has increased but so has their access to cash. However, profits are marginal, and often mothers can hardly feed themselves and their children.[45]

When it comes to decision-making a married man is the legitimate boss of his compound. Nevertheless, the power to make decisions within the household is recognized as depending highly on personality and the kind of decision. Some people, both men and women, are known to be resistant to another person's authority. Within the household, legitimate power varies among the wives; the first wife is supposed to be the chief of the others, but her authority is not always respected by husbands or co-wives. A man's authority to decide on the marriage of the second daughter of his sister is reduced; as is his say on the marriage of his own daughters. Some males use violence to impose their will or to punish for assumed wrongdoings. Women tend to apply manipulation, but they may also use violence. Further, both women and men use ritual power to carry out their own will.

The quality of emotional relationships women have with others is both dependent on structural principles and individual preferences. "The matrilineal puzzle," understood as a conflict of interests between a woman's husband and her brother, is not prominent in Papel women's discourses. A husband's reluctance to perform the costly, but essential, beating-the-drum ceremony for his unfaithful or unruly wife at her death can, however, easily give rise to disagreement between the husband and his in-laws. The relationship between a maternal uncle and his sister's son is more notorious. Marital quarrels concerning matrilineal descent are well recognized. Interestingly, husbands may complain about their wives being too loyal to their own kin in general, but without referring in particular to their brothers-in-law. Women, on the other hand, lament their husband's lack of interest in their own children, and at times they blame it on the matrilineal inheritance. However, most women attribute marital antagonism to the husband's failure to follow the rules of polygyny, that is, respect the authority of his senior wife and otherwise treat all wives equally. Furthermore, men's withdrawal from providing the livelihood for the family is, for women, a real source of conflict.[46] The contemporary practice of extramarital relationships, practiced by men and women, also contributes to marital discord, as does heavy drinking and the related violence. Divorce, or rather physical separation, is common with subsequent disagreements. A wife's choice to leave her husband depends on the possibility of taking the children with her, or the quality of relationships with co-wives, and the availability of alternative places to go. Children are important for women, both in practical and emotional terms.[47] They help their mothers extensively while young and support them in marital conflicts. Grown-up children may even compensate in case the husband is unwilling to carry out his responsibility to give their mother a proper funeral. Finally, both women and men value friendship, particularly with age mates. Friendship is an indispensable source of amusement and fun, but also for mutual help and emotional support, for example at significant events such as marriages and deaths.[48]

In this chapter I have focused on Papel marriage, the division of labor, decision-making, and relations between spouses and co-wives. The matrilineal kinship structure of the Papel is not a totalizing system; however, it is important in women's lives. The matrilineal inheritance is in decline, not as a principle, but rather through the destruction of the inherited property itself, the rice fields.[49] Nonetheless, when it comes to ritual practice the Papel are recognized to be rigid and uncompromising. Women must marry according to the custom of their people and they must have a proper funeral to secure their afterlife and the safety of the matrilineage. Women's daily life is more marked by being a wife than a sister, despite husbands' frequent absences. Mothers are increasingly taking economic responsibility for the provision of the family, and their children are typically affectionate and loyal to her, an issue that will be examined in forthcoming chapters.

In the next chapter, "Burdens of Birth," I will examine mothers' reproductive experiences and their considerations about having children. When
discussing marriage women frequently refer to their good or bad luck with
husbands. Bearing children is in a way also described as a risky business
about suffering and gratification.

2

Burdens of Birth

The phrase "burdens of birth," *(kansera di padi)*, is commonly heard in Biombo. With time, I come to realize that burdens of birth are not restricted to delivery but included other events related to childbearing as well. Delivery, which is considered to be a frightful and dangerous event, is described as a particularly painful and tortuous experience. "Women suffer because they give birth," I am repeatedly told. But also: "Mothers love their children because they have to endure the pains of birth."

Pain has different meanings in different cultures and eras (Johannisson 1996; Kleinman et al. 1992; Kleinman, Das, and Lock 1997; Morris 1991). Before the introduction of anesthesia in Western societies pain was thought of as a natural and unavoidable part of childbirth (Poovey 1987). According to Catholic doctrine, pain during childbirth was women's punishment for original sin. Yet, control of pain in childbirth with the application of technology and extensive use of medicines spread rapidly with the introduction of hospital births (Cosslett

1994, Davis-Floyd and Sargent 1997a). In the United States in the 1940s, wealthy women who had allied themselves with physicians held that "the progressive, 'modern' way of giving birth was to divorce oneself from outdated servitude to biology by giving birth in the hospital under total anesthesia" (Davis-Floyd and Sargent 1997b:9). However, since the late 1960s many feminist researchers have criticized the excessive use of painkilling drugs and advanced technology in birth. The critics have also denounced the male domination of childbirth, which has curtailed the agency of women in childbirth, both as mothers and midwives.

As a reaction to the extensive use of technology and drugs a return to more "natural" childbirth practices was advocated (Fisk 1997, Holmqvist 2000, Jordan 1983, Morris 1991). After it was considered a woman's right to give birth with pain relief, it has become virtuous for a Western mother to endure the pains of birth. According to Tess Cosslett (1994) natural childbirth, sometimes idealized as painless,[1] is predicated on the assumption that women are essentially mothers, that childbirth is innate or instinctive, and that birth should occur without medication and technical intervention.

Midwifery has been given notable attention in the anthropological literature on childbirth, and knowledge needed for birth assistance is explained as either acquired, instinctive, or evolutionarily adapted (Davis-Floyd and Sargent 1997b, Jordan 1983, MacCormack 1982, Trevathan 1997). Research on midwifery emphasizes the role of traditional birth attendants in giving emotional support to women during labor.[2] The physical anthropologist Wenda R. Trevathan (1997) suggests that emotions related to childbirth, such as fear, anxiety, and uncertainty, have led women to seek company from other women during childbirth as an adaptive survival strategy; thus, she argues, only in a few cultures do women give birth alone. According to the anthropologists Robbie E. Davis-Floyd and Carolyn F. Sargent, Trevathan's research "shows the benefits to mother and child of continuous woman-to-woman contact, of safeguarding—rather than regulating—the process of birth as it unfolds, of providing a supportive environment, and of allowing uninterrupted time after birth for the formation of a strong mother-infant bond" (1997b:9).

The popular maternal bonding theory, which takes mother-infant contact directly after birth as essential for maternal affection, holds that mother love originates in childbirth. This theory was established in the early 1970s by two American pediatricians, John Klaus and Marshall Kennell.[3] Klaus and Kennell were influenced by John Bowlby's attachment theory, which was grounded on Freudian thinking about the primacy of our early emotional relationships with parents, particularly the mother, for the formation of individual personality (Eyer 1992, Hrdy 1999).[4] Bowlby concludes that maternal emotional and nutritive responses are provoked by infant behavior, which is instinctual and adaptive for their survival, analogous to imprinting in birds. Maternal bonding theory uses female sheep and goats as a point of reference, but sheep and goats reject their offspring if separated from them immediately postpartum.[5] Klaus and Kennell argue that, because of the hormonal status of mothers after giving birth, the first minutes and hours of life are a "sensitive period" through which maternal affection is established. In contrast, Bowlby is concerned with how infants gradually became attached to their mothers. Thus, Bowlby argues that mothers should not be separated from their children during the first three years to achieve a secure attachment. Both attachment theory and bonding theory attribute disturbances in child development, as well as child abuse and neglect, to inadequate maternal attachment or bonding, and both theories have been used to advocate changes in routines in maternity wards and child care institutions (Crouch and Manderson 1995, Eyer 1992, Hrdy 1999).[6]

In the 1995 revised edition of their 1976 publication, Klaus, Kennell, and Klaus want to convince anxious parents who are unable to have contact with their infants directly after birth that "all is not lost" (1995:88). According to Klaus, Kennell, and Klaus, "it appears that there are numerous built-in human systems that tie the mother and father to their baby so that the development of the relationship seems almost fail-safe" (88). At the same time, though, they argue for the importance of early contact for effective bonding. As a final conclusion, Klaus, Kennell, and Klaus admit that they have tried to express cautiously their "convictions concerning the long-term significance of this early bonding experience. . . . We believe that there is firm evidence for the benefits of early contact between parents and infants immediately after birth. Less than an hour alone together in private is almost certainly inadequate" (88–89). So, the idea of a "sensitive period" for attachment is still on the agenda. While fathers are said to become "attached to their new infants in their own ways" (74) the mother is described as equipped with a "whole system" that allows her "to communicate with her infant in ways that can bypass the logical and rational areas of the brain and allow the mother to take in and sense the baby at a deeper, more primitive level" (86).

In the 1995 edition of their book, Klaus, Kennell, and Klaus not only emphasize the need for immediate contact between mother and infant after birth for establishment of maternal affection, but also that emotional support during birth is "an essential ingredient for every laboring woman. It is needed to enhance not only the mother's physical and emotional health during childbirth but also the special relationship that ties parents to each other and to their infant" (1995:42).

Maternal bonding theory has been heavily criticized. The sociobiologist

Hrdy argues that "bonding" in terms of biologically-based affection established during a "sensitive period" after birth is unlikely to evolve in primates.[7] She argues that in humans, "unlike sheep, bonding right after birth is by no means essential for the development of love. It can, however, facilitate the process" (1999:488). Hrdy takes maternal responses to infants to be adapted and biologically based and she emphasizes innate maternal responses to infant cues.[8] At the same time, Hrdy argues that establishment of maternal affection is a gradual process in line with Bowlby's attachment theory. Empirically, maternal bonding theory has been difficult to verify. Researchers have produced contradictory results and studies have failed to demonstrate that children who did not have an early contact with their mothers immediately after birth are in higher risk of neglect or abuse (Field 1996). Studies in support of bonding theory have also been disqualified on methodological grounds and ideological bias (Eyer 1992, Lamb and Hwang 1982, Myers 1984).

Let us now turn to Biombo. What are Papel mothers' experiences of the burdens of birth, a concept that not only includes delivery but also menstruation, pregnancy, and breastfeeding? Is Papel birth assistance sisterly and supportive, as some would expect of "natural" childbirth without influences from modern technology and medication? Do Papel birthing practices somehow contribute to maternal affection in line with maternal bonding theory? Or, do Papel mothers have an alternative theory of the origin of mother love? All these questions will be addressed in this chapter, but first I will examine the reasons Papel mothers give for having children, despite the fear and pain of giving birth.

Motives for Having Children

A Papel girl is not only born to become a wife but mother as well. Women and men want to have many children. It is difficult to determine an ideal number of children women want to have. However, many times I have asked mothers how many children they would prefer to have. Most women respond by saying: "You never have too many children." No woman mentions less than four children as an appropriate number, and most likely the answer is "no less than x" or "y is enough." They say for instance, "no less than four, two females and two males," or that "six is enough." Several times women mention that six children is a good number, and according to the Papel custom a husband should pay his father-in-law a cow when his wife has given birth to six children.[9]

The reasons women give for their eagerness to have children of both sexes are numerous and difficult to rank in order of importance. One day a woman may emphasize that without children her funeral will not be a proper one, or that a life without children is not worth living, the next day she may argue for the importance of having someone to take care of her in her old age or that she needs her children's help.

For a Papel woman it is important to add members to her lineage through childbearing and not to break her line of descent. However, for a further continuation of her descent line, beyond her own fertility, she has to give birth to daughters. Only the children of daughters will belong to her lineage while the children of sons will belong to the lineage of their own mothers. Thus, a man's line of descent depends on his sisters' fertility, not his own. Women sometimes complain that their husbands lack interest in their own children because they do not belong to his lineage and will not inherit from him. Instead, men are said to be more interested in their sisters' children. Yet, as mentioned before, the relations between an adult man and his heir, that is, his oldest sister's son, are not always good.

Children help their mothers with their work. Young unmarried daughters are particularly helpful to their mothers. They assist with the daily work and take care of younger siblings. Sons are also important because they belong to the household until later in life when they may inherit from their mother's brother. Adult men maintain the rice fields, or at least they did in former days, and they build houses. In this patrilocal society, sons are crucial for bringing new women and grandchildren into the household. Adult children are expected to contribute to the economic, physical, and emotional well being of their parents in old age. Carlo's mother argues, as do many mothers that "women suffer because they give birth, they must endure the pains of birth, but in turn children are obliged to respect and take good care of their mother." Men want sons of their own as well because they contribute to their livelihood. Daughters are also appreciated by men, because "daughters always take better care of their aged father than do their sons or daughters-in-law."

However important daughters are for helping their mothers and extending their line of descent, the most common reason given for a woman's eagerness to have daughters is that they wash their mother's body at death.[10] The whole body of a cadaver must be thoroughly washed with warm water and soap. A sister's daughter or some other woman from the same womb can substitute for a real daughter, but it is shameful to be washed by a woman belonging to another lineage. "Only a woman belonging to your lineage should wash your body. If not, the woman who will wash you will proclaim that she has washed the genitals of a woman belonging to another lineage. It will not be nice," Apili explains. At death even if separated, wives wash their husband's body along with his daughters. Sons are important for a proper funeral of both of their parents, but not in terms of handling the corpse; sons offer a cow or some other animal.

Having many children enhances a woman's social status during her life and after her death.[11] The opinion of women who have many children is taken seriously, I am told. Once when I am discussing the burdens of birth with an elderly woman she suddenly she asks me how many children my mother had. I tell her that my mother gave birth to eight children and she already has fifteen grandchildren. All have survived.

"She must be a powerful woman," the woman says.

"A powerful woman? Why do you think so?" I ask.

"A woman with so many adult children has power," she states, and then she asks: "Who would argue against a woman with so many children?"

Giving birth to many children who survive increases a woman's position and earns her respect, both within and outside her own lineage, but also in relation to her husband and co-wives. Women say that children are more likely to take the side of their mother in times of conflict between the parents, something I have witnessed several times. Men complain that in such situations their wives may assert that fathers have nothing to do with the children because children belong to their mothers.

Besides practical, economic, social, and ritual aspects, both women and men mention emotional reasons for having children. It is considered a pleasure to play with an infant. The mother, father, or somebody else may sit cuddling an infant, or go around and rock it in their arms just for the pleasure of it. Infants, even at two or three months, are thrown up into the air for enjoyment, or they are helped to jump or dance. Infants are cherished, or as Maria puts it: "Even boys like to play with a beautiful child." Most people like young children. But mother love is something more than just liking a child.

The Kriol word most commonly used to express love is *misti*, which is also used to ask for things or to express a want or a desire for something. A man *misti* a woman, or vice versa. People also *misti* money, beer, or bread, or whatever they might need. In general terms, Papel mothers *misti* their children. Yet, mothers do not often verbally express their feelings of love for a particular child, nor do they repeatedly state their love to the child. Mothers express their "feelings of longing" *(sinti saudadi del)* for a child that is absent because they have "grown accustomed to it" *(kustuma del)*, another way of expressing affection.

Mothers often emphasize how they must suffer for their children, but also that they will be rewarded for their suffering. Mother love is an emotion that emerges from a relationship based on give and take. Mothers gain status, promise of a proper funeral, and enjoyment from having children. In return mothers endure the burdens of birth, symbolized by the pains of delivery. The events included in the burdens of birth are interrelated, that is, menstruation, pregnancy, birth, and breastfeeding.

Menstruation

For the first time in Biombo I hear that a woman will not become pregnant or menstruate without sexual relations. Some urbanized women say however that this is not a fact, but they firmly maintain that village women still believe this. Indeed, they are right. Many village women tell me that a woman who does not "see a man" (*oja omi,* that is, have intercourse with a man) will not menstruate. Therefore, some mothers are reluctant to admit they have begun to menstruate while still breastfeeding a child. That would mean that they have had sexual relations, which is forbidden during breast-feeding.[12] For instance, Abonjaté, in her forties, is still breastfeeding her two-year-old son when I ask her if she has menstruated since she gave birth. "No, not yet," she says. "I have not had moon yet because I have not seen a man."

To menstruate is expressed in Kriol as to *tene lua,* or to "have moon." The explanation is simple: "When you menstruate you look at the moon and then you know when you can expect to have your next moon." The expression to "wash moon" *(lava lua)* is also used. Women say that through menstruation the body expels dirty, unnecessary blood. However, women say that the expression to wash moon has to do with the fact that the special cloth used for menstruation has to be washed when they menstruate.[13] The idea that a group of closely related women, that is, co-wives, sisters, or friends, might menstruate at the same time is not considered.[14] Every woman has her own moon independent of other women, they affirm.

There are variations in women's physical experiences of menstruation.[15] Some women say they have no problems at all when menstruating while others experience pain. I have never heard any general comments about ill-tempered menstruating women. When I ask a specific question about eventual changes in a woman's temper related to menstruation, the answer is "no, no . . . not with menstruation . . . but pregnant women may be in a difficult mood." Physical experiences vary. A few women even cry because of severe pain, particularly during the second day of their menstruation. The time frame varies also; there are women who menstruate for only two or three days, while others may continue for more than a week. The amount of blood expelled is also said to vary.[16]

There is no celebration of a girl's first menstruation; instead, she may feel shame. Segunda says that because many village women and elderly women still believe that menstruation is impossible without sexual relations an unmarried girl will try to hide the first menstruation from her mother. When she finds out, the mother may accuse her daughter of having sex and punish her harshly. An unmarried girl may also be ignorant of what is going on and become afraid, as some girls are first informed of menstruation at their marriage ceremony.

There is no ceremony performed when a woman becomes "expired" *(passa prasu)*, that is, when her menstruation ceases and she can no longer bear children. The term *passa prasu* is also used to indicate the expiration date of medicines and certain food items. This seemingly derogatory expression nonetheless does not have an entirely negative meaning. A woman who already has an appropriate number of children of both sexes at the time of menopause is respected and no longer needs to worry.

At a party I attend Apili, in her sixties, is in a really good mood; she dances the best she can and has great fun. The other women, still of childbearing age, sit and discuss their problems with tiresome husbands, the lack of rice, and sick children. "Look at Apili, now she has a nice life. She has many grown up children. She has a lot of energy. She has no more worries about difficult births, and children who become sick and die," one of them comments.

Pregnancy

Women do not share news of their pregnancy right away; only after two periods have been missed it is time to tell the husband about the eventual birth.

"After missing two periods of menstruation a woman should inform her husband," Augusta explains to me. If the time of pregnancy does not coincide with the husband having had sexual relations with his wife, he may accuse her of sleeping with somebody else. The time of birth can later result in a similar suspicion. Still, some men do not always keep accurate track of their cohabiting. "Some men are not so smart, they drink a lot and then they do not remember what they do," Quinta says. Quinta tells me about a neighbor who had a difficult time with her last pregnancy. Her husband is a heavy drinker and he accused his wife of sleeping with another man. His wife answered that he was a very stupid man who did not even remember what they did. "What a quarrel," Quinta laughs. "That woman gave birth to a little girl and her husband is still drinking." Nonetheless, most husbands react positively to the news of their wife's pregnancy.

For a woman of fertile age it is normal, and in most cases preferred, either to be pregnant or breastfeeding a child. Pregnancy is considered to be a healthy state; nonetheless individual changes in physical and psychological well-being are recognized. Some women have difficult times during pregnancy, particularly during the first part. A few women may feel bad during the whole period. Nausea and vomiting during the first months are well known. Pregnant women in general, but particularly those who suffer from nausea, desire special foods, often with a strong taste, like green mango with salt. Some women find certain foods repulsive and they may feel disgust from a particular smell.[17] Most women say they generally feel well and do not suffer any special problems during pregnancy. "A little tired. That's all," is a common response. A few women admit they are constantly tired during pregnancy, however, without being sick.

Despite her condition a pregnant woman is supposed to participate in all normal daily activities; she should fetch water and firewood, cook, take care of children, work in the fields, and go fishing.[18] Women who suffer bad health and more serious fatigue during pregnancy can expect help from co-wives, mothers-in-law, or daughters. "It is better to be on good terms with your co-wives," a mother of six children says when we see her neighbor, who is pregnant in her last month, carry water on her head. "But not all women have co-wives," she says. "Formerly it was more common with co-wives. Today some women do not accept having co-wives, therefore they have nobody to help them when they are in need."

Sitting too much is bad for a pregnant woman, and if she does not bother to move around and work she will have a difficult birth, Maria explains. I have heard comments about lazy pregnant women, and even the phrase "lazy like a pregnant woman" used to describe someone who is not working hard enough. Augusta and Quinta, who work together, are not always on good terms. Quinta likes to hang around and chat with neighbors and passers-by, and she is away from her work for an hour or two when she goes to the marketplace or somewhere else to arrange things. "Quinta is lazy like a pregnant woman," says Augusta, who is pregnant. Then she begins to complain that a pregnant woman is always expected to carry on with her work: "A woman can't expect any help because of her pregnancy." At the same time Augusta knows that she will not be able to fully participate in the coming cashew season because she will be in her last month. "This year I won't benefit much from collecting cashews," she says.

Even the mental health of pregnant women varies. It is considered normal for a pregnant woman to worry over the approaching birth. People are well aware of the high risk of complications that may occur during delivery for the mother, her child or both.[19] Everybody knows or has heard about someone who died giving birth. A few women are said to become a bit crazy while pregnant. They become easily upset and some stop talking to other people. At the same time many women express their satisfaction at being pregnant; they like to become big and say they have a lot of energy. They look forward to becoming mothers.

To suffer infertility is considered a major misfortune or *mufunesa*. Infertility is most likely to be interpreted in religious terms; it may be seen as a sign that a person should become a religious specialist.[20] An infertile woman will raise others' children, however, it is still particularly important for a woman to add new members to her lineage. Therefore, infertile women or women who have only given birth to sons want to raise a girl who belongs to their lineage. A man's infertility is less likely to be recognized than that of his wife, as she is likely to take lovers or become identified as the infertile person in the marriage. If the husband finds that his wife is barren he can neither claim another woman from her father nor ask for divorce. "The only solution for him is to hope for better luck with his next wife," says Maria. "A man cannot separate from his wife solely for the reason that she is infertile." A husband who mistreats his barren wife is considered to be poorly educated and worthless, Maria informs me. If a man treats his barren wife badly, possibly in the hope she will leave him, it simply demonstrates that some women have bad luck with their husbands.

While infertility is a major tragedy, some pregnancies are surely unwanted. Among these are premarital pregnancies, pregnancy before the previous child has terminated the appropriate breastfeeding period, pregnancy occurring in the absence of the husband, and pregnancies after a woman has given birth to a desired number of children and another may hamper her health. It is also considered inappropriate for a woman whose daughter is married and has given birth to a child to become pregnant herself.[21]

There are various measures known to avoid unwanted pregnancies. Women who have gone to school or live in the *prassa* know about the intrauterine device (IUD) and contraceptive pills. To arrange to have an IUD women have to go to Bissau. Some women maintain that there are no problems with an IUD, while others argue that it eats up the body and makes one thin and tired. A few women know about the pill but they find it too complicated to use. In addition, the pill is thought to be hazardous to one's health. In the villages sexual abstinence during the breastfeeding period appears to be the most common method of family planning, and modern contraceptives are not well known. Some women tie an amulet to their waistband to avoid unwanted pregnancy. Herbal medicines such as hot pepper boiled in red wine are known to cause abortion. Some women say it is possible to arrange an abortion at the National Hospital in Bissau but I have never met a woman in Biombo who had one. I am told that abortions are traditionally considered to be ethically wrong by the Papel. The Catholic policy against abortion and family planning, other than natural methods such as having intercourse only during the safe periods of the menstrual cycle, is familiar to the Catholic women, but sometimes they obtain contraceptives through Protestant missions.

The risk of pregnancy can be reduced if a woman has intercourse with many men during a certain period of time, as the "mixture of blood" (*mistura di sangi*) from several men will somehow hinder conception or cause abortion.[22] Women who arrange contraceptives without the knowledge of their husband can thus risk being accused of adultery. Similarly, a husband may accuse his wife of promiscuity if she has weaned her youngest child and for some reason does not become pregnant again. Two adult women, already mothers to many children, complain to me about their reputation as promiscuous. One of them says she has never slept with a man other than her husband, but because she has not become pregnant for five years her husband has accused her of unfaithfulness. The other woman has arranged contraceptives without her husband's knowledge: "He would never accept it because he wants me to give birth to more children," she explains. She sleeps with her husband, and occasionally with other men, she says.

Preparation for Birth

It is a common knowledge that a pregnant Papel woman can ease her birth if she follows certain precautions. There are some food restrictions. A woman who eats monkey bread *(kabassera)*, the fruit of the baobab tree *(Adansonia digitata)*, will give birth to a "dirty" child that should be washed with water containing monkey bread seeds. A woman who eats a lot of hot pepper will give birth to an infant with closed eyes. To open up the eyes they should be washed with a medicine prepared with smashed leaves from the hot pepper plant soaked in water. If a pregnant woman eats eggs her infant will be born with a white tongue that must be washed with red palm oil. Pregnant women are also advised to avoid eating the fatty hippopotamus meat or tuna fish, as both contribute to a difficult delivery. In case such meat is eaten a bone from the respective animal or fish should be put into water and the laboring woman should drink it to ease the birth. These and other food taboos are not strictly adhered to; if they are broken there are ways to counteract the negative effects.[23]

A pregnant woman should not have sexual relations with men other than her husband since the fetus is said to die if there is a "mixture of blood." Sexual relations with the father of the child are not considered to have a negative effect on the unborn child. Women who miscarry are sometimes accused by their husbands of having extramarital relations and killing the fetus with "mixture of blood." Many women have at least one miscarriage but a few women repeatedly suffer such misfortune. Miscarriage is often attributed to sorcery, and as such it is only curable within the Papel tradition; however, God may also decide to take back someone who wanted to return from the other world without permission.

The concept of prenatal consultation at a mission hospital or a health center is familiar to most women. The mission hospital in Quinhamel is run by the Catholic mission, which began its missionary work, education, and delivery of health care in the area in the early 1950s. Catholic nuns run this popular hospital, which is often referred to as "the house of the nuns," or in Kriol as *kau di irma* (*irma* means "sister"). The two nuns who have been working at the hospital during most of my stay have resided in Guinea-Bissau for many years and speak fluent Kriol. A couple of Guinean nurses and other locally trained staff work at the mission hospital; however, the nuns, who were also trained nurses and midwives, do most consultations and treatment. Only mothers who reside in the Quinhamel area are supposed to have access to the services, which are also sought by women from Bissau. When pregnant, a woman is advised to attend the scheduled prenatal consultations regularly and give birth at the hospital. Afterwards her infant is vaccinated and attended to when sick. There is no requirement for the mothers to be Catholic.

Besides the mission hospital in Quinhamel, there is another Catholic mission hospital in the region and one Protestant mission hospital. There are also seven state-run health centers in the region, which are staffed with two to five nurses and sometimes a midwife. All the nurses and midwives at the health centers have been trained in Guinea-Bissau and most of them come from other parts of the country or from the city of Bissau. The language used is Kriol, and only a few of them speak Papel. The recurrent shortage of drugs at the health centers affects the work negatively.

I interview eighty-seven mothers of children less than five years of age in a village situated in more than ten kilometers from the mission hospital. While almost all have attended prenatal consultation, fewer than half of them participated more than once, compared to almost all women (97 percent) who live in a village on the outskirts of Quinhamel.[24] The village women prefer to go to the Catholic mission hospital for prenatal care rather than to the nearest health center some four to five kilometers away. When I ask the mothers why they attend prenatal consultations at the mission hospital but not at the closer health center, they say they are grateful for the drugs the nuns give pregnant women.[25] Mothers also mention that if they don't attend prenatal care at the mission the nun would later refuse to consult the child in case of illness.

Mothers who do not follow the schedule for prenatal consultations or lose their prenatal cards have to pay fines the next time they come to the mission. "*Irma* is difficult," Impina says. She is pregnant and goes regularly for prenatal care at the mission hospital, which is five kilometers away from her village. When I see Impina she is upset. "Yesterday I went for a consultation but *irma* refused to examine me because I had lost my consultation card," she says angrily. Impina explains that the week before, when she traveled to Bissau, all her money and documents including her prenatal card, were stolen. Impina knew she had to pay a fine and therefore she had arranged for the money required. She gave the money directly to the nun, who refused to accept it. The nun refused to give her a new card or to attend her. She did not give Impina the drugs she usually received. Instead the nun scolded Impina and told her to come back only when it was time for birth. Impina became furious and refused to leave the mission. She waited there until the sun was hot, but the nun was firm and did not examine her.

Many pregnant women have problems with the nuns. Nonetheless, they prefer to go there for prenatal care. Irene is pregnant for the third time and she is not feeling too well.

"Ohoh, I have a pain in my stomach when I eat too much, my mouth is all damaged and I sleep badly," she complains.

"You drink too much," her neighbor responds.

"Ohoh . . . oho . . . you better not tell *irma*," Sábado says and explains to Irene that *irma* does not like pregnant women to drink alcohol.

"Good, now I know, I will not tell her," Irene says and laughs. "I have already enough problems with *irma*. Last time she demanded that I should go for an analysis. I didn't. Now I don't know what she will do next time I go there."

Burquenha enters the discussion. She argues that it is much better to go to the rice fields, as is the Papel custom, and tramp in the mud, than to go to the mission or the health center for pregnancy control. In the old days, she explains, women who felt bad and were tired during pregnancy went to the rice fields to exercise before giving birth. "I still do so. When you go in the mud you feel your body becomes light and the tiredness comes out of your body," Irene says. Sometimes in late pregnancy women also go to an elderly woman who massages their abdomen with red palm oil and changes the position of the fetus so that it will be born headfirst.

Women describe pregnancy as tiresome, but not as particularly dangerous. However, the death of an expectant mother, even if her death is not related to her pregnancy, is seen as transmissible. When a young pregnant village woman died after mistreatment from a man she had refused to take as a husband, all the other pregnant women in her neighborhood performed a ceremony, which was described to me. During the night the pregnant women concentrated at crossroads, where a calabash filled with water and a rope used to climb palm trees had been placed. The women danced naked, ripped their waistband and threw it away.[26] Then they washed themselves with the water and finally broke the calabash. This ceremony was performed to prevent additional deaths of pregnant women in the village.

Birth

There are several places for a woman to give birth: at home, her parent's home, the health center, a hospital in Bissau, or at the mission hospital. In addition, some women give birth alone, either in the bush or at home.

Regional statistics for place of birth indicate that distance to the mission hospital and the reputation of a particular nurse or midwife at the nearest health center are important factors a mother considers when choosing a place to give birth.[27]

Birth in the Village

Women who give birth in the village are most likely to give birth, as they say, in their "husband's home." Those women who have bad relations with their mother-in-law and eventual co-wives, I am told, often prefer to give birth in their parent's home, or at the health center or mission hospital because they are afraid of being bewitched. In the villages, an elderly woman, most likely a mother-in-law or a co-wife, will assist a woman in labor. Only two or three other women are present. Children, men, and young women who have not given birth are not allowed to be present. "A girl who assists birth will not want to give birth herself," says Maria. "Many girls say they will never give birth because they are afraid of the pain."

When the pains start a woman pretends that nothing is happening.[28] Only when she feels she is close to giving birth will she tell others about her condition. A woman should not cry or show signs of discomfort during delivery. There is a saying that if a woman cries at her first delivery she will cry every time she gives birth. Prolonged births are feared and the mother will be urged by the assisting women to give birth quickly and without complaining. Women are said to be in control of their own birth, and prolonged births are thought to result from a fear of pains. The assisting women may beat a woman whose birth becomes prolonged in order to force her to give birth more rapidly. A woman who cries too much may also suffer beatings or verbal abuse. Various herbal medicines are recommended to speed up the delivery. Attempts may also be made to get the child out by pushing on the mother's belly. A woman gives birth sitting on her knees. If the afterbirth is not expelled, a cloth is tied over the mother's belly and a pestle put into her mouth to force it out, explains a village woman. The umbilical cord is cut when the afterbirth is delivered; otherwise there is risk it will not come out. The afterbirth is then buried inside the hut.

After birth, the child will be washed and then smeared with red palm oil by the assisting women. The mother takes a warm bath with herbal medicines. She will also consume some of these to get rid of the excess blood from her body. Thereafter, the mother, covered with a sheet, will sit for a while over a bucket with hot water and some medicines to clean her lower abdomen. Finally, the mother will rest, with her back turned toward a fire to keep her body warm and be served food.

The mother will be informed about her child's sex, but she is not expected to engage in any kind of communication with her newborn. After a rest, the length of which depends on the situation and the time of day, the mother can breastfeed her infant if she wants to. However, there is no hurry because she is not thought to have enough milk to satisfy a newborn during the first one to three days. Another woman preferably breastfeeds the infant to keep it satisfied while waiting for the mother's milk to come in.

Some women give birth without crying while others cannot bear the pains without shrieking. Later, a mother who cried out during birth will be mocked. Everybody, men, other women, and even children, will ridicule her. "You bleated like a goat," people will tease. Birth can become a source of shame but also pride. To give birth is a question of courage, and those mothers who are courageous enough give birth alone.

Giving Birth Alone

It takes me some time to realize the significance of giving birth alone. While working with the hypothesis that women give birth alone to avoid being beaten during delivery, I unsuccessfully seek out women who are willing to tell me about eventual beatings during their delivery. The informants assure me that women who have a prolonged birth and "do not behave correctly" are beaten to speed up the birth or make them silent.[29] But no one admits suffering beatings herself.

Quinta is the only woman who has admitted to me quite honestly that her mother had hit her, but first after she had given birth.

Quinta tells me that she has given birth seven times and three times alone.

"Why did you give birth alone?" I ask.

"Ohoh. You know, last time the pains came suddenly and there was no woman at home," she explains. Quinta's mother arrived just in time to help her to cut the umbilical cord. Then, Quinta tells me, her mother struck her, not because she had whined or because the birth was delayed, but because she had not gone to the hospital to give birth, as her mother had told her to do.

"But why should women give birth alone?" I insist.

"Those women who give birth quickly can give birth alone," responds Quinta.

"Is it possible that women who are afraid of being beaten during delivery prefer to give birth alone?" I ask.

"Yeah, it is possible . . . but . . . no . . . if they are afraid of giving birth they would also be afraid of giving birth alone," Quinta responds thoughtfully. Then she explains that it is a matter of choice when women, who already have demonstrated their valor to give adequate birth, give birth alone: "You understand, those mothers who give birth alone without any complaints are respected." Quinta is one of them. Giving birth alone is honorable.[30]

Nonetheless, the actual place of birth sometimes depends less on choice than the situation at the time of birth. Giving birth alone is often explained as unplanned: "Nobody was at home," "My mother-in-law went for a visit," "No woman was nearby," or "The birth came suddenly." For instance, a village woman explains to me that she gave birth alone to her fifth child when she went to fetch water at the well. She knew her time was close but the pains came suddenly and the infant was born rapidly. Her child was born alive but died before she returned home. Sometimes giving birth alone is due to bad planning. Elsa, who left her home alone to give birth at the mission, waited for too long. She gave birth to her fourth child alone under a tree on the road.

Only a few women admit they had intentionally given birth alone. Abipsol is one of those. "I just want it that way," she says. Then she explains that since her mother-in-law died she has always given birth alone; she got used to her mother-in-law and now she does not want to give birth in the company of another woman. Now that Abipsol is pregnant for the twelfth time she prefers to give birth at home and alone. She is well, she has only a little pain in her back, but she has never suffered from nausea or any other problems during her pregnancies. Abipsol assures me that she has no worries about her next birth. "Every time I give birth I get a little tired. That's all," she says. When I meet her next time she has given birth to a son, again alone and without any complications.

"Is he your last-born *(kodé)*?" I ask, and look at her little son sleeping in her arms.

"I don't know," she responds. "I still want to have one more daughter." After twelve births Abipsol has seven sons but only one daughter is alive.

Those women who intentionally give birth alone know they are good at giving birth. Those women who are afraid of the pains and want to avoid mockery and beating during birth, as well as women who have a bad relationship with their mother-in-law and co-wives may prefer to give birth at the health center or the Catholic mission.

Giving Birth at the Mission

When the mission began to assist births women were not willing to give birth there, Segunda tells me. "They did not like it that the placenta was thrown away, and they also felt ashamed to give birth lying on their back in front of the nun. Now we are getting used to it," she affirms.[31] Segunda maintains that the conditions at the mission hospital are much better than in the village. The village women who assist births do not know much about it, she says: "They kill the child with violence and make the mother tired. To put a pestle into the mouth of a mother to get out the afterbirth is dangerous." Segunda says that some women are afraid of giving birth and they fear the pains, which may cause delay in birth and the death of a child. "These mothers should give birth at the hospital," she argues. Segunda tells me about her cousin; three times her newborn died during childbirth because she was afraid to give birth, the fourth time she gave birth at the hospital and the child survived.

Women who give birth at the mission hospital often go there without informing anybody. They want to avoid being caught by sorcery on the road. Mothers also say that it is thought of as a sign of fear to go to the mission hospital for birth, and that afterwards they will be teased for giving birth there. The women will try to come to the hospital as late as possible. Some women wait too long and give birth on the road. Helena, who lives only a twenty-minute walk from the mission, had to give birth to her youngest child in Ana's house on her way to the mission hospital. Pregnant women who have attended prenatal services but live too far away or are unable to go can send for the mission ambulance.

I have asked many mothers why they have given birth at the mission hospital. Only rarely do they refer, as does Segunda, to better conditions in terms of health care. However, as Segunda's suggests, some mothers say they want to try the mission after having a difficult birth at home or after a child has died in delivery. One mother admits she was simply afraid of giving birth and therefore she chose the mission. Commonly mothers say they just want to try, sometimes with a comment that the nun gives clothes to the newborn child and a T-shirt to the mother, which are appreciated. However, the most cited reason for giving birth at the mission hospital, a reason mothers also give for attending prenatal consultations, is that the nun will possibly later refuse to treat the child if it is not born there. These mothers are planning for the child's future, securing access to the nun's "strong medicines."

When I ask Nina, a mother of four children and pregnant for the eighth time, about where she will give birth, she answers that she does not know yet. Nina has ambiguous feelings about her pregnancy. After she stopped breastfeeding her lastborn, she slept with her husband for a year or more without becoming pregnant. She thought that God would not give her any more children, but suddenly she missed her moon and realized she was pregnant. Nina admits she would like to have one more daughter, but she is worried about her health and afraid of giving birth again. Nina was very tired during her last pregnancy. Her second co-wife was away breastfeeding at her parents' home, but her third co-wife, a young girl from a neighboring village, was a great help to her. Then Nina decided to give birth for the first time at the mission hospital, as did her younger co-wives. She was nervous and the delivery was terrible. She admits it was not easy to give birth in the village with her husband's aunts scolding her for crying and pushing her to give birth quickly, "but anyway giving birth in the village was better," she concludes. In addition, Nina felt ashamed to lie on her back and give birth in front of the white nun. "The nun will fine me if I do not show up for birth this time, she will not examine my child," Nina argues. She does not want confrontation with the nun: "She has strong medicines for children."

Until recently the nuns gave the newborn infant sugar water at the first dawn and all infants were placed in a particular room. Mothers initiated breastfeeding twenty-four hours after birth or later. There are new routines now, I am told, and mothers are supposed to initiate breastfeeding soon after birth and the infants are not given other liquids.[32] However, they are first washed and weighed and then given to their mothers to breastfeed. Newly delivered mothers with whom I discussed their birth at the mission hospital both confirmed and contradicted these changes in routines. However, all the infants had their own beds that were placed in their mother's rooms. Mothers stay one or more days at the mission depending on their own and the newborn's health.

A woman who has just delivered should stay indoors for the first days after birth and not engage in work. She should also have somebody to help her take care of the infant, comfort it, and keep it clean day and night, particularly before the milk comes in. Once the mother has recuperated after birth and breastfeeding has been established the infant will sleep with her in bed. Women emphasize, however, that these routines depend on access to additional help, which varies depending on the number of and relations with co-wives, other women in the household, and older daughters.

During the time a mother stays indoors after birth, she should eat boiled monkey bread (kabassera) or rice with sour milk and red palm oil, all cooked on new stones. Care must be taken that the food does not boil over; otherwise the breast milk will become "light" (levi). During the first month after giving birth it is considered bad for a woman to carry heavy things like water and firewood. Thereafter, she is expected to continue with all routine work in the household as before, in addition to taking care of her newborn child. A mother's exhaustion from a crying baby who will not allow her to sleep at night is not considered as a legitimate reason for additional rest, and some women complain.

I have attempted to identify mothers who have suffered from postnatal depression, but without success. Both women and men consider it quite legitimate that a mother whose child has died, or a mother who has suffered from birth complications becomes somewhat downhearted. Such a woman has certainly reason to become worried, in particular if the cause of her misfortune is still not identified (see chapter 4). Grief, worries, depression, and even madness are all recognized as plausible if unfortunate reactions to misfortune. But after a birth without any particular problems, all mothers

are happy, Segunda assures me, though, she admits taking care of and feeding a newborn is not always so easy.

Breastfeeding

The initiation of breastfeeding is normally somewhat delayed after birth,
irrespective of the place of birth. Colostrum is described as a watery liquid
with a grayish or yellow color. It is considered neither good nor bad, but its
quantity is too small to be considered sufficient food for the newborn. Colostrum will not, however, be expressed and thrown away. It is preferable
for a wet nurse to breastfeed the child while the mother waits for the milk to
come in. To prepare for successful breastfeeding someone will be sent out to
fetch sapaté leaves (Leptadenia Hastata), often when a woman is already in
childbirth.[33] The leaves will be pounded and mixed with ground rice and
boiled to a lump. They enable the milk to come in more rapidly. Women
often eat this food regularly, for example, once a week, to produce an abundance of milk. Despite delayed initiation of breastfeeding after birth all
mothers manage well to establish lactation. Children are breastfed on demand and any indication of a child's discomfort is quickly responded to by
offering the breast.

   The Papel do not attribute any particular qualities to breast milk or the
act of breastfeeding that morally obligates mothers to breastfeed their children. If a mother can afford to feed her child appropriately without breastfeeding, she can do so. However, in Biombo alternatives to breastfeeding
are lacking, thus all mothers are obliged to breastfeed. When asked if she
likes breastfeeding one woman responds typically: "It is not a question
whether you like it or you don't like it—it is just something you do." Nonetheless, some women express pleasure at breastfeeding while others tell me
they dislike it; they find breastfeeding tiresome or say it restricts what they
can do. However, all agree that breastfeeding is essential for the child's survival and it is the mother's obligation to breastfeed: "The mother has to suffer for her child."

Breastfeeding Precautions

A lactating mother has to take care to produce a sufficient amount of quality milk. Women emphasize that a mother should eat plenty of food to have
enough good milk. However, mothers do not equate inadequate milk production with a lack of food. Only one mother, an obese woman in her thirties who is still breastfeeding her well-nourished two-year old son, relates
her lack of milk to hunger. She tells me that she used to have a lot of milk,
but when she went through periods of hunger her milk disappeared. The
mother explains how the last year's famine was extraordinarily difficult and
how her breasts dried up for several weeks.

No food is considered to make breast milk bad except fresh lemons in large quantities. Lemon juice is said to enter the milk, which makes the child skinny and sick. The same will happen if a child eats many fresh lemons. Palm wine fills the breasts with milk. Some mothers who drink distillate alcohol, or *kana,* say it causes their milk to flow easily, while others say it dries up their breasts. Otherwise it is not considered a problem for breastfeeding or pregnant women to drink alcohol. Zinha, a young mother, complains to me about her lack of milk: "You know, my husband has not gone to extract palm wine for some days and now my breasts are dry." She shows me her breasts and expresses a few drops of milk to demonstrate her point. Zinha is aware of the nun's disapproval of alcohol consumption for pregnant and breastfeeding mothers, as are most mothers who regularly go to the mission. Zinha assures me that she would never dare to tell the nun about how much she likes to drink palm wine, in particular when she is breastfeeding a child.

A breastfeeding woman is expected to abstain from sexual relations with her husband or any other man. Sex would cause her milk to become bad and her child to have diarrhea; the child's stomach would swell with blood. Breaking this rule is considered a serious transgression in the villages, but compliance in urban areas is less common. If a child often has diarrhea and does not thrive properly the mother's family will suspect that the mother is having sexual relations with her husband. They may demand that she come and stay in her natal home for a certain period of time, or in some cases during the entire breastfeeding period, which can last for two years or more.

I have never met a mother during my stay in Biombo who did not have any milk at all.[34] Lack of milk is, however, a problem a few mothers encounter. Twelve out of eighty-seven breastfeeding mothers whom I asked about the quantity of their breast milk claimed they had insufficient milk. One of these mothers has always had insufficient milk; her two-year old son is thin and sickly. A mother of twins and two women with infections in their breasts say they also lack sufficient milk. Two more mothers explain their actual milk deficiency as temporary; their respective children are over one year of age. Four more mothers claim they have little milk, but all had well-nourished and healthy looking children, a fact they acknowledge when I ask about their children's health.[35] Two additional mothers say their milk is both bad and insufficient; their children die within the year.

Breastfeeding women often encounter problems such as inflammation, infection, and "worms in the breasts" *(bitcho na mama),* which can all be treated locally. "Worms in the breasts" and breasts with abscesses are massaged with red palm oil and heated with a dry lemon warmed over a fire. Sometimes an abscess is opened with a bit of glass from a broken bottle to get out the pus. Mariama, an elderly woman knowledgeable about treatment of women's problems such as infertility and breastfeeding complications, maintains that most breastfeeding problems can be resolved, but that patience is needed. According to Mariama, a minimal level of intelligence on the part of the mother is also required. When I ask her what to recommend to a neighbor who is a young mother with a serious infection in her breasts, she shrugs her shoulders. Then Mariama comments that some women are too stupid for proper treatment to be completed.[36]

Mothers repeatedly emphasize that they have to breastfeed their children to enhance their chance of survival; they have to suffer for their child. For instance, one mother shows me how milk leaks from a hole in her breast every time her infant suckles. She has inadvertently made that hole many years ago after attempts to open up an abscess. Despite profound pain due to abscesses and inflammation, I have never met a mother who had terminated breastfeeding for that reason.

Bad Milk

Breast milk is considered to be good in itself and an appropriate food for infants, but there are some mothers who have bad milk *(ma liti)*. These mothers are said to have hyena's milk *(liti di lubu)* or hot milk *(liti kinti)*. A mother whose first child is thin and sickly is likely to be suspected of having bad milk. The same applies to a mother whose children die one after another in the first months of life. In such cases the milk can be tested.[37] The mother will express milk into her hand, a calabash, or a spoon and she (or her *dona* or her mother) will put an ant into the milk and observe if it survives. The father of the child is rarely present. If the ant survives it is said to demonstrate the good qualities of the milk; if not, the milk is considered to be bad. Still, the result may be ambiguous.[38] Among fifteen mothers who say they have had bad milk according to the test, five still argue that their milk is most likely good or at least acceptable, while four mothers who verified their milk quality as good still suspected their milk to be bad. Some mothers will only put an ant into the milk when they have a reason to suspect it's bad, while others test their milk when the first child is born. It is not considered to be the mother's fault if her milk is bad.

It is uncertain to what extent it is possible to cure bad milk. A Papel woman in my neighborhood is known to cure bad milk, but two mothers who have tried her treatment tell me they both gave it up because her medicines had such a terrible taste. An elderly woman recommends that mothers drink water soaked with leaves from *po di veludu (Dialium Guineense)* every day instead of normal water to cure their bad milk.

Women disagree about the consequences of feeding a child with bad milk. Some say the child will die if it drinks such milk; thus the child must be given cow's milk or powdered milk. The child can also be breastfed by its grandmother or some other woman. If that woman does not already have breast milk she will allow the child to suckle and the milk will come in little by little. There are no known medicines that cause the milk to flow, only persistent suckling.[39] However, most women say a mother with bad milk should keep on breastfeeding, but also take care not to breastfeed too much and complement her milk with other foods.

All the mothers I meet who say they have bad milk tell me that they continue to breastfeed. In addition, they say it helps if the mother eats nutritious and tasty food, such as boiled rice with a sauce made from the fruit of the oil palm or a peanut sauce. Paulina, a middle-aged mother, tells me she has always had bad milk. Therefore, she has tried to breastfeed her children only a little and introduces them to other foods in the first month. Sometimes she has been lucky and managed to obtain cow's milk. But in certain periods, she explains, it has been difficult to find appropriate food so she has had to give more breast milk. Paulina admits she would have liked the nuns to give her a bottle, but she has never dared to ask for it. "The nuns would not understand my problem," she says.

Bottle-feeding

All mothers know about the bottle as an alternative to breastfeeding a child. They have primarily come to know about it through the Catholic mission. At the mission twins and orphans are offered a bottle and powdered milk by the nuns. Some years ago, even the mother of a single child who had breast-feeding problems or a badly thriving child could receive a bottle from the nuns. None of the mothers I meet can afford to buy powdered milk themselves. It is far too expensive.

Less than about one-fifth of 120 village children in my village survey have been fed with a bottle one or more times. None of the mothers has exclusively bottle-fed her child, nor used it as the principal source of feeding. While about two-thirds of the mothers who have tried a bottle used it for a short period of time because of temporary lack of milk, health problems, or multiple births, one-third of these mothers have tried bottle-feeding just for fun. The bottles in use are few and circulate between mothers who want to try. The bottles come from the mission or are bought in Bissau, often by the father of the child. Bottles are more frequently used by women in more urban areas, and still more so among those who have a better education.[40]

In general discussions about bottle-feeding, women argue it must allow the mother to leave home for work sooner after birth. They maintain that bottle-feeding is also suitable for mothers who lack or have bad milk. However, mothers who have tried bottles tend to find them less attractive and more complicated to use. The most common problem is to find appropriate food to put into the bottle. Three types of food are put into the bottle: prepared powdered milk, a watery maize gruel, and juice from monkey bread *(kabassera)*. Another common problem with bottle-feeding is that the child often refuses to take it. This is never said to occur with breastfeeding. When I ask a middle-aged village woman if there are children who refuse to take the breast, she looks amazed and says: "No, a healthy child will always take the breast. Only sick children, and maybe a few children big enough to be weaned may refuse to take the breast."

Fernanda, a young mother of two children, explains that she bottle-fed her first-born son for some weeks with porridge to complement her milk after her breasts became badly infected. Now she has given birth to her second child and she breastfeeds it without any problems. "I will not use the bottle again because now I have plenty of milk and it is good," she says. "A bottle is not good for a child and you never know what food to put into the bottle next time your child is hungry." Julia, also a young mother, tells me a similar story. She gave the bottle to her first child because she became sick. When she was better several days later she started to breastfeed again and stopped using the bottle. She prefers to only breastfeed her second child because she finds it tiresome to use the bottle: "You have to wash it all the time and suddenly you have nothing to put into it." In addition, she argues that breast milk is better than bottle milk: "It gives more energy."

Not all mothers agree with Julia's opinion that breast milk is better than bottle milk. Some mothers say that powdered milk is neither better nor worse than breast milk. "It is all milk," Celeste says. "It must be good to feed a child with bottle milk, otherwise the white people would not use it for their children. The nun would not give bottles to orphans and twins if it was bad." It is a general opinion that white people do not breastfeed their children, and this is repeatedly used as an argument for the good quality of powdered milk.

I discuss bottle-feeding with a couple of mothers of twins who successfully use it to complement their own milk without negatively influencing their own milk production. Elina is not so lucky. I am directed to her house because she is known to feed her twins with a bottle. During the first months after birth of her twin boys she had enough breast milk, she explains to me, but at approximately five months of age the nun gave her a bottle and explained its use. Bottle-feeding functioned reasonably well. She emphasizes that her main problem is to find food for herself and other household members dependent on her. Elina used to go fishing but it is not manageable with twins. Her husband is away working in another part of the country with one of Elina's four co-wives. The two younger co-wives have already left the compound, and Elina is now alone with her elder son, the baby twins, the daughter of a co-wife, and an old co-wife her husband inherited.

Some weeks later Elina comes to my house and I learn that she has survived by begging. On Fridays she strolls between compounds and begs for help. "I have no other choice. You understand? I can't go fishing," she says embarrassed. "These Fridays are like a dance, you do not think so much about what you do—you just move automatically." The five- or six-year-old daughter of her co-wife carries one of the twins. She is short of stature and thin, and she almost disappears behind the cloths that cover the infant tied on her back. I give Elina some food. The next time I meet Elina is at the market place a couple of months later. She tells me that one of her twins has died and her second one is terribly thin. "For some reason now I have too little milk, and the nun refuses to give me more powdered milk because now I have only one child left to feed," she complains. Elina shows me one of her flat, empty breasts as evidence. I encourage her to visit the nuns and give her some money.

Still, time passed and I do not see Elina. Finally, she knocks on my door. The nuns have persistently refused to give her milk powder for her son, and he is thinner than ever. I weigh him; he is 5.0 kilograms at fourteen months of age. I decide to give him the "magic formula" I have successfully used in similar cases. I make a daily dose of a mixture of milk powder, sugar, and oil. In addition, Elina is still breastfeeding him. The boy increases rapidly in weight for some weeks. Unfortunately he begins to develop diarrhea, which improves as soon as he stops taking the milk mixture. I change strategy and give Elina money and food. Elina's son gains weight little by little but he does not start walking until he is two and a half years old.[41]

Termination of Breastfeeding

In Biombo, a mother has to breastfeed her child to secure its survival. All the mothers I have met breastfed their children, but they differ in when they begin to introduce other food to the child and in how long they continue to breastfeed.

Exclusive breastfeeding, which means that the child receives only breast milk, is extremely rare, if it happens at all.[42] Most infants get water to drink from an early age, even in the first days of life, but the introduction of other food varies. An infant will not be given normal adult foods, that is, boiled rice and sauce (often fish boiled in lemon and hot pepper), before the child has teeth. Elderly women say that in the past children first learned to eat other foods when they could sit. Nowadays, young mothers start giving other foods even in the first month and they breastfeed for a shorter time. Younger infants are typically fed rice boiled until soft with a little sugar, butter, or crushed groundnuts, or gruel made of black maize with sugar or dry bananas. All women agree that the breastfeeding period is shorter today than in the old days. The Papel mothers used to breastfeed for at least two years, they say. Indeed, the average time of breastfeeding is almost two years for the children included in my village survey, and only rarely do mothers breastfeed for less than eighteen months.[43]

There are children who breastfeed for more than two years. The last-born child *(kodé)* is beloved and often spoiled and is likely to be breastfed longer than other siblings. Sometimes *kodé* is allowed to breastfeed until she or he refuses the breast. Zilda's *kodé,* a four-year old girl, is still breast-feeding. The girl looks both happy and healthy. When I ask her if she still has milk Zilda does not respond but expresses a long spurt of milk from her breasts as a demonstration.

Only if a child is healthy and doing well, or at least the child has learned to walk and ask for water and eat common food, is it considered appropri-ate to stop breastfeeding. Children who have been sickly or do not grow properly are breastfed longer than healthy children. In such cases, people say, the mother "has to suffer" *(ten ke sufri)* for her child. Such is life. Lack of other food is also given as an explanation for extra long breastfeeding periods. Still, occasionally mothers say they keep on breastfeeding only because their husband is temporarily away so they are in no hurry to stop.

While some mothers say they keep on breastfeeding because they like it, others say they terminate breastfeeding because they disliked it. Often they express their dissatisfaction with breastfeeding by saying that they are not good breastfeeders. Ana, a young mother, says that she wants to breastfeed her newborn only for a year and a half.

"It is enough," she says. "I don't like breastfeeding."

"It is only because you want to see a man *(oja omi).* I will keep on breast-feeding for at least two years," teases Ana's senior co-wife, who has a child of eighteen months. "I like better to breastfeed than to do other work."[44]

A mother does not always decide alone when to stop breastfeeding. Fathers also have their opinion. When I ask about who decides when to stop breastfeeding a child, the answers vary. A group of men to whom I put the question all agree: it is the father who decides. When he wants to sleep with his wife he will demand that she stop breastfeeding. However, he will do this only when he considers the child big enough. I take up the same issue within a group of women. Some agree that it is a decision to be made by the husband. Others say that it is the decision of both the parents. Still others say the mother has to decide; they assert that mothers will not stop breast-feeding just because their husbands demand it. If mothers want to breast-feed longer they will argue that the child is still not big enough or that it needs to be breastfed longer because of an illness. An elderly village woman tells me that parents often do not agree on when to stop breastfeeding, and who decides depends on who has the strongest will. "When you hear through the window at night that your neighbors are quarrelling, every-body knows what the problem is," she says.

In the village survey I ask mothers which parent decided when their last child was weaned. The most common reason that mothers give for terminating breastfeeding is their wish to have more children (65 percent). In particular, young mothers and mothers who want more children of either sex express their desire to become pregnant again as early as possible. Some women say they, just like their husbands, would like to resume sexual relations. The second most common reason (20 percent) the mothers give for their termination of breastfeeding is that their husband had demanded that they stop. Only one respondent indicated the decision to be a common agreement between the parents.

When a child is weaned it stops sleeping with its mother and often it will be sent away to stay with its maternal grandmother for a period of time. Some children stay away only long enough "to forget the breast," one to four weeks, while others stay for months or years (see chapter 3). Breastfeeding is stopped abruptly from one day to another. Children react differently to this situation; a few children are said to cry heavily and it takes them a couple of weeks to become adjusted to the new situation. Others adapt quickly.

Meaning of Mother Love

What have we learned about Papel women as mothers? What are their experiences of the burdens of birth?

Women's individual experiences of menstruation, pregnancy, birth, and breastfeeding vary but common traits can be found. A woman should not menstruate too often in her lifetime. In strict terms, menstruation indicates sexual relations without pregnancy. Pregnancy, sometimes tiresome, is most often welcomed while birth, painful and dangerous, is feared. Breastfeeding is a mother's obligation: whether she likes it or not, it is a prerequisite for child survival.

Western discourses on natural childbirth often stress the emotional sisterly support of women giving birth in the past or in far away places. However, when a Papel woman gives birth in her village assisted by those women who are considered to be qualified, such support is unlikely. There is no lack of agency attributed to a woman in birth, which in turn may hold her responsible for the prolonged and complicated birth. The role of the assisting women is to force a mother not to let her fear of pain interfere with the birth. Too much crying out is likely to result in physical assaults and mockery. In contrast, women who get no support at all, that is, those who give birth alone, are admired and respected for their courage. Nonetheless, after birth all mothers are expected to rest and be well taken care of, and they should neither be preoccupied with the practical arrangements of the infant nor do they engage in communication with their baby. Early initiation of breastfeeding is not seen as important.

Despite lack of emotional support during birth, lack of early contact between mother and infant after birth, and the somewhat delayed initiation of breastfeeding all the Papel mothers I met established successful breastfeeding.[45] According to a study on breastfeeding among the Papel in Biombo from the 1990s, 98 percent of mothers breastfeed for more than a year and 87 percent for more than eighteen months (Aaby et al. 1997). In a striking contrast to the Alto women described by Scheper-Hughes (1992),[46] most Papel mothers have confidence in their ability to produce an abundance of good quality milk for their child. In Biombo, after a breastfeeding period ranging from 18 to 30 months, the decision to terminate is normally consciously taken in accordance with the physical maturity and health of the child. The child's physical well-being and survival are emphasized.[47]

Both maternal bonding theory and Papel mothers associate mother love with the event of giving birth, but with different meanings. The proponents of maternal bonding theory argue that mother love depends on biological processes triggered by early mother-infant communication, which they describe in terms of irrationality and primitive sensation.[48] They also emphasize emotional support given to mothers during birth as important for maternal affection. For a Papel mother, neither early mother-infant communication nor emotional support during labor is seen as important for mother love. In contrast, mother love is seen as originating in suffering the burdens of birth. Mothers endure the fatigue of pregnancy, the pains of birth, and the obligation of breastfeeding in order to have children, who will extend their lineage group, enhance their social status, help with work, contribute to their emotional well-being, take care of them in old age, secure them a respectable funeral, and ease their entrance into the afterlife. Papel mothers express mother-infant relations in terms of reciprocity: mother love is a question about give and take.

In this chapter I have described the Papel mothers' concerns about having children and their experiences of menstruation, pregnancy, birth, and breastfeeding. Values attributed to reproduction and motherhood are essential to understand mothers' eagerness to have many children. Scheper-Hughes (1992) pays limited attention to these issues. Surprisingly, in a book so full of painful discussions, the pains of birth or other physical experiences of reproductive events are scarcely treated.[49] However, reproduction in the Alto is clearly marked by contradictions and ambivalence, and pregnancy appears all too often to be an unwanted, even forced, condition. While Scheper-Hughes emphasizes the primacy of poverty and high expectancy of child mortality in the development of maternal indifference, she also suggests that women's lack of control over reproduction might be an explanation for maternal neglect (1992:428).[50]

Whatever produces maternal indifference, Scheper-Hughes argues that cultural ideas about the nature of children and interpretations about diseases and afterlife make maternal neglect ethically possible. These themes will be treated in the next two chapters. In the following chapter I will focus on ideas related to the concepts of children and their needs. How do these influence or reflect mother love, child care, and survival?

3

Conceptualization of Children

The Papel maintain that an infant born into this world has the soul of a person who has died. Fernanda is in her forties and has been a widow for many years. Her youngest son is twelve, and her oldest daughter is already married and has given her a grandson. Fernanda is very fond of him and she keeps me continuously informed about his intellectual achievements. "He is very clever. He is eighteen months old and he already knows most people and many things by name. He speaks a lot and he plays a lot. He wakes up also early in the morning, exactly as his grandfather used to do. My neighbors say he has the soul of his grandfather," she tells me. "If I was not a Protestant I would believe that."

Alma Gottlieb (1998, 2000a, 2000b, 2004) has persuasively illustrated how beliefs in reincarnation among the Beng in Ivory Coast shape their conceptualization of infants. For the Beng, infants come from the world of the dead as a reincarnation of someone who has died. The entry to this world is gradual and it takes several years to complete. It is considered the parents' responsibility to identify and satisfy their infants' needs to prevent them from returning to the afterworld. According to Gottlieb, infants are treated as active agents with their own will and desires, and "their agency is seen not only as biological but also intellectual, since they are attributed a high level of consciousness that must be decoded by an elite group of adults with special translation skills" (1998:131).

Beliefs in reincarnation are documented in West Africa, parts of Asia, the Middle East, and among native North Americans (Gupta 2002:38).[1] Akhil Gupta argues that reincarnation compels us to reconsider ideas about children, their agency, and childhood as a specific period in life since "age classes that so shape the experience of childhood in the West are neither natural nor universal" (52). This is precisely what the recent body of literature on children and childhood has stressed, though without reference to reincarnation. Earlier childhood and children's studies have been criticized for ignoring children's agency (Caputo 1995; Gottlieb 2000b; James, Jenks, and Prout 1998; Prout and James 1990b; Wulff 1995). The critics have also called attention to the shortcomings of ethnocentric assumptions and the emphasis on developmental psychology and its consequent obsession with age stages and the 'natural' physical and mental maturity of children. Furthermore, anthropologists engaged in research on infants, children, and youth have focused on their relative invisibility within mainstream anthropological studies, similar to the former disregard of women. In addition, Gottlieb (2000b) points out that most works on children are concerned with older children rather than infants.[2]

Anthropological studies on the conceptualization of infants and their care indicate great cross-cultural variation (DeLoache and Gottlieb 2000, Hewlett 1991, Jahoda and Lewis 1989, LeVine et al. 1994, Prout and James 1990a). These tend to propose that care of infants and children as well as rearing strategies are informed by parental conceptions about children. However, similar conceptions may not always lead to similar child care practices and educational efforts. For instance, a pregnant Tongan woman refers to the fetus in her womb as a child with its own nature, intentions, and will (Morton 1996). The paramount aim of childrearing among the Tongan is to educate the child, who is thought to be naturally stubborn. Through harsh physical punishment, which begins after the first birthday, children are taught to be obedient and show absolute respect to those who are older. Great efforts are made to teach children to speak in respectful language. The Gapun villagers in Papua New Guinea have similar ideas about their children, but their child-rearing practices differ (Kulick 1992). The

Gapun consider their children to be aggressive, selfish, and willful and thus not easily taught. Acquisition of language, knowledge, and other capacities are seen as an autonomous rather than socialized processes and care of children is permissive and physical punishment rare.[3]

Scheper-Hughes (1992) suggests a causal relation between the Alto concept of the infant and mothers' neglectful care of children. She emphasizes the Alto mothers' delay in ascribing to their infants "such human characteristics as consciousness, will, intentionality, self-awareness, capacity for suffering, and memory" (412). Infants are surely seen as human, Scheper-Hughes argues, but less so than older children and adults, and therefore "it is entirely plausible that Alto women who have lost one or more young babies do not feel the deep sorrow and grief that our theories of attachment, separation, and loss suggest must or should be there" (415–16).

According to Scheper-Hughes, the Alto concept of the individual leads mothers to delay assigning humanness to their infants. The Western notion of the "individual" remains remote in northeast Brazil, she argues, where "family, kinship, and other social roles define one's place and social identity" (1992:414).[4] Scheper-Hughes claims that Alto infants are conceived of as interchangeable rather than as unique individuals. This lack of individualization is reflected in child care practices and maternal affection. Scheper-Hughes argues that only when an infant gains its status as fully human with a personal name does it have the "right to the affections and passionate attachment of his mother. Until that time the affection shown the infant and young baby is general and nonspecific" (415).[5] Physical contact between a mother and infant is scant: holding is minimal and most often a young child is found lying on its back. Infants are normally only breastfed for a few days, and they sleep with their mothers only for the first weeks. In the Alto, infant care is often the responsibility of young children, as mothers engaged in paid employment are normally not allowed to take infants to work. Thus, at times mothers are obliged to leave their infants alone at home. Fosterage is also common in the Alto. Rather than relate the habit of foster care to maternal indifference, as she does in earlier publications, Scheper-Hughes (1992) explains fosterage as a mother's strategic choice when there aren't better alternatives.[6]

Scheper-Hughes argues that Alto naming practices reflect mothers' conceptions of infants, both in terms of when and what the child is named. Infants are frequently not baptized for a year or more and sometimes only after the child becomes seriously ill. Instead, a child is simply referred to as "baby." Anyone can suggest a name for an infant and if it doesn't stick another name will be proposed later. Because infants are seen as replaceable, "a newborn can inherit the name of an older, deceased sibling, and several children in the same family may be given a variant of the same personal name" (1992:414).[7]

Once more, let us turn to Biombo. How do Papel mothers think of their newborns? Do they attribute human nature, individual personality and agency to infants? How do they take care of infants and children? Why do mothers so frequently put their children in foster care? Are the Papel naming customs informed by mothers' perceptions about infants and/or shaped by the high child mortality?

Nature of Newborns and Child Care

The Papel believe in reincarnation: when an infant is born the soul of a person who has already died is reborn in its body. In rare cases, the soul may be replaced by a spirit during pregnancy, resulting in the birth of a nonhuman child (see chapter 5). Thus an infant is either born as a reincarnated person *(pekadur)* or, in exceptional cases, as a nonhuman spirit or an *iran.*

Though a normal newborn Papel infant is considered to be a human being at birth, there is no consensus as to whether the baby can see or hear.[8] A few mothers say infants are capable of seeing immediately after birth, but most hold that this may take a week or more. Elderly women say that young mothers today claim their infants see earlier than was the case in their youth. No child is born blind, I am told, as a person can only become blind later from disease, sorcery, or old age. Children can occasionally be born deaf, I am told. Mothers observe that their infants will turn their head if they clap hands, but they do not always take it as an indication that they hear. Many maintain that an infant will learn to hear properly within one to three months. One mother explained to me that at about two months a child knows his or her mother by smell and will recognize her voice a little later. Mothers I talk with all agree that infants feel pain, and the fact that they cry when vaccinated was frequently used as an example to illustrate this.

An infant should never be left alone and most of the time they are in physical contact with the mother or another caregiver. Access to caregivers varies depending on number of and relations with co-wives, older daughters, co-wives' daughters, and other elderly women. During the daytime the infant is carried on the back of its mother, some other woman, or a younger girl. Occasionally boys may carry infants or young children on their back. Men do not carry infants in this manner. During the night the infant sleeps with the mother. It is preferable that a newly delivered mother has another woman, often her mother-in-law, a co-wife, or her own mother, close at hand to help with the infant, even during the night. The first weeks after birth a woman is not expected to leave her home for work such as fishing or going long distances to fetch firewood and water.

Women say infants are different when it comes to their daily care: some are easy to take care of, while others demand a lot of attention. Some infants eat, allow themselves to be washed, and then they sleep most of the time. Others are demanding and cry a lot, particularly during the night. To hear an infant cry is not only considered to be disturbing but also bad for the infant. When an infant starts to cry its mother will immediately offer it the breast. If she is not close a nearby person will quickly try to soothe the child by comforting it, rocking it, or gaining its attention. An infant who cries too much may become frenzied and get cramps, I am told. Further, if an infant cries during long periods of time the crying becomes a bad habit, since the infant gets used to it. In the villages, a *prassa* woman says, people believe the navel will extrude and become thick if the infant cries too much. To start carrying the infant on the back early, at two to three weeks after birth, is felt to reduce the risk of an extruding navel, commonly observed but considered undesirable and ugly.

Young infants are not considered mature enough for training; instead it is a mother's responsibility to interpret and satisfy the needs of the child. Infants cry for various reasons: hungry or sick infants sleep badly and are often difficult to comfort, mothers say. "Infants are not all the same," argues a mother of twins when she explains to me their different behaviors. One of them is very demanding, but he is healthy, his mother says confidently. However, some children cry all the time no matter what is done to comfort them. If this happens the mother will visit a diviner, who through divination identifies whose soul is reborn in that child. "By crying too much such infants are asking for a designation of whose soul has returned in their body," a female villager explains. Once that person has been identified the infant stops crying.[9] While mothers appreciate when their infants are quiet and satisfied, they would not boast of their own lovely and beautiful infants and tempt fate.

Mothers prefer to have their infants nicely dressed, warm, and clean. Young children are washed at least once a day. Mothers are observant of dry skin or scabies. Scaling on the head of infants, not normally harmful, is dissolved with red palm oil or olive oil. Lice must be kept away. Rags are used as diapers for younger infants, but those who can afford it may use imported cloth nappies bought in Bissau. Mothers say they feel when the child on their back needs to evacuate or urinate: "You feel its movements." For toilet training, an infant is allowed to sit on its mother's feet with legs apart around her ankles and defecate on the ground. The feces are then wiped up with earth and thrown away.

Children get their first teeth at varying ages. Discomfort during tooth cutting is recognized but not considered serious. It is a problem, however, if the first teeth appear in the upper jaw *(dinti di riba)*. In such a case the mother is not allowed to cook for her husband and will move to another house. Otherwise her husband will become sick, and if he has sexual relations with the mother he will die. Provided the cause of the father's problem is identified early and a washing ceremony performed the father of the child can be saved from death. In the old days everything the parents owned had to be thrown away, for example, clothes, bed, and vessels. Today the bed will not be thrown away but only its cover, a thread from a skirt, and other items: "Things are too expensive today," Maria explains. "Most infants carry an amulet to prevent the first teeth appearing in the upper jaw and thanks to God it doesn't happen too often."[10]

An infant should learn to control its body. Mothers are observant of infants' physical maturity, in particular their ability to sit, crawl, or walk at appropriate ages. Mothers, or responsible caregivers, massage young infants to stimulate their physical development and, when appropriate, they start helping them to sit, crawl, and walk. Preferably a child should sit at four to six months, crawl a little later, and walk at one year of age. An infant born with an observable physical impairment, or an infant who does not learn to sit or walk at the expected time is at risk of being suspected of having been born without a human soul (see chapter 5).

The ages at which children begin to talk vary; some are quick learners, others not. In the villages children's first language is Papel. On the other hand, at the *prassa,* where the population is more ethnically mixed, children are likely to speak Kriol first or at the same time as Papel. Even if both parents are Papel, many prefer to speak Kriol with their children as "children have to learn Kriol, but they will learn Papel if they need it." Parents recognize that these children may not learn to speak Papel properly. "Nobody is born to speak a certain language. If a child whose parents belong to one ethnic group is brought up with another group the child will learn the language and custom of that group, not that of the parents," Juana argues. Children learn the language they hear when young, and it is recognized that they learn languages quicker and more easily than adults do.[11] The first words children are held to utter are "mother" *(mame),* and "breast" *(mama).* Then they begin to ask for other food and water. A clever child who masters a language at a young age is noticed. Elina's son has been sickly and he is severely undernourished. At two years of age he is still unable to walk, but he speaks fluent Papel: "He knows the words for everything," his mother says proudly. "He is always with me and we talk together a lot, so of course he learns to speak earlier than a child who spends more of its time with other children." Education is recognized as important in order to learn a language but qualities regarded as inborn are also important.[12]

Personal character and intelligence are, in part, understood as transmitted to the infant from the former owner of the soul. Physical appearance, for better or worse, may also be transmitted to the child from the reincarnated person. An elderly man and his teenage daughter provide an example.

The girl, who is a little chubby, is neatly dressed. I notice her face is severely deformed and wrinkled, the nose can hardly been seen, and her mouth is just a small, round hole. I ask her father if she got burnt as a child.

"No, she did not. She is a person who died, and that person got burnt," he responds.

"So she was born with her face like that?" I ask.

"No, she was born normal, but she became seriously ill and all her face became destroyed. Later, little by little she became better but her face never recovered," he responds, and stretches out his hand to give me an indication about his daughter's age at that time. Apparently she had been four or six years old.

People maintain that infants inherit both personality and physical appearance through the soul that is reincarnated in their body. That soul is essential for their human status. My attempts to detect a still more complete humanness with increased age or linked to particular events after birth were not successful.

Rearing through Play and Punishment

Personal character is inborn, but learning is still a prerequisite for a fruitful future. Parents, or their substitutes, are responsible for bringing up their children properly and for teaching them to become hardworking and honest people. Intelligence is also valued, as is verbal competence; however, both are recognized as contributing factors to deceitfulness.

Children are trained to acquire certain physical abilities. Infants are hardly able to walk before they have learned through imitation to rhythmically swing their hips and clap hands. Play is also used to teach infants to behave correctly. Give-and-take games are common: a young child will be offered an item, or piece of food, but then asked to give it back.[13] If the child agrees to give it back the action will be acknowledged kindly, and the item will be returned to the child. If the child keeps the item, unwilling to share it with others, it will be commented on. The child may also be hit lightly on its shoulders or cheek, or a hand waved in front of its face as a sign of disapproval of her or his unwillingness to share. From an early age infants hear "I will hit you" (n'na sutau) when they do something inappropriate. Beating as a way of teaching is introduced gradually. The seriousness of the warning is revealed when children become older.

Physical punishment is seen as an essential instrument to teach boys and girls older than two years proper behavior. Mariama explains to me the main conventions for disciplining children:

> You should never beat a child that is not yours, or one you are not responsible for. It is a humiliation when other people hit your child—that way they

say that you have not brought them up properly. It is your obligation to educate your child. If it does not behave well you have to beat it, but you
should only beat your own child, you understand? If another person beats
your child you feel insulted.

However, not all women like to beat their own children. Some women
lament their situation, as does Nhora, who is in her fifties. She finds it difficult to physically discipline her own children and still more so her grandchildren. Nhora argues: "Children are the product of their upbringing. To
have success in life children have to be prepared not to become lazy and deceitful, you understand? Because I do not have the heart to beat my children
they never help me. My children never help me. Because I don't beat them,
I have to do all the work myself."

Women do not agree on whether beating is a good thing or not. Juana
says she prefers to talk to her children rather than physically discipline them:
"When you beat children a lot, they may become still worse. Some children
never develop properly because they are beaten too much," Juana remarks.

I often hear women declare that men are more inclined to physically
punish children than women are. Janette, a young mother of three, argues
that women are less likely to beat children than men because when women
beat children or observe other people beat children they remember the pain
they suffered when they gave birth. "When my husband beats my child I feel
the pains of giving birth," she says. I find myself within a group of women
who all agree that men use physical punishment more than women. "A
child loves its mother more than its father," they agree. "But a child is more
afraid of the father and obeys him better." Nonetheless, I frequently observe
women beating children, but have hardly ever witnessed a man beat a child.
However, I regularly see elderly men brandishing sticks and running after
groups of misbehaving kids. Men are possibly responsible for the rare but
serious punishments, while women take care of the routine upbringing.[14]

I do not register in my field notes all cases of child beating because
it is too common an event. I often see women hit children, normally four
to twelve years of age. Indeed, often upon my arrival beatings stop with a
comment that it will continue after my departure. Sometimes children are
beaten quite harshly, sometimes with bare hands but more frequently with
some object such as a wooden stick, a shoe, a stool, a bundle of straws, or
whatever is at hand. Some children are hit only once or twice, others are hit
many times. Most often children respond with intense crying and shouting.
It appears that the few children who do not cry are hit more intensely and
for a longer time than those who whine. Most of the time beatings are intended to punish wrongdoing, such as when a child hits a younger toddler,
refuses to obey, destroys or loses something valuable, spills water, steals, lies,
wets the bed, or soils clothes. Children who refuse to take their medicines

are often forced to do so with violence. Some children who have a habit of eating earth are beaten. When I ask a mother whose daughter liked to eat soil whether there aren't other ways to make her stop eating dirt, she responds: "The only way is to beat her, then she will cease to eat dirt."

The beating of children is not always justified as just punishment or as necessary for educational purposes. Some people are known to be very heavy-handed with a particular child or to children in general. A mother of a ten-year-old girl beats her a lot. She complains about her daughter's bad manners, at the same time she shouts ugly words about the child's father who lives in a nearby village. The villagers have various interpretations of the unjustified abuse of the girl. A female villager tells me how the mother had hit her daughter until she could not cry anymore. Even at that point she continued to beat her. Still worse, she was not at all embarrassed when people turned their heads to see what was going on. "I live on the other side of the village and I still get disturbed by hearing those awful beatings. That woman must be sick in her head," she says. A male villager explains the maltreatment differently: "The problem is that the mother does not love her daughter," he argues. Still another female villager highlights the unresolved conflict the mother has with the daughter's father. To take vengeance on someone through maltreatment of a child is a recognized practice, she says: "After a divorce I would never leave my children with my husband. He will treat them badly only because he hates me."

In those cases where children are severely abused, mental illness, lack of love, and hatred may all be viable explanations. Infants and younger children are rarely victims of physical violence, while children older than four to five years are frequently punished physically when misbehaving.

Another way mothers provide children with a firm and good upbringing is to send them to be fostered for a period of time. Children are said to be more likely to learn to work hard and behave better when brought up outside the parental home. Let us therefore look at the fosterage practices. Who are the most common foster parents? For what reasons are children sent to stay away from their mothers? What do mothers think about leaving their children with others?

Fosterage

Many children stay away from their mothers for a period of time during their childhood. Most of the time this is a question of fosterage but not legal adoption (juridical substitution of parenthood). The expression used is "to give" *(padi)* or "lend" *(pista)* a child.[15] Children are normally not fostered before they are taken off the breast, and only in case of a mother's death or other extreme situation is a newborn left to stay with a woman other than its mother.

According to the village survey I conducted in 1995–96, about one-third of mothers who have at least one weaned child younger than five years has one or more of her children staying with others.[16] About three-fifths of all these children stay with their maternal grandmother or *dona*. Close relatives, mostly maternal or paternal aunts, take care of about one-fifth of the children, and another one-fifth stay with their father and *madrassa,* their mother's co-wives. Children younger than five years stay with their maternal grandmother or on rare occasions with a mother's co-wife, while all children who stay with aunts and other close relatives are nine years or older. The mothers I interview are more likely to have their own children fostered than to foster others' children.

Mothers most commonly give two reasons for fostering. Nearly half of respondents say they need someone to feed and/or take care of the child, and roughly two-fifths say they have given a child to their own mother because it is the custom to do so. The custom that a woman gives a child to her mother is frequently expressed in religious terms. Mother's mothers claim they have the right to take one of their grandchildren, and should a woman refuse to give her own mother a child, then death, illness, or bad luck, may befall her.[17] Elderly women also often take care of additional grandchildren to help their daughters terminate breastfeeding, work, or manage a difficult situation. The *dona* may live in the same village as the mother or in a nearby village but sometimes they live far away. Children often weep for their mothers for the first few days but normally acclimate rapidly. Several times mothers say to me that the *dona* and the child have became used to each other and therefore they would not take the child back.

Divorce is the third most common reason for children not staying with their mothers.[18] The first husband or the husband who has paid the bride price formally has rights over all the children of his wife. Nonetheless, a mother will not easily leave her children with him if she is on bad terms with her co-wives. Most men are neither willing to have their children brought up with another man, nor are they willing to live with children their new wife has by a former husband. Therefore, a woman will probably not bring her children from a previous relationship with her to live with a new man. She will leave the children with her own mother or somebody else, most likely an aunt (her own sister or a sister of her husband) or a paternal uncle of the children.[19] No mother says she had given a child to one of her brothers, though he is likely to live in the same compound as his mother. A man will preferably not foster a sister's son who is likely to become his heir. "A man should help his sisters to bring up their children," António affirms, "but he will not take his sister's son to his home and bring him up. The sister's son only comes to stay in his house after his death."

Mothers express a variety of feelings when asked about their willingness to have their children fostered. Some mothers mumble, "there is nothing to do about it" *(djitu ka ten)*. Others maintain that the child will be better off or that the child will only stay away for a short period of time. In fact, the amount of time a child stays away is most frequently seen as temporary or uncertain. Children may stay with a *dona* only for a couple of months or until they are grown up. The biological parents will keep personal contact with their child and the foster family. To adopt a child, that is, to register it officially as a child of one's own, is known but uncommon. The emotional relations that children have with foster mothers vary; most people express their profound affection for all their mothers, be it *dona, madrassa,* an aunt, or other woman. Not all foster children are so lucky, and some suffer harassment, hard work, beatings, and even hunger. However, in turn, mothers say these children learn to work hard and become better prepared for real life than children brought up only by their own parents or *dona*. Indeed, though mother's mothers are the most common foster caregivers, they are considered to be bad educators.

A *dona's* love for her grandchild is taken for granted and she is assumed to do her best to ritually protect her grandchild and to feed her or him the best she can. However, my informants agree that a *dona* loves her grandchildren too much and spoils them.[20] Juana explains:

> Djuma has spoiled her teenage granddaughter. The girl never does any work and when she does not want to go to school she will lie to her *dona* that she has a headache and her *dona* feels pity for her and allows her to stay at home. The girl is fooling her *dona* and in the end she herself will suffer; she neither succeeds with her schoolwork nor does she know how to do any work worth the name. The old woman will not be able to protect her granddaughter for her whole life.

Women are also concerned with other problems. Grandmothers are sometimes aged, their health may be frail, and they lack awareness of changed times, especially regarding health care. If the mothers live far away, in Bissau or in another distant village, they are unable to intervene if the child becomes suddenly sick. This may leave the child in a precarious situation. The other women in the compound will not take the child to the health center or advise her or his *dona* to do so because it would make them responsible if the child dies. The Papel are normally careful not to interfere in the affairs of other people, particularly if relations are constrained. Witchcraft accusations are common and nobody wants to become involved when death is a possibility.

In Biombo I often notice newly weaned children staying with a relative or a *dona*. The conditions of these children vary. An elderly woman tells me that her grandson is surely much better off with her than with his mother. "His mother is at the marketplace in Bissau all day long; from early morning to late night she sells bread. That is not a good life for a young boy," she says. Her grandson, who is two and a half years old and somewhat small for his age, looks happy and his grandmother is proud of him. "He is very clever. He will stay with me for some years, maybe until he starts school. He has already had all his vaccinations, and I always take him to the mission hospital when he is sick."

Poor three-year-old Zinha is not so lucky. Her grandmother is old and confused. Zinha coughs all the time and looks thin and neglected. She has no vaccination card and her grandmother never takes her to the mission hospital or the health center.

"The old woman is more in the other world," explains a neighbor. "She does not follow the new times."

"But why don't some of the other women take Zinha for treatment and vaccination," I suggest.

"No, you won't do that without permission. In case the girl dies you would be made responsible," she responds.

If a misfortune befalls a mother's lineage, she may fear it will cause her child's death while he or she stays with the mother's mother; the *baloba* might see the child and take it to punish a maternal family member for ritual failure (see chapter 4). At the same time, a child staying with a *dona* is protected from a jealous co-wife who might want to kill the child with sorcery. In extreme cases, such as repeated child deaths of unknown causes, a mother may decide to give her child to a person living far away from matrilineal hazards and envious co-wives. Such a person could even be someone belonging to another ethnic group. Yet another alternative to protect the life of children is to give a girl as a *katandeira*.

When a particular mother or a group of women belonging to the same lineage lose many children, senior lineage members can visit a *baloba* (a kapok tree where an ancestral soul has settled) belonging to another lineage and ask for help. With the mediation of the *balobeiru* of the respective *baloba* they will ask the ancestral spirit to ensure that their lineage women give birth to many healthy children, making the lineage numerous and powerful. In turn, the senior representatives of the lineage will promise to send a girl from their lineage to serve the *baloba,* that is, to become a *katandeira*. A *katandeira* has a lifelong obligation to "fetch water" (*kata iagu,* and hence the name *katandeira*) and cook rice to offer at the *baloba,* and the *balobeiru* has the right to wed the *katandeira* or arrange her marriage. Several years later, when it becomes clear that the *baloba* granted the lineage members' plea (that is, when children stop dying so often), the contract must be fulfilled. At that moment, mothers are not always willing to give their daughters as *katandeira,* however, a mother who has lost many children is the first candidate to do so. If she does not agree to send a daughter away she will risk losing still more children as a punishment for her rejection (see chapter 4).

Two mothers tell me they have given girls to serve *baloba* in distant villages.[21] When I ask Juana if it is a good thing to become a *katandeira* she emphasizes that it is respectable and sometimes favorable in economic terms:

> You know, Helena's daughter is a *katandeira*. She is much better off with the *balobeiru* than with her mother. She eats good food and travels a lot. She is respected because she serves a *baloba*. People are also a little afraid of her because of that. The *balobeiru,* an old woman, is very kind to her but she has no children of her own and she treats the girl as if she were her own daughter.

Juana admits that not all girls are as lucky as Helena's daughter. Some *balobeiru* are drunkards. Some may marry the *katandeira* themselves while others give them to their sons or somebody else. Juana tells me about a famous *balobeiru* in a neighboring village who used to have many *katandeira*. They all had a good life because he was wealthy and he always had plenty of rice. But when he died his successor turned out to be a scoundrel. Now he marries all the *katandeira* himself. "He treats his wives badly. One of his sons wants to take the *balobeiru* to court for having killed his mother. But that *baloba* is strong and you have to give a *katandeira* if you want some help. There is nothing to do about it. That's our custom," Juana argues, but then she adds: "But this custom will disappear. Today many mothers refuse to give their daughters as *katandeira*."

The custom of giving girls as *katandeira* illustrates a concern for child survival at the lineage level. Similar concerns, however, on a more individual level, are reflected in the general fosterage patterns of the Papel. Mothers emphasize the positive aspects of fosterage such as better social or economic conditions for the child, and their own opportunities to "look for life" or "make a living" *(buska bida* or *fasi bida)*, that is, engage in work or a new relationship. The negative aspects of fosterage are similarly related to mothers' anxieties about the health and well-being of their fostered children.

Let us now look at the Papel naming practices. Are these informed by conceptualizations of infants and young children and the high child mortality rates?

Name Giving and Meaningful Names

Most people have a Papel name, which in Kriol is called *nomi di terra* and mainly used at home, and another (often Portuguese) name called the "white man's name" *(nomi di branku)* or "city name" *(nomi di prassa)*. The surname is that of the father, or more exactly that of the mother's husband, likely to be the father. In addition, some families, often Christians, or families with a Portuguese connection since the colonial time, have a Portuguese surname or middle name.

In the course of my fieldwork in Biombo (see the introduction) I register all 700 inhabitants living in a village. At that time I thought I understood the name-giving practices of the Papel. Two young men who know all adult villagers and most youngsters by name assist me. Aware that more than one name is often used for the same person we decide to use the name most frequently used in the village, or both the Papel name and the white man's name. Our census runs smoothly and I feel confident of our work.

Some weeks later I identify through my census mothers of all children younger than five years of age in the village. When I interview these mothers some of them say they or their children have different names from those we have registered. In a few cases the children's surnames are also said to be different. Some mothers want me to register them with a new white man's name. "I like that name better now," one mother explains. Occasionally mothers say their Papel name is not wholly wrong but that another name is used more frequently. The surnames of the mothers are all correct. To sort out problems with the children's names is more complicated, partly because this time I want to see their vaccination card. Sometimes a child is registered with a different name from that on the vaccination card, and now the child's mother proposes still a third name. What is the problem?

There are various reasons for the discrepancies in children's first names. The white man's name is typically used for bureaucratic, official purposes. Thus, when a mother goes to the health center for the first time with her newborn she may announce whatever white man's name crosses her mind, and she does not always remember it later. The mother may also decide to change her child's name. During the census, one father informs us about his children's names and insists that we register the white man's names. But since these are seldom used he does not remember which of his children has what name. Another father informs us of the name of his child, but the mother apparently does not like that name, and therefore asks me to register her child with a new one.

The discrepancy in children's surnames has its roots in the fact that many women marry older men and thus they often become widows at a young age. The husband's sister's son will inherit these widows or they will remarry or find a lover and continue to give birth. Some of these women use their late husbands' surnames for all their children, even those born after the husband's death. One mother prefers to register her infant with her own family name, Nank, the family name of the royal lineage. Still other women whose husbands have not inherited from their mothers'

brothers, prefer their infants carry the family name of the husbands'
matrilineage, but when a man inherits from his mother's brother he will
change his surname and take the surname of his own lineage, that is, the
name of his mother's lineage.

The problems I have in keeping the villagers properly registered reflect
the somewhat ad hoc name-giving practices. There are children who get
their name(s) right at birth, others may be without a name for months, and
others start with a particular name but end up with a new one. The same
person may be called by a variety of names depending on who addresses
her or him, when and in what social context.[22] This can cause problems, for
example when a person who has moved dies and the death is announced on
the national radio. It is not always obvious to rural people what names their
relatives use when outside their home village.

There is no special name-giving act. When a child is born, little by little
those who are interested, most likely the child's mother, father, or *dona* just
begin to use a name, often a Papel name. If there is more than one name
suggested, the one most frequently used is usually accepted. However, sometimes no consensus is achieved about the child's name, and thus two or
more names will be used. Fernanda's youngest daughter still goes by two
names. Her father gave her a Papel name and at first it appeared to be the
only name in use, however, after three to four months her mother and older
siblings started to use a Portuguese name. Two years later she goes by both
names but her Portuguese name is clearly more frequently used.

Most Papel names have a particular meaning, and many can be used for
girls as well as boys. For instance the Papel name Batada, "you were late to
come," reflects the fact that a child's mother had waited a long time for her
first child to be born. The name Adoline has the meaning "what will you
offer me?" Both names are used for girls and boys. To name a child after
an influential person or someone who is likely to contribute to the child's
livelihood is common. Some children are named after a foreigner close to
the family (there are two Joninas in Bissau and one little girl was given my
name in Quinhamel, but tragically she died at about six months of age).
Children may be named after a deceased relative, though not if that person
died young or in unfortunate circumstances for fear the child may be fated
to suffer the same destiny. People also avoid names of those who died a
tragic death at an early age in consideration of the mother, for whom the
name and child would be a painful reminder. Twins should have similar
names such as Erica and Erique, Augusto and Augusta, or Paulo and Pau-
lino. Adults, or older children, may get nicknames in accordance with their
personal character. An elderly, hot-tempered man is referred to as Mala-
gueta (a Kriol word for hot pepper), and a young man as Uit (a Papel word
for bull). "Uit, he is a fighter," a female villager explains.

Mothers who have lost many children sometimes prefer to wait before naming their newborn. "They are afraid that the child will die," Maria says. "They do not want to lose another child with a real name. A nameless child is easier to forget." A mother who has lost one or more successive children can name the next one born Impors, a Papel word that signifies child.[23] There are still mothers who prefer to use names that indicate their fear that the child might die or the modest hope that the child will at least survive. The Kriol name Elsó (the corresponding Papel name is Otokonono) means "the only one." The Kriol name Amisó (in Papel Anssumai), means "only me." Such names symbolize a mother's hope of keeping one child. Kriol names such as Mortu (death) and I Na Muri (the corresponding Papel name is Pekers, meaning "she or he will die") have been consciously chosen to avoid tempting fate.[24] All these names indicate that the mothers have lost many or all of their previous children.

The name-giving practices not only reflect a concern for the child's survival and its future but also the emotional and material benefits the child will hopefully give its mother. Names are chosen to describe circumstances, not tempt fate, pray for mercy, build or strengthen alliances, et cetera. Finally, some names are chosen simply because they are liked.

Conceptualizing Children and Child Care

This chapter covers the Papel mothers' ideas about their infants, their child-care practices, and naming customs. The question is whether conceptions about young children influence childcare and educational practices. Are these conceptions as well as maternal dedication also reflected in the naming customs?

Beliefs in reincarnation clearly mark conceptualizations about children and their humanness, personality, and agency. Papel conceptualizations of infants and their child care practices stand somewhat in contrast to those of Alto mothers as described by Scheper-Hughes (1992). Papel mothers view their newborns as human at birth, each one having a particular personality, in contrast to the Alto concept of infants as not yet fully human and without an individual personality. The infant care practices of the Papel involve a great deal of holding, co-sleeping, rapid response to crying, and devoted care, very much in line with descriptions of child care practices elsewhere in Africa (Leiderman et al. 1977, LeVine et al. 1994).[25] Massage and training secure physical capacity and attention is given to physical and mental development. An infant should never be left alone. In contrast, Alto mothers have little physical contact with their infants, who sleep in their own cot and small children may be left alone at home. They also show a lack of responsiveness to infants' individual needs and a general indifference to their survival. In Biombo, the mother is the most important caregiver during the first two years of life; however, as in Alto, the mother is not the only care-giver as elderly women and young girls, and even boys, frequently assist the mother, especially in caring for weaned children.

Scheper-Hughes's description of the Alto mother's concept of children and its contribution to neglectful child care and lack of mourning for child death is persuasive. However, I argue that conceptions of infants' gradual achievement of humanness and individual personality do not necessarily imply mothers' lack of interest for their survival. The infant's potentiality for full humanness and individual personality can be reason enough to care for its survival; if the infant survives it will become a beloved son or a daughter with his or her own personality, wants, and preferences. As will be discussed in next chapter, losing something that never fully developed can be cause enough for grief.[26]

There are some similarities concerning fosterage practices and naming customs in the Alto and Biombo.[27] In both societies children are fostered when mothers' circumstances do not allow them to adequately take care of their children. Additionally, in Biombo, the institution of *katandeira* is aimed at preventing child deaths. Both societies practice delayed naming and use impersonal terms such as "baby" for certain infants. Papel naming practices are clearly shaped by the high level of infant mortality, but they in no way reflect maternal indifference to child survival, rather the contrary.[28]

Richard D. Alford's cross-cultural study of naming and identity is re-vealing about causes for delayed naming of infants (1988).[29] Alford admits that his

> initial expectation was that the period of naming would largely be a product of infant mortality. Societies with higher infant mortality would name chil-dren later, as one way to reduce the attachment to a child who might well die; and societies with lower infant mortality would name children earlier, since the risks of attachment were lesser. (1988:34)

To Alford's surprise, only in a few societies did he find so-called "risks of attachment" as an explanation for delayed naming. Reasons other than avoidance of grief for delayed naming were more frequently given. Alford's study shows that in some societies parents wanted to avoid the attention of injurious spirits; in others parents maintained that named infants were more likely to die or that an infant might be too weak to bear a name—to burden a child with a name would cause illness. Still others perceived the naming of an infant as a statement about its possibility of survival; because that would tempt fate, it was better to postpone naming. Alford also found that naming frequently coincided with certain achievements of the child such as weaning, crawling, or teething. One more reason for delayed naming was to wait for the child to demonstrate its individual personality to be able to give it a more appropriate name.[30]

As demonstrated in Alford's cross-cultural study, delay in naming infants is often likely to be related to parents' wishes to protect their infants, and an early naming is believed to endanger the child's life. Ethnographic evidence also shows, however, that delayed naming is sometimes used intentionally to reduce grief. Alford refers to the Kanuri people in Nigeria who name their infants eight days after birth because they prefer "to reduce their grief" if the infant dies (1988:34). Catherine Lutz describes how the Ifaluk in Micronesia prefer to delay naming for ten days because newborns are known to die easily: "It is better that a newborn who dies do so nameless; without a name . . . there is less to forget," they argue (1988:106). However, an Ifaluk infant is considered a person while still in its mother's womb and there is no indication of Ifaluk mothers' lack of attachment to their infants (see Lutz 1988:105 –9). Similarly, a Papel mother who has lost many children may prefer to let her newborn infant die unnamed because it is considered easier to forget. Forgetting can be a bereavement strategy, and it should not be confused with fear of attachment or maternal indifference. The Papel custom not to give the same name of a child who died young in order to avoid reminding the mother about the tragic death reflects the strategy of forgetting as a way of coping with grief.

The Papel concept of infants and child care practices are influenced by the belief that an infant is born with a reincarnated soul and thus conceived of as a human being with an individual personality. Nonetheless, conceptions that do not attribute humanness and individual personality to newborns do not necessarily bring about maternal indifference, neglectful care, or a lack of grief when infants die. Furthermore, delayed name giving and use of unattractive or impersonal names is likely to be an indication of maternal concern for infant survival, not of indifference. I suggest that mothers' statements that a nameless child is easier to forget should be taken as a bereavement strategy rather than an avoidance of attachment.

As will be discussed in the next chapter, which treats mothers' interpretations of diseases and death and their ideas about the afterlife, forgetting is a long-term bereavement strategy that Papel mothers use in their attempts to keep on living despite the deaths of their children.

4

Diseases and Death

Juleta, who is in her forties, is one of those women who has lost many children, but she also has many left. When I meet her for the first time she has six children who are alive; she has lost six. Juleta gave birth to three children with her first husband but only the first-born daughter is alive. Then her husband suddenly disappeared and she had seven more children with a new husband; four of them have died. Juleta left that man and now she has a lover. He is the father of her two youngest children. Juleta's lastborn, a healthy and well-nourished one-year-old girl, is always referred to as Kodé, a term Juleta uses to indicate her intention to stop having children. "Six is enough," she says, and expresses her gratefulness to have both sons and daughters.

One day Juleta comes to see me. She has a problem: she has not "seen moon," or menstruated, for too long a time. Juleta says she feels how her body has changed. "Please, Jónína, help me with an abortion," she begs. To arrange an abortion is not an easy task. I hear from a friend in Bissau that at the National Hospital no abortions are performed because "there are no gloves" *(luva ka ten)*. Luckily, a week later Juleta passes by my house and happily declares that she has finally "seen moon." An abortion is not needed any more, but now she wants me to arrange contraceptives for her. "I can't have more children," she tells me, and begins to complain about her bad luck with men. She has to feed all her children alone and pay for their school, health care, and clothes. To arrange contraceptives for Juleta appears no easier task than an abortion: the intrauterine device (IUD) is too dangerous and women feel bad when they take the pill, she tells me. A condom (*kamisa di bentu* or "shirt of the wind") will not work either. "Something else. I am in a hurry. My Kodé is sick. Her body is all hot," she explains and leaves. A few days later Juleta passes by again and reminds me about the contraceptives. Again she is in a hurry—Kodé is still sick. The nun gives Kodé some medicine every day, she says. The next evening, Kodé dies.

The following morning I attend Kodé's burial together with two other women. When we come closer to the place of the funeral, the home of Juleta's first husband's maternal uncle, we hear the crying. My companions enter the compound; they walk straight, always looking forward and not greeting anybody. Juleta sits with extended legs in front of the house and cries violently. She does not notice our arrival. We enter the house where a group of women cry. Kodé lies on the floor, wrapped in black shrouds. Her maternal grandmother comes and takes a seat beside the body and cries; she talks and strikes her hand in the air. When we go outside a few men and some twenty women are there already. People enter the compound continuously. The women are crying silently. Juleta and a few other women run around hysterically. They all have naked breasts and are without shoes. They cry and shout "Kodé, Kodé, Kodé." The dead child's maternal grandmother joins them. Her father stumbles around heavily drunk, crying and talking to himself. A pig enters the yard looking for food; a cat sleeps in the sun and chicken scratch around. A group of children stand silently on the periphery. We sit for one hour or more and a woman sitting next to me comments, "The sun is getting hot." At that point, a group of men begin to prepare a bier for *djongagu* to identify the cause of death. That makes Juleta cry still louder. A group of elderly men enter the house and carry Kodé out and place her on the bier. Two young men lift the bier up and halt in front of an elderly man who asks Kodé for the reason of her death. The bier moves ahead, indicating a negative response to all his questions. Then other people ask and the bier still indicates no. Finally, the girl's maternal grandmother poses her question and the bier moves backwards. The *djongagu* identifies Kodé's maternal aunt, who died several years ago, as responsible for her death. Everybody is completely silent, observing the bier. There is no crying. Then, the bier halts in front of Juleta, who cries violently. The bier is finally carried away to the grave behind the house. Only men follow but many of the women, together with Juleta, cry more intensely than ever. Suddenly, everybody leaves the yard, without greetings, without affirming words of comfort.

On the way back I am told that God was punishing Kodé's maternal aunt for having done sorcery so she was obliged to take children belonging to her womb to the other world. When I come home and begin writing my field notes, I suddenly hear weeping from the mission hospital, a sign that yet another child has died. The rain pours down, it is September, famine time, the most dangerous time of the year for young children.

Juleta cries for several days. Juana visits her and tries to make her understand that she cannot keep on crying, she "must begin to forget." Ana brings her food several times and tries to console her, but to little avail. Ana tells me that the very same day Kodé died, Juleta had taken her to a *djambakus* who diagnosed her with "sudden pain" *(pontada)*. He refused to treat the child and told Juleta to go elsewhere for help. "You understand that he knew she was dying. It is difficult with *uso* [tradition]. When you know she is dying you will not enter into the matter because, if she dies, you run the risk that people will say you killed that girl," Ana explains. Later, a male villager indicates that Juleta spent far too much time on seeking care within *uso*, she should have taken Kodé straight to the nuns the day she died, as he had told her to do.

Some weeks later Juleta travels to see her brother. She hopes he has enough rice to give her some. When I see Juleta after a couple of months at her arrival back in the village she looks better. "Everything is fine," she answers when I ask about her situation. Juleta tells me that she is hoping to have one more child. Aware that she is close to the end of her fertile period, Juleta argues that she menstruates every month and that her age mates are still giving birth. "Jónína, you know, every time I see an infant I want to have one more child," she says sadly. A mutual friend tells me that Juleta always cries for her last-born. "*Kodé* should not die. You know, everybody wants to have a *kodé*. The first child is also very much beloved by its mother, but that child dies easily," she explains. Juleta desperately wants to have her *kodé*, but three years later she has still not become pregnant again.

Worldwide, too many women share their lot with Juleta. In 1999, approximately 10.5 million children died before reaching their fifth birthday, and 98–99 percent of these deaths occurred in low-income countries (Ahmad et al. 2000). Africa accounted for 36 percent of these deaths and the continent has the highest child mortality rate in the world. In Africa, 150 children out of 1,000 live births die before they reach the age of five years, and for sub-Saharan Africa the average is 175.[1] The burden of mortality is still unequally distributed among and within African countries. The difference between the lowest and highest child mortality rates within Africa is more than tenfold, and mortality rates for particular ethnic groups are considerably lower for those with access to power and economic resources (Brockerhoff and Hewlett 1998).

In Europe and Northern America child mortality declined dramatically in the nineteenth century and the first half of the twentieth. However, this decline was not always linear, and the death of children aged one to five years dropped faster and more continuously than for younger infants (Bengtsson 1996; Bideau, Desjardins, and Brignoli 1997; Corsini and Viazza 1997; Garðarsdóttir 2002, Lithell 1999; Rollet 1997). After an almost 60 percent drop in global child mortality rates for children under the age of five years during the second half of the twentieth century, the decline in child mortality has slowed down during the two past decades. Recently child mortality rates have even increased in some countries, particularly in Southern Africa (Ahmad et al. 2000).[2] The diseases that most commonly lead to child deaths are acute lower respiratory infections, diarrhea, measles, and malaria. These diseases are aggravated by malnutrition in more than half of the cases (Gove 1997, Rutstein 2000, Smedman 1999). About 70 percent of these deaths are preventable and can be treated at low cost. The underlying factor contributing to the high death toll is a lack of appropriate and accessible health services for pregnant women and sick children, which is compounded by socioeconomic factors.[3] Deficient environmental conditions, such as limited access to safe water and sanitation and decent housing, make an already precarious situation even worse. Furthermore, child survival is shown to improve with better education of mothers.[4]

There has been an upsurge within anthropology of writings on children and youth suffering from inequality, discrimination, poverty, and war (Argenti 2001; Blanchet 1996; Croll 2000; de Berry and Boyden 2002; Glauser 1990; Hecht 1998; Kitzinger 1990; Miller 1997; Nieuwenhuys 1994, 1996; Peters and Richards 1998; Richards 1996; Scheper-Hughes and Sargent 1998; Stephens 1995). On the other hand, the alarmingly high infant and child mortality common to everyday life in so many poor communities has been given less attention.[5] Guided by the perspective of political economy, writings on children and youth in adversity are often concerned with global processes, though they often, but not always, also give consideration to the local history, cultural context, and individual experiences. Scheper-Hughes's book *Death without Weeping* (1992) is an exemplar of an ethnography that takes into account the complex historical, political, economic, and religious background while it remains highly concerned with the local culture and everyday life of individuals.[6]

According to Scheper-Hughes (1992), whenever Alto mothers speak about why children die—in general terms—they name poverty, hunger, bad water quality, lack of shoes, and deficient medical care. Money would solve all these problems, they say. However, when speaking about the deaths of their own children, no mother names poverty and hunger as the cause of death. Instead, the women distinguish between child deaths they view as natural, that is, coming from God or from nature, and deaths they suspect are caused by sorcery, the evil eye, and magical possessions. Mothers attribute most of their own children's deaths to natural causes and name diarrhea as the most common killer of children. They also mention measles and respiratory diseases as common causes of child death. At the same time, mothers often emphasize the cause of death as being located inside the child, who is seen as "born already wanting to die" (315).

Alto mothers want infants to demonstrate a fighting spirit: "active, quick, responsive, and playful infants were much preferred to quiet, docile, inactive infants, infants described as 'dull,' 'listless,' and spiritless" (Scheper-Hughes 1992:316). An infant who does not thrive risks being classified as a "doomed" child, one that has the feared "*child sickness*" (364). Such an infant is generally regarded to be "as good as dead," or "better off dead" (365). Local faith healers and the elderly praying women do not cure this disease, as children become damaged if they survive. Hence mothers are afraid of a cure and hope for a quick death. If a child is suspected of having the feared *child sickness,* she or he is taken to a hospital often as a precaution against gossip that the mother neglected the child (in fact, 70–80 percent of all child deaths in the Alto occur at home). Nonetheless, Scheper-Hughes affirms that a mother who turns away from a "doomed" child is not blamed and she would not hold herself responsible for her infant's death even though it may be hastened by withholding fluids, food, and care.

The Alto mothers do not weep for their dead infants: they do not mourn by remaining silent, nor do mothers show signs of delayed grief. Instead, a mother may feel relieved and say that she has not had enough time to love the infant who died before revealing a personality.[7] Furthermore, Alto mothers find it comforting to think about their children as angels in heaven. At the funeral of a child neither joy nor grief is expressed, and the infant is not the focus of discussion. According to Scheper-Hughes, men are rarely present, but "female relatives, neighbor women, and children often mill about" (1992:419). No special clothes are put on. Some adults, but never the mother, may follow the procession to the graveyard. Sometimes children bury children. The priest does not give a blessing, toll a bell, nor accompany the procession to the cemetery. Scheper-Hughes argues that the observed indifference of Alto mothers toward the death of their children is but "a pale reflection of the 'official' indifference of church and state to the plight of poor mothers and children" (1992:272). She claims that the noted indifference to children's survival at all levels in the society contributes to "normalization" of child death. Scheper-Hughes maintains that in many poor countries "the naturalness of infant and child mortality has yet to be questioned." There, "child death may be viewed less as a tragedy than as a predictable and relatively minor misfortune, one to be accepted with equanimity and resignation as an unalterable fact of human existence" (275).

In Biombo child death is a common event: one-third of all children born alive are likely to die before they reach the age of five years. Most adult Papel women have experienced the death of a child—some have lost many children and a few mothers have lost all the children to whom they have given birth. The requisites of the neglect thesis, namely, extreme poverty, high fertility, and child mortality are present in Biombo. The question is whether the deaths of some Biombo children may somehow be caused by negligent care due to maternal indifference for infant survival. Is there a "normalization" of child deaths in Biombo?

In order to answer these questions I begin this chapter with a discussion of diseases, death, and the afterlife. This leads us to a consideration of the accessible alternatives for health care and categorizations of the most important of the children's diseases. What health care alternatives are available to mothers? Do mothers have the necessary resources to seek care? Do mothers have confidence in the health care alternatives at hand? Do all mothers always recognize the danger of their child's disease? Finally, I discuss maternal grief. The question, however, is not whether Biombo's mothers grieve, but rather, why mothers grieve for their dead children. Is maternal grief related to interpretations of the cause of death as good or bad? Does the belief that the child has been granted a pleasant afterlife help the mother to accept its death and free her from grief?

Diseases, Death, and Afterlife

I discuss diseases, death, and the afterlife with Mário, an elderly village man, late in the afternoon at his compound. Mário does his best to help me understand that diseases, death, and life in the other world are all intertwined. He emphasizes that diseases have various causes and should be cured accordingly but that ultimately God is responsible for and involved in every event, even diseases and death. Mário explains: "Only those people who are called on by God, those who die from God's diseases, will inhabit the other world . . . but those who die suddenly will not find a place there, as they were not called on by God. You know, people who die badly will come to the other world but they will be driven away and they may settle in a *baloba*. God wants it that way, that *baloba* tells people what God says."

"But a child that dies . . . will that child go to the other world?" I ask.

"Children who die will enter the other world without problems because they have not done anything wrong," Mário maintains. "Children who die will meet their grandmother or father in the other world and they will take care of them. But children will return to this world." Mário maintains that people who die will be reborn in the other world in another form; their body will decay in the earth but the soul *(alma)* will enter into a new form in the other world.

Later I discuss the same question with Impors, a middle-aged village woman, and Pekers, an old *balobeiru*. Pekers is unwilling to speculate about the other world. "I have not seen the other world . . . I will only know when I die," he argues. However, a little later he tells me a story I had already heard several times. The story is about the death of an old Papel man who constructs a barrack in Manjaco land and waits there for his family to come. Pekers explains: "You understand, the soul goes to the barrack but the body will stay in the earth. Those who die in old age from God's diseases will stay there in the other world. But a person who dies *kru* [raw, uncooked] cannot settle in the barrack. That person will sometime be reborn here in this world. Their soul is here still but we can't see it."

Pekers emphasizes that the Papel still follow the original law, which states that people who have pain in their body go to a *baloba* and ask God for help. "God makes everything. It is God who brings us people to this world. It is God who maintains us here. Without God we would be only dirt on the earth," Pekers maintains.

Like Pekers, Impors argues that we do not know what happens when we are dead: "We have never seen what is in the other world." She also maintains that a person who dies suddenly may go there but such a person will not be allowed to settle because God has not called on that person.

"But children, do they enter the other world? Can a child be called on by God?" I ask.

Impors clarifies: "A child will never die from one of God's diseases. Children can stay for a while in the other world, but they all return. They may return to the womb of their last mother or to the womb of some other woman but a child will always return in the same lineage."

People agree that a child who dies will be reborn in this world, but in the meantime the child will stay in the other world. However, people do not agree on the form a person takes in the other world. Some say that there must be similarities between these two worlds and therefore those who die in this world must be born as infants in the other world. Others say people in the other world have the same appearance as they did when they left this world. Still others say they don't know. Finally people do not agree on whether a dead infant will be reborn in this world by the same mother, or even within the same lineage.

Juana tells me that there are mothers who cut a piece from their dead child's ear to recognize it again when it becomes reborn to her or to some other woman. Juana is inconsistent when she talks about the form of a person in the other world. One day she is quite determined that children who enter the other world will be reborn there as infants. Another day, I ask her if there is any difference between adults and infants in the other world. She answers that it is not always easy to be a child in the other world. However, if a child already has its *dona* there its life will not be bad. "You understand that the *dona* will take care of her grandchild. If she is already in the other world there will be no problems," she argues. Other people have expressed similar concerns about possible caregivers of children while they are in the other world waiting to return. Mpone argues that most children have some close relative in the other world to take care of them. She adds that in the other world people will not remember anything from this world: "Therefore, children who die will not weep for their mothers. But the mother, still in this world, she will remember her children who have died. She misses them and she weeps."

Most people assert that a child never dies because God has called on it. They also say that a child never dies "only from a disease." However, those who live in the *prassa*, often Christians who have attended school, may say that a child can die because of a simple disease. Once, when I try to understand the causes of child death, Segunda firmly argues that a child can indeed die from a "disease only."

"You mean that there are some children that die from a disease only? Most people seem to say that in the end the problem was a kind of combination of sorcery and other disease. Isn't it?" I ask.

"Yeah, most do, but some children die only from a disease," Segunda assures me. She tells me that her neighbor's daughter recently died "only from a disease." The girl was one year old and had just begun to walk when she became sick. One of the nuns at the mission hospital insisted on performing a medical analysis but the mother did not go to the laboratory; she had no money. Later when the child's health deteriorated the nun punished the mother by refusing to examine the child unless the mother paid a fine. The mother had no money and she went home with her daughter. "The girl died three days later from that disease. She had anemia . . . all white. It was only a disease. For sure," affirms Segunda.

A person's funeral reflects the nature of her or his death. Those who have never been engaged in sorcery and die old when God calls on them will find peace in the other world. The funerals of such people are joyous, but they are nonetheless called "weeping" *(tchuru)*. Animals are slaughtered and the beating-the-drum ceremony is performed to facilitate the entrance of the soul of the deceased in the other world. Funeral attendants laugh, drink, eat, and dance to celebrate. When a rich, respected, old person dies there may be a party for several days, and the body will not be buried until three to seven days after death. In contrast, untimely and sudden deaths are bad deaths that occur against the will of God. Such are the deaths of children. The burial must be carried out quickly; there is no beating-the-drum ceremony and no animals are slaughtered.

Despite this, children's funerals are highly emotional events. Children should be buried as soon as possible after death—in the morning if they die during the evening or night, otherwise in the afternoon. Neighbors, both men and women attend but women tend to be more numerous. The child's body is washed by an adult woman and then wrapped in a shroud. A mother never washes her dead child's body nor is she involved in wrapping it in the shrouds. The same applies to women closely related to the child. If the mother or the father of the dead child has lost other children, or if there is a suspicion that sorcery was involved, the identification ceremony for the cause of death, *djongagu,* will be performed. Children are buried outside the house, normally in the courtyard since "children do not yet have a house of their own." Older people or people with their own house may be buried inside their house or more likely in front of the doorstep. During the following days neighbors and family members who are unable to attend the funeral will come to express their bereavement. Then the mother will leave for her parents' home, where she may stay for a couple of weeks. There, she is expected to calm down and begin to forget her child.

Health Care Alternatives

Papel mothers and fathers consider diseases *(duensa, **pamaka**)* to be a huge problem for children. Nonetheless, diseases are thought to be curable if they are diagnosed correctly and treated adequately and quickly. In other words, there are no fatal diseases. Various alternatives for treatment are at hand depending on the seriousness of the respective disease. A distinction is made between two main categories of health care: that of *uso* or *mesinhu di terra* (local medicine), and *mesinhu di branku* (the white man's medicine.) The term *mesinhu* (medicine) is used for drugs, amulets, and other protective items, for instance to protect cars from accidents and valuables from thieves.[8]

An indication of an infant's disease is a "warm body during the night" (*kurpu kinti di noiti,* often recognized as malaria), listlessness, crying, vomiting, and loose stool. These symptoms are normally first noticed by the mother or another caregiver. The first action likely to be taken is an extra offering to the spirit of the compound. The head of the household, the child's parents, or the *dona* will offer to the *iran* of the compound a little *kana* (distillate from cashew wine or sugarcane brew) and boiled rice. Mpone explains: "When your child is sick you take rice in a calabash or clay pot, and *kana,* or rice and red palm oil and give it to the *iran.* The mother and the father go together, but the mother cooks the rice and carries it to the *iran.*" Women and men emphasize the importance of ritual to prevent diseases. An elderly man explains to me the importance of regularly performing an offering ceremony at the compound's *iran* to prevent children's diseases:

> When people do not respect our customs and do not continuously perform this ceremony children become sick. You must take some food to the *iran* otherwise children will become sick and die. Even if a child gets "the white man's medicines," it continues to be sick and will die if you only take it to the hospital. If you go to a *djambakus* to make a divination to know the problem and perform this ceremony the child may also die. If your child dies anyway, you still have to keep on and perform this ceremony to save other children.

Frequently, before any help is sought outside the home, some local herbal medicines are often used. A variety of plants are used for medical care and knowledge about these herbal medicines is widespread. Access to these herbs is often free because someone within the family, a helpful neighbor, or the mother or father themselves likely knows where to find the herbs and how to use them.

In case recovery is delayed or the infant's health becomes more precarious, the next step may be a visit to a *balobeiru* or a *djambakus* for divination *(bota sorti).* A divination offering is considered reasonably cheap, requiring about 500–5,000 pesos (5 –50 U.S. cents), in addition to a little rice and 300–500 milliliters of distillate alcohol. When the disease is suspected to be life-threatening and resources permit, several diviners may be visited. Healers and diviners who belong to other ethnic groups can also be consulted; their divinations are considered more independent since they do not know the family involved. If more than one diviner is visited the total outcome is evaluated, but sometimes the results turn out to be contradictory. After the diagnosis is established, one will seek a *djambakus* or a healer who specializes in resolving the problem at hand. According to *uso,* people should pay in accordance with the contract made with the respective *baloba, kansaré,* or *iran.* Payment can be a chicken, goat, pig, *kana,* rice, or cloth depending on the seriousness of the request and the economic situation of the person involved. Today some diviners and healers are considered to be more scoundrels or money-makers than respectable professionals; sometimes they ask for payment in advance instead of waiting until the patient is better, which is the custom.

While trying to cure the child's disease with *uso,* the mother may simultaneously decide or be urged to by her husband to take the child to the mission hospital or a state-run health center.[9] Both men and women agree that it is the responsibility of the mother to take her child for nontraditional treatment. "Only if you come home and see that your child is sick and its mother has not taken it for treatment, you will have to tell her," explained a father with whom I discussed health care for children.

"The white man's medicines," or *mesinhu di branku,* are considered to be effective for treatment of certain symptoms. The prices for these medicines have increased considerably during the last decade. During my stay the mission hospital had a fixed price for a consultation (5,000 pesos or about 50 U.S. cents), which included necessary medicines. For comparison, only one medication might cost ten times more in a drug store in Bissau. Many mothers remembered the days when Western-style medical care, when available, was free of charge for all. At the state-run health centers in Biombo health care was still free of charge for children, but these centers were frequently out of drugs. At that time the only possibility was to buy the prescribed medicines in a pharmacy in Bissau, but there they were expensive, ranging from 3 to 10 U.S. dollars, besides the cost of travel to Bissau.

Most health care alternatives, other than routine or emergency offerings to the *iran* and herbal home treatment, require extra resources such as time, transport, and money. When it concerns spending scarce resources on any kind of health care, mothers always insist on their children's health as a priority. "You know, a human being is always worth more than money," mothers routinely say when asked about their willingness to pay for health care. When I confront mothers with the possibility that they might not have the money to pay for health care, some argue that they will try to borrow money, or they will sell a chicken, pay with rice or *kana,* or they will just somehow find a solution. One such alternative is to go to the nun, a nurse, or a healer and ask for mercy: "You never know, they may feel pity for your child and treat it anyway." Many mothers admit, however, that it is difficult to seek health care without money, and in such a case there is sometimes not much to do about the situation: "The child has to suffer," they say. Men insist, as do mothers, that a child's health always is a priority: "Money is nothing. Human life is everything." Nonetheless, women frequently lament their husbands' unwillingness or inability to help with money when a child needs health care, particularly white man's medicine.

Interpretations of Child Death

Mothers are most likely to explain health problems, which they see as related to the Papel *uso,* as sorcery or ritual failure. Sorcery is considered to be the most important reason for a child's death. It is seen as a serious and expanding problem. Because of envy, hatred, vindictiveness, or simply bad intentions some people decide to use sorcery to hurt a rival or someone they dislike. A child is often the chosen victim.

Roughly 15 percent of children aged two to four years old are said to have been bewitched at least once in an interview survey I conduct with mothers in two villages. This is probably an underestimation since mothers are not always willing to discuss their suspicions of sorcery because they are often rooted in constrained personal relations. In addition, mothers are aware that the nuns at the Catholic mission openly oppose all treatment other than Western medicine, which may make them reluctant to admit to a white person that their children have been victims of sorcery. Furthermore, fathers and elderly people sometimes consult a *djambakus* for problems attributed to sorcery without the mothers' knowledge.[10] Nonetheless, many mothers explain to me in some detail their children's symptoms when bewitched and their subsequent treatment. However, no mother mentions who the responsible person might be.

The characteristic symptoms of a bewitched child are difficulty in breathing and fever, symptoms similar to a respiratory infection or severe malaria. Such a child is considered to be at a high risk of death and can only be healed within the framework of the Papel culture since the origin of its disease has its roots there. White man's medicine may cure the symptoms but for a lasting effect the child must be cured by *djambakus*. The *djambakus* consulted will first diagnose the child with divination and then give the child some medicines. Foreign, dangerous objects have been incorporated into the body of a bewitched child. These objects, such as hair, bones, bloody flesh, and stones, will be drawn out from the child's body. An amulet is then furnished for preventive purposes.

A person who wants to bewitch the child of an enemy or a child belonging to her or his lineage may perform the act or the person may seek help from a *balobeiru, djambakus,* or so-called *darmadur* (a person who offers, from the Kriol word *darma* meaning "to offer") or some other knowledgeable person willing to use ritual knowledge for such nefarious work. Such work is performed at night.[11] Women as well as men are involved in sorcery, but there is some disagreement about whether men or women are more inclined to use sorcery. Apili tells me that in former times men mainly practiced sorcery. "Women did not have the heart to kill other people's children because they gave birth themselves," she argues. "But, today envy has taken hold of most people and both men and women kill with sorcery." Segunda argues that women are more vengeful in their nature than are men, and thus they are more likely to be involved in sorcery. To be effective, a person who shares the same lineage as the victim must perform the act of sorcery. Juana claims, however, that nowadays, with the increase in people's greediness and enviousness, people use sorcery to kill even those who do not belong to their own lineage.[12]

A co-wife's jealousy is the most frequently mentioned reason for killing a child with sorcery. However, it is risky to bewitch and kill the children of one's co-wife. God will later punish the person for such work. Apinto, who has given birth to nine children, has lost four of them. She tells me that they all died after a short period with fever and difficult breathing. She does not know why they died, she says. A neighbor woman is more talkative. She tells me that Apinto's mother, who died several years ago, is taking all her grand-children to the other world. God is punishing Apinto's mother for having killed her co-wife's children and thus God forces her to kill the children of her daughter. If a woman who has killed her co-wife's children has no daughters, she will be obliged to take children from the same womb, for in-stance, her sister's children, she clarifies.

All descriptions of sorcery encountered in my research indicate a con-scious act performed on behalf of a person who commissions the act. Notions of unconscious witchcraft do not appear to have a place in Papel culture. For instance, Maria has never heard about such an event, and she seems not to understand my question about it. When I ask Juana about un-consciously committed bad work she, like Maria, is bewildered, but sud-denly appears to grasp what I am after. She tells me about an old woman who had a beautiful grandchild who suddenly became sick and developed a hunchback. The old woman became identified as having bewitched her own grandchild and thus causing the disease. She accepted the accusation, but she said she did it against her own will. "Everybody just laughed at her," Juana says, and adds that it is a very rare event that people unwittingly use bad work.

Any chronic disease that is not cured despite repeated visits to a *djam-bakus,* the mission hospital, or a health center may finally be interpreted as a warning about failure to fulfill ritual responsibilities. The mother herself or somebody belonging to her matrilineage is normally to blame. Life is not always easy and delay in ritual fulfillment may be a result of difficult practi-cal circumstances, a lack of the necessary resources, or a shortage of time. However, sometimes the wrongdoing is caused by forgetfulness or lack of responsibility. Children often become sick as a warning for such ritual fail-ure. They will become better only if the relevant ritual failure is identified and fulfilled.

At times it is difficult to identify whom to blame for neglecting ritual performance. It is not necessarily the mother who is at fault; it could be her brother or other maternal relatives. In such cases, mothers sometimes find themselves and their children to be innocent victims in events beyond their own sphere of influence. One day Segunda tells me about a young mother in Biombo who lost two children during the same day, and still one more child a week later. The first two children who died at the National Hospital in Bissau were six and ten years old. The mother had "gone to her father's home to calm down," Segunda explains. A week later the husband came with the dead body of her third child; now only one of her children remained. After a series of divinations the family of this unlucky mother found that her younger brother had made a contract with a powerful *baloba*. He had bought a car for public transport and had requested success in his business. All went well except that he forgot to pay back the *baloba* for the services so that the *baloba* took three of his sister's children as a punishment. "Now they have made the necessary ceremonies," explains Segunda. "An ancestral spirit is pitiless if people do not fulfill their promises." That is why mothers sometimes do not like their children to stay with their own mothers; they are afraid that if *mufunesa* falls on their lineage the ancestral spirit will see their child and take it.

Mothers are, however, not always innocent when their children die.[13] When a ten year old girl in a neighboring village became sick she was interned for five days at the mission hospital with a high fever; when her situation became critical she was referred to the National Hospital in Bissau where she died. Some months earlier, the girl's mother had gone off to "carry calabash" *(karga kabas)*, a ceremonial pilgrimage that all Papel people must perform once during their lifetime. The mother was to go by foot to all the *baloba* belonging to her lineage and make offerings, but she became very tired and left out one *baloba*. According to a divination performed, the ancestor spirit residing in that *baloba* became angry and killed her daughter. Younger mothers may also lose their children as a punishment when their elderly maternal kin members do not fulfill the *karga kabas* ceremony for the well-being of their lineage.

Mothers may blame themselves for a child's death if they refuse to give a daughter as *katandeira,* a woman who serves a *baloba,* as a return for ritual services requested by her lineage members (see chapter 3). A mother explains to me that she lost two children for that reason. Both of her children died suddenly, without becoming sick. Such an abrupt death of a child, apparently without any prior disease, is seen as a punishment for an extremely serious ritual oversight. Mothers describe such castigation as cruel and unjust. There should be some space for action, they argue. Children who have suddenly died without a prior disease were often six to fourteen years old and described as well-nourished and healthy looking.

Children who die during the first days after birth are sometimes said to have died without any disease symptoms. The death of a newborn is often attributed to sorcery or ritual failure, but certain newborns return quickly to the other world, by their own desire, or because somebody in the other world has sent them over to bring things back from this world. Mothers who lose one infant after another directly after birth, without any sign of a disease, may become suspicious that they are victims of an infant who "comes and goes" *(bim-i-bai)*. While infants in general are described as innocent, not yet capable of doing much harm, *bim-i-bai* infants are described as deceitful.[14] Preventive action can be taken to stop the infant from such tricks. The mothers can mark the ear or cut a part from the ear of her live newborn. The child is said to be more likely to stay with the mother rather than risk embarrassment for such an ugly ear when returning back to the other world. A suspected *bim-i-bai* infant can also be buried naked, with the aim of not satisfying its intention to return with something valuable to the other world. Only elderly women are allowed to be present at such a funeral to prevent the child from entering some woman of a fertile age. The body is sometimes even burnt to extinguish that child forever.[15]

The Animal Diseases

I am told that the Papel only recently learned of the animal diseases or *duensa di limária di matu,* which are named after forest animals. Diseases such as forest goat disease *(frintamba),* ant-bear disease *(timba),* sheep disease *(carne),* monkey disease *(santchu),* and cat disease *(gatu)* belong to this category of diseases.[16]

The widespread acceptance of these animal diseases illustrates the influence that medical knowledge from other ethnic groups, in particular the Balanta, has had on Papel medical practices. "Thanks to God we got to know about the animal diseases from the Balanta. Before we learned about them our children died a lot from these diseases," a mother explains to me. The Balanta are recognized as those who know best how to cure the animal diseases. The same applies to the diseases "sudden pain" *(pontada)* and "soul stolen" *(alma furtadu),* which can also attack children.[17] No lasting cure can be given for these diseases at the mission hospital or the health centers, though certain symptoms can be temporarily relieved. Nowadays there are many Papel, mostly women, who have learned to treat these diseases. The animal diseases are in no way caused by an *iran* or cured with an *iran's* help, which is important for the Catholics. The Catholics take *iran* to be the devil, and thus only associated it with evil actions, in contrast to the Papel religion where an *iran* is seen as a source of good and bad, depending on human intentions.[18]

There is a series of animal diseases that are considered to be more or less serious for infants. It is important to note that these diseases, with their origin among the patrilineal Balanta, do not reflect concerns related to matrilineal descent. Rather the causes of these diseases mirror anxieties about relations between humans but also between humans and animals, especially where both mothers and fathers play a role. For instance, those who hunt monkeys or eat monkey meat run the risk that their child will contract the monkey disease. An elderly man explains to me that his wife, who likes to eat monkey meat, performed the washing ceremony for the monkey disease before she gave birth in order to protect her child. "A child with monkey disease will refuse to take the breast and become thin. The hands become crippled, the face wrinkled, the eyes glassy, and the hair texture coarse, like a monkey," this man says, demonstrating to me with his hands and face. "But that disease does not often kill; the infants become thin only until the washing ceremony is performed." A mother of a thin and sad looking little girl tells me that her daughter probably has the monkey disease. She says that she has taken her daughter many times to the mission hospital without improvement. "I suspect *santchu* got her, you know, her father likes to hunt monkeys," she explains. I have seen many children who are suspected of having the monkey disease or are said to have had it and were cured. Monkey disease has symptoms very similar to those of *gatu,* the cat disease, and the treatment is the same.

The cat disease attacks children a little later than monkey disease. It begins with acute diarrhea and vomiting; over time the child becomes malnourished, experiences persistent diarrhea, and begins to cry like a cat, hence the name. The cause of cat disease is a disrespectful behavior shown to a cat, dead or alive, by one of the parents or even the child. A pregnant woman who passes by a dead cat should symbolically cover the cat with a thread from her clothes to prevent her child from getting the disease. Likewise, children should bury a dead cat as a preventive measure. Young men who kill and eat a cat run the risk that their children will get the disease, Segunda explains. "You know, young men sometimes kill a cat and eat it, just for fun. When their children are born that cat will catch them. Today Papel eat cats, in the old days we never did." Segunda laughs and then she adds. "Actually, a cat is tasty. It tastes like a rabbit."

Cat disease is the most common of the animal diseases. In my survey I found that nearly one-fifth of all children one to four years old in a more *prassa*-like village has had cat disease compared to one-tenth of the children in a more remote village. I have seen many children who have had cat disease, and their mothers all tell me similar stories: The children usually get diarrhea and begin vomiting, most likely between six months and two years of age. The mothers take their children repeatedly to the health center or the mission hospital where they are given some medicines that sometimes temporarily cure certain symptoms such as diarrhea. However, the children always relapse. Finally, the children are taken to a person who knows how to diagnose and treat cat disease.[19] The washing ceremony is performed at the homestead of the parents. Neighbors bring some money or a little rice that is cooked with sour milk and red palm oil and serve all participants, including all the children in the neighborhood. After the ceremony the children gradually become better.

The risk that a child will die from monkey or cat disease is considered to be low, in particular if given treatment in time. When a child with one of these diseases dies, despite proper treatment, the death is commonly explained by *djakassidu,* a mixture of the respective animal disease and sorcery or some ritual neglect.

Measles

Measles *(sarampa, **pubuka**)* is recognized by many people as one of the most dangerous of all children's diseases. It is a disease that "jumps" *(ta kamba)* from one child to the next, that is, it comes in epidemics. Mothers say that measles epidemics are less frequent today than in the old times, and some mothers attribute this to the routine vaccination of children. Indeed most mothers appreciate vaccinations and many recognize their preventive role against diseases and refer to fewer children dying from measles than before as evidence.

The symptoms of measles are well known: fever, rash, red eyes and tongue, harsh cough, and ulcers in the mouth.[20] Every person gets measles only once in a lifetime, people say, normally as a child. However, adults or youths who have not yet had measles may also get it, some say. Measles enters the community in a mystical and deceptive manner, as Impors explains:

> Measles come with a doll-like child in beautiful clothes. Some children or even adults, who have the ability, so-called *pauteiru* [clairvoyants] will notice that child and talk to it, and say like that: "Aha, you are beautiful. Come to my house," they say. Because they like that child they take it home, or the child may run after them and enter the house. That child brings with it that disease, and that disease jumps from one child to another.

There are preventive measures that are taken during a measles epidemic. When a child is sick with measles it is particularly urgent that some of the old people of the household make an extra offering and ask for help. Children carry amulets or leaves from a particular plant in the hair for protection. When measles are only present in one or a few compounds of the village, all children from other compounds are forbidden to go there. However, when a child in one's household has measles it is considered too late to keep that child isolated from the others: "If one child has measles the next child may get it depending on its luck."

A difficult measles epidemic concerns the whole community. When many children die, the women of the village gather at the village *kansaré*, which is normally situated in a barracks in the outskirts of a village.[21] The women will make an offering and dance; some of the elderly women will sleep there during the night until the epidemic is over. The villagers will contribute with money, rice, or *kana*. A bottle of *kana* will also be placed at the entrance of the village for protection and the old people will kill a goat or a chicken at the site of a mighty *iran*. Indeed, when measles comes to the village all the villagers should ask the *iran* for help, but those implicated have more reason to do so. For instance, a mother who has been in Bissau where children are thought to get measles easily, should go to *djambakus* and ask that the disease does not catch other children, or if it does that those children will become better. If no child dies the mother has to fulfill the offerings she vowed to make. When the epidemic is over and if nobody died an animal should be killed, *kana* offered, and a ceremony performed to thank the *iran*.

Besides these kinds of measures, children with measles are treated according to the Papel *uso* as well as with the white man's medicine. I visit a number of children sick with measles who are treated with a multitude of herbal medicines, as well as the white man's medicine.

The White Man's Medicine

The white man's medicines are considered effective to cure certain diseases and some symptoms. The white man's medicine is said by many to be appropriate for children while it has less to offer to adults, a view especially held by elderly people. "Old people get their cures at the house of the *iran* but children should go to the house of the nuns," an elderly father answers typically when I ask him about alternatives for health care for adults in comparison to that for children.[22]

The public health centers, the mission hospitals in Biombo, as well as the hospitals and pharmacies in Bissau are the main dispensers of the white man's medicine. Mothers admire the effectiveness of drugs such as chloroquine (for malaria), antibiotics, and aspirin. These medicines can even be bought at marketplaces without a prescription.[23] Both men and women emphasize that it is the mother's responsibility to take her children for immunizations and treatment at these health institutions. A woman will not take the sick child of a co-wife or another woman to a health center without being authorized to do so; she will not risk being made responsible if the child dies. Papel women are fairly free to travel, alone or in the company of others, and to avoid exposing themselves to sorcery they often prefer to travel without informing their husband or other women in the compound.

However, the mother of a sick child is usually reluctant to go to a health center or a hospital without an elderly woman. If her child dies she does not want to carry it home dead on her back. A woman of fertile age who carries a dead child will risk losing all her children unless she and her husband perform a costly ceremony.

The mission hospital is considered to be the best way to get access to the white man's medicines, but mothers of sick children must learn to deal with the nuns, which is not an easy task. To communicate effectively with the two nuns who run the hospital demands special knowledge, self-control, and tolerance of abuse. The nuns require discipline. "*Irma* is tough (*duru*)," people say. Mothers have to come to the hospital according to a certain schedule for vaccinations, prenatal consultations, and curative care. A child is supposed to be nicely washed and to wear clean clothes when taken to the mission hospital. If the child is seriously ill it is better to convince the nun that the disease has advanced rapidly. A mother who delays a consultation for a sick child risks, as a punishment, that the nun will refuse to treat her child. Any sign of treatment within *uso*, such as scar over the spleen (a common treatment for big spleen, *bassu* or the habit of putting olive oil in the hair of a child to get rid of scaling, is considered by the nuns not only to be inappropriate treatment but even a cause for penalty.

The lightest punishment for wrongdoing is scolding. The nuns also charge fines (about 50 U.S. cents), which are seen as fairly tough when money is scarce. It is somewhat more difficult to tolerate being beaten by the nun on the face or shoulders, or having one's ear twisted. The hardest castigation is when the nun refuses to examine the child. I am told the nun may at times accuse mothers of deliberate bad treatment of their children, and even with the intention of killing their own child. These accusations are recognized as outrageous and senseless. Likewise, mothers feel humiliated when the nuns interpret their children's undernourishment as negligence, ignorance, or a deliberate withholding of food, rather than a consequence of disease. A mother who has a dirty vaccination card or, still worse, if she has lost it, may decide to first visit the nearest public health center to get a new one. The health center nurses are more willing to negotiate the price and form of payment. If mothers are lucky they sometimes can get a new card for free.

As already discussed, mothers appreciate certain white man's medicines and most are willing to tolerate what they consider to be mistreatment and abuse in order to have access to them. However, when it concerns general child care and nutritional issues mothers are not as happy with the help given by the nuns. One day when I meet Juana she is not happy at all. She tells me that the nun bought a lot of millet (*miju pretu, Sorghum Vulgare,* in Latin) in Fulani land then ordered that it be made into porridge. Now the nun has a bag of porridge at the table by the side of the weighing scale. For each underweight child the nun orders the mother to buy that particular porridge for 20,000 pesos (about 2 U.S. dollars). If the mother does not have the money the nun keeps her child's vaccination card and orders the mother to go home and find the requested money. Juana continues:

> The *irma* believes all children are thin because they do not get enough food, she does not understand that sometimes there is enough food but the child is sick and refuses to eat. And you can't explain this to her. She doesn't listen. She doesn't understand. She always talks to black people like they are children who don't know anything. She says that we blacks treat our children badly. We mothers, we are used to taking care of children and we know that it is not only lack of food that makes them thin. Besides many mothers know how to make a better porridge than the one the *irma* tells people to buy. Our village is full of that porridge that nobody wants to eat. You know, one woman said she did not want to buy any more of that porridge, that she had much better porridge at home and she went home to fetch it. That porridge was delicious with a good smell from peanuts and bananas. It was dry. It didn't have that humid smell. *Irma*'s assistant said at once she wanted to learn to make such a good porridge. But *irma* does not understand anything. She herself knows everything. She thinks she has nothing to learn and she thinks everybody is stupid and that we mothers do not care about our children—*irma*—she who has never given birth herself.[24]

The health center nurses are normally considered easier to handle than the nuns. The nurses work more with outreach activities in the villages, for example, administering vaccinations. However, the chronic shortage of drugs at the health centers results in prescriptions for drugs that are only available in drug stores in Bissau. In addition, the mothers often consider the nuns, who are white, to know better how to cure with the white man's medicines than do the blacks. Like the nuns, the health centers nurses also use punishment to teach mothers what they consider to be appropriate health care. Fines are common, but the mothers can often negotiate payments with the nurses. Some mothers like to bargain, but this easily results in mistrust as some get service for free while others pay, and the prices vary. At the mission hospital there is no negotiation; most prices are fixed and official.[25] Mothers' judgments of the health centers vary, as does the popularity of individual nurses. The fact that some of the nurses at the public health centers are frequently absent from their work while others may be rude further erodes trust in the nurses.[26]

The Protestant Spirit

I have never heard a mother explain the Catholic nuns' capacity to cure children with reference to their spirit, or their religious practice. Instead, most people say that the nuns cure children because they have "strong" drugs. When life becomes difficult, with disease and death threatening the family, mothers sometimes turn to "the Protestant spirit" *(spiritu di protestanti)* for help.[27]

Those people who convert to a Protestant religion have to dissociate themselves from *uso*.[28] They are not supposed to participate in any kind of ceremony that does not belong to the Protestant religious practices and they are not allowed to drink alcohol. In return, they are told they are immune to sorcery and ritual punishments. Isabel, barely twenty years old, the mother of a one-year-old son, decided to join the Protestants. Isabel's two-year-old daughter died some eighteen months ago. She tells me that her daughter was taken away from her through a "satanic act." Moreover, her daughter's death is only one of many tragic events that have happened to her family. Therefore, Isabel, her younger co-wife, and her husband all have decided to escape their destiny within the Papel *uso* through conversion to Protestantism. When I ask her whether her husband is allowed to have more than one wife she maintains that a man with more than one wife may keep all his wives when he becomes a Protestant, but he is not allowed to arrange for additional wives. Then Isabel repeats that she wants to escape the burdens of *uso*, which have already taken her firstborn child.

Dominga, who is about fifty years old, has decided to see whether the Protestant spirit would help her. Her misery is total, she maintains. Dominga's husband died a couple of years ago; one of her sons is good for nothing, the other is somewhat better but chronically ill. Her teenage daughter is only interested in amusing herself. Dominga's *kodé*, a five- to seven-year-old girl, is thin and sickly. Dominga herself is extremely skinny; she often takes off her worn T-shirt to show me her bony body and sagging breasts. "I can't work much with such a fragile body and empty belly," she argues and asks me to feel her stomach with my hands. Dominga's maternal family does not help, she says: "They are all too busy feeding their own children. We Papel are like that. We only think about our own nearest family." Dominga has been sick with some abdominal problems for some time. She has gone from one *djambakus* to the other and one *baloba* to the next without any help. She has been to the health center, has had an analysis carried out at the laboratory, and taken some white man's medicines, but without improvement. One day she tells me that she has become a Protestant. "I want to try that, you know, that might help," she argues. When I ask if she does not have faith in the Catholic mission she responds abruptly that it is not easy for poor and illiterate people to join the Catholic mission. Dominga argues it is worth trying the Protestant spirit, at least for a while. Both *uso* and the white man's medicines have failed, and her mother was buried several years ago. Dominga has nothing to lose.

Frequently I ask mothers if they have visited the Catholic church. Many respond that they would like to but they have not yet had the opportunity, they do not have time, or they do not have the proper clothes or shoes. Indeed, nobody living next door to the mission can miss the passage of well-dressed church visitors every Sunday morning. Education is another obstacle; to become a Catholic one has to acquire a certain amount of knowledge, which is only accessible through written texts. An illiterate person must therefore find help from somebody who reads and can explain these texts.

Many women claim the Protestants are easier to join than the Catholics, and one's economic and educational background is less of an obstacle. However, the Protestants demand that members quit all of the Papel ritual practices, something that places Elina in a dilemma. Elina has seriously considered the possibility of joining the Protestants in hope of a better life. She has given birth to seven children, but only two are alive. Elina, in her late thirties, lives alone in her husband's compound with an old inherited co-wife; her husband is in the south with a younger co-wife. Elina's younger boy, whose twin brother has died, is severely malnourished and sickly and he does not walk at two and a half years of age (later he was washed successfully by a Balanta man for the chameleon disease, one of the animal diseases). The older boy, who is six years old, is also seriously ill (later he was diagnosed with tuberculosis and was also successfully treated, this time with white man's medicine). Elina is worried about her future. Repeatedly she discusses her bad luck with children and her lack of daughters to carry forth her mother's lineage. "I am the only child of my mother who has given birth and I have to have at least one daughter," she says. "And my sons are always sick." I point out that the Protestant mission in her parents' village might help her with medicines for her sons.

"They might help me, but if I go to the Protestant mission hospital (*Kristus*) I cannot assist in the funeral of my parents," she answers.

"But aren't you allowed to go there for help without becoming a Protestant?" I ask.

"Yeah, but many of those people who go to *Kristus* cease to participate in our funerals for whatever reason. I won't take that risk now. Maybe later, when my mother is buried."

Elina's reproductive history of many child deaths and with her precarious social and economic situation, makes the Protestant faith an attractive alternative. Nonetheless, her responsibility to give her mother a respectable funeral does not allow her to convert—not yet.

The most attractive power of the Protestant spirit, as expressed by Papel women, is its capacity to neutralize misfortune related to their own traditions. Isabel, Dominga, Elina, and other mothers with whom I discuss child death are considering whether their children might have a greater chance of survival if they were to convert to another religion.[29] They all find it tempting to try, but the pros and cons have to be evaluated thoroughly before any decision is made.

What Counts as Negligence?

The many mothers with whom I discuss children's diseases and death all express a clear concern for their children's survival. In practice, these mothers have all sought a multitude of treatment alternatives for their children, with Papel or Balanta *uso* or with white man's medicine. Some have even abandoned their own religion in an attempt to save their children. No mother has expressed relief at the death of her child. No mother has argued that her child was too poor, too damaged or too sick to live a worthy life. However, I observe a few sick children who could possibly be classified as suffering neglect. In what follows I present three stories of mothers who did not take their children to the mission hospital or the health center when they were apparently fatally ill. Why did their mothers not seek care?

One young mother, Pi, reacts differently than other mothers when I discuss the death of her daughter. I had previously registered Pi as a pregnant mother of two children. Some eight months later, I discuss her children's health in more detail. On the road to Pi's house, a male villager informs me that her two-year-old daughter died three months ago. He is unwilling to give any further information about the circumstances of death; "I don't know, I was not there," he says. When I arrive, Pi's third born, a boy six months old is obviously sick. However, his mother first maintains that he is healthy, but then she admits that he has had a fever for the last two days. "But he is getting better now," she tries to assure me. I invite Pi to take her son to the mission hospital, but she says she prefers to wait and see until the next day. "He is better. He takes the breast," Pi says, but then starts joking about her lack of milk because she was dead drunk the day before. I ask Pi if she drinks a lot. "Until I drown," she responds and laughs. Pi is agitated and I anticipate difficulties in entering into a more serious discussion with her. When I finally find an appropriate moment to ask her about the death of her daughter the boy defecates where he is crawling in front of us. A pig immediately appears for a meal. Pi shouts at the pig and makes a lot of noise to drive it away. She cleans up the feces with a piece of rusty corrugated iron and throws it behind the house. She explains, still laughing and shouting after the pig, that her daughter became sick with a fever when she took her to Bissau. In the same afternoon she returned to the village with her sick daughter. The girl had a fever for an additional two or three days. Pi explains that her daughter died at six o'clock in the afternoon. No care at all was sought because she did not think her daughter was seriously ill. I notice that Pi's children are unusually poorly vaccinated. Her five-year-old daughter has been vaccinated only once (for tuberculosis) and her six-month-old son has no vaccination card yet.

Another day I hear a woman accuse a mother of killing her child by refusing to seek health care in a hospital. I just finish interviewing Ampo, a mother who participated in my survey, when Francisca arrives. She takes a seat and is more than willing to join us. Francisca laughs and comments on everything and everybody. She suddenly tells me that Ampo refused to take her child to the hospital. "You know, her child was seriously ill for many days and finally the child died because she refused to take the child to the health center for care," Francisca says, right in front of Ampo, who only shrugs her shoulders. Indeed, before Francisca came, Ampo told me that she never took her children to the health center or to the nuns, either for treatment or vaccination. When I asked why she responded first with "nothing" but then admitted that she had more confidence in *uso*. Ampo explained to me that her youngest daughter had been bewitched and that a *djambakus* had drawn things out of her eyes. She died anyway. Ampo had spoken about the death of her daughter in a low voice with her eyes fixed on the ground, as do many mothers. Later, I interview Ampo's younger co-wife. Her children are all fully vaccinated and have been taken to the nuns for health care but they have also become bewitched and treated accordingly. When I leave the compound the two women accompanying me say that Ampo is not clever at all as she does not want the white man's medicine.

I often meet and chat with Diminga, who is in her late fifties. She has given birth to seven children; three have died. The first two of her children died within a week after birth many years ago. Diminga never goes into any details about their deaths, but several times she tells me about the death of her sixth child, her second daughter. The girl died at the cashew time some ten years ago. "That girl was always thin and always sick but anyway she had learned to walk and talk a little bit," explains Diminga. One morning Diminga had noticed that the girl had a fever. She used to take her daughter to the nuns when she was sick, but this time she did not; it was in the beginning of the cashew season and Diminga was working hard collecting cashews every day. Diminga left her daughter with older siblings at home as usual. When she came home late in the afternoon the girl was very ill, but it was too late to go to the mission hospital. The girl died during the night. Diminga obviously still fights with the thought that she should have left work that day and taken her daughter to the nuns.

Was it Diminga's unconscious intention to allow her daughter to die? Is her history an instance of neglect? Ampo refuses to take her children to the hospital when sick; they are only treated with *uso*. Is it negligent health care or a sign of detachment if a mother never takes a sick child to the nuns? Is she not intelligent enough, as the other women maintain? Pi maintains she did not seek care when her daughter was dying because she thought the child was not seriously ill. In addition, she shows no sign of grief when discussing the death of her child, unlike most mothers. Does Pi neglect the care of her children? Does she consciously or unconsciously want them to die? Is she not clever enough to recognize a serious illness? Or does her heavy drinking prevent her from understanding the danger of her daughter's disease? Or is her drinking a sign of grief? Indeed, Diminga is a heavy drinker too; only lack of access to alcohol or her badly failing health keeps her occasionally sober. How can I conclude whether or not care is negligent or if grief is absent in particular cases like these?[30]

Maternal Mourning

When I discuss mothers' reactions to child deaths I am frequently told that weeping for those who die is something people do not only in this world but in the other world as well: "When somebody dies in this world we cry and those in the other world laugh. When a child is born in this world we laugh but those in the other world cry." Such is life. Papel mothers mourn children's deaths. It is obvious. To ask why is, in a way, senseless. Even so, I struggle with the question. The reasons women and men give are practical, social, economic, and emotional. The reasons why mothers cry for their dead children are just as obvious as why women want to have children.

When I ask Ana why mothers cry when their children die she answers: "Mothers cry because they are worried. They do not know why their child died. A child has never done anything wrong and thus they should not die." A child's death always indicates a problem whose origins must be identified in order to prevent additional deaths, she emphasizes. Augusta responds differently: "Mothers cry because when their children die they have nobody to help them when they become old. That's why they cry." Other women refer to emotions. "This is your child. You love that child. Of course you cry," says Maria. Mpone argues, as do many other women, "you cry because somebody you have grown accustomed to has died." Some women refer to the pains of birth and all the physical suffering mothers go through to have a child. Segunda argues, "Mothers love their children because of the pains they endure during birth. That is why they cry over the death of their children." Impors holds similar ideas: "Of course mothers cry when their children die. Both because of all the pain and burdens of birth and to have to wake up in the night and take care of the children and give them food. And all that." Then she is silent for a moment and adds, "but mothers also want their children to become adults and to have a good life. And when that wish can't come true mothers weep."

Juana is also concerned with broken promises and lost dreams for the child's future. One day I tell her about Scheper-Hughes's book *Death without Weeping*. First she is doubtful and finally she laughs: "Everyone has his or her customs." Not to seek care when a child is sick is senseless, she argues, and Juana says she does not believe that there are mothers who will not cry when their children die. "Don't people feel sorry for the child who dies young?" she asks. Juana reminds me that the nuns sometimes blame mothers for coming too late to the hospital with their children. "They argue that the mother wants her child to die. I do not understand that way of thinking," she says. I show Juana a picture from Scheper-Hughes's book of children who carry a dead sibling for burial. To allow children to bury children was the most aberrant thing she had ever heard of. Juana sighs; there are so many things in the world she does not understand.

Broken promises are also given to explain mothers' distress for miscarriages and stillbirths. People say that women are not supposed to cry in public when they have a miscarriage; indeed, they may not even tell people about a miscarriage if their pregnancy is not yet common knowledge. Women say they give birth to a dead child when "its body is complete." A mother whose child is born dead or a mother whose child dies directly after birth should not cry, according to Juana, but then she stresses that for sure they cry in private. "You understand," she explains. "That child never came to be." Still, Juana reminds me that these mothers have gone through pregnancy and suffered the pains of birth, for nothing.[31]

The above-mentioned reasons given for mothers' grief refer to child death in general, not the death of particular children. Like Scheper-Hughes, I kept my own records of reproductive histories through interviews with mothers and caregivers.[32] I maintain that for a Papel woman the experience of child death is the very part of her life she is striving to forget. I am not sure if all the women either wanted to or even could recall their total number of pregnancies. If they could not, it was due to emotional constraints, not because of poor memory or indifference. Mothers are reluctant to discuss the death of their own children. Occasionally, mothers say that they will become too sad when counting their dead children; thus they prefer not to discuss their deaths. A few mothers cut off the discussion, claiming that they do not remember.[33] Those who tell their story frequently become visibly disturbed. A few women start to cry, particularly elderly women. Some mothers who know how to speak Kriol prefer to discuss their children's deaths in Papel. When I ask mothers how many children they have, many mothers first count their children who are alive and I have to ask them specifically about those who have died. Some mothers who have many children alive are even reluctant to count them all so as not to boast in front of a less successful co-wife. The mothers count their children in birth order, and when going from one child to the next they say "who next took the breast." Mothers refer to their dead children in birth order, often calling attention to the child's sex, but they never use their names. I never ask a mother about the names of their dead children; I feel I have already asked too many uncomfortable questions.

I also discuss child death with many fathers who become emotional when they are reminded about their dead children. A young father tearfully tells me about the death of his two-year-old girl who died from cholera.[34] The child got diarrhea in the evening, but the mother did not tell anybody about it. Next morning the girl was seriously ill, and he ran with her to the health center some seven kilometers away. He was too late. The girl was severely dehydrated and the nurse had difficulties setting up an intravenous infusion for treatment. She died within few minutes of her arrival at the health center. The father is upset and angrily he blames his wife for not having informed him about the illness earlier. On my way back from the household, a woman tells me that the father had spent that night with his new second wife, and therefore the mother did not want to disturb him by telling him about the illness.

Nevertheless, fathers are not considered to be as emotional about their child's death as are mothers. At a community meeting on women's burdens in life, a young mother comments that a father does not care so much when his child dies, as he wants to sleep with his wife the next night. "It is the mother or *dona* who treats the sick child. Fathers are worthless. That is why children cry more when their mother suffers or dies than when their father suffers or dies," she says.

Grief is so evident that preventive measures are taken. When a mother loses her child, in particular if this has never happened to her before, she is supposed to stay in her parental home for a couple of weeks "to forget her child" and "calm down." As discussed in the previous chapter, name-giving practices are affected by mothers' strategies to forget their dead children. A child whose mother, father, or *dona* dies, is likewise assumed to grieve. During the funeral ceremony of a mother, her young children are to run under the bier carrying the corpse of their mother, which is used to identify the cause of death, a ceremony aimed to help them to forget her more quickly. In addition, a child may carry an amulet for the prevention of grief. A young child whose mother has died is said to die easily because of the ravaging consequences of the child's grief for the mother. It is recognized that people experiencing grief lose their taste for food and become thin. However, eating too much and becoming severely overweight is also attributed to sadness among adults, as is excessive drinking.

It is taken for granted among all Guineans that both parents mourn their dead children. Once, I discuss child death and the afterlife with two Fulani men who are Muslim. They present somewhat different ideas about

the afterlife and cause of death than do the Papel. One of them says that according to the Islamic law people should not cry when a child dies because
that death is the will of Allah. He maintains that in Senegal, where he lived
for several years, people did not cry. "Here in Guinea-Bissau we all cry anyway. That's our habit. Children have a good life in the other world and
therefore we should be happy. But we cry anyway," he says. Then he explains
how he himself cried when his young daughter died: "I cried when my
daughter died. I loved her. I had become accustomed to her. I wanted her to
become an adult and happy." The other man agrees: "It is normal to cry
when a child dies. Not only for mothers but also fathers and other people."
However, mothers are particularly vulnerable, he maintains, because of "all
burdens of birth and everything else." The man says that according to Fulani belief all children go to the better place, *gloria,* with all those who have
done nothing bad.[35] He assures me that the life in *gloria* is a good life; "in
gloria there is nothing lacking, neither food nor water. You understand that
a mother and a father whose child dies will be compensated for their suffering; if they end up in the bad place their child will come and take them over
to *gloria.* Anyway they cry. Such is life."

Within the Papel culture, mothers whose children die, and in particular
those mothers who have lost all their children, have an indisputable reason
to grieve. A mother weeps because she has lost someone she loves. That love
is based on affection related to knowing and becoming accustomed to the
child, but it may also be a loss of something that never came to be. Emotional distress attributed to suffering from the burdens of birth for a child
who never flourished is clearly expressed. A mother may be worried about
not having children to take care of her in her old age, in practical, economic,
and emotional terms. Furthermore, she may be worried about future births
or the lives of other children she may have. The cause of death of her child
must be identified and acted upon so as not to risk other children's lives.

Diseases, Death, and Maternal Dedication

In this chapter I have described the nature of children's diseases and alternatives for their cure, as well as considerations about mothers' grief when
children die. Do mothers' interpretations of their children's diseases and
death somehow influence their efforts to seek health care and shape their
emotional reactions to the death of a child? Does an inevitable, or even favorable, cause of death and a pleasant afterlife reduce mothers' grief? Does
a frequent event tend to become normalized and no longer tragic? How can
an anthropologist decide whether or not neglect or grief is present?

For a Papel mother the etiological classifications of diseases are crucial
to the choice of health care. Distinctions are made between symptomatic

and explanatory treatment, similar to what Susan Reynolds Whyte describes among the Nyole in Uganda. According to Whyte, "the symptomatic idiom brings the power of substances (in terms of pharmaceuticals and African medicines) to bear on problems," while "the explanatory idiom identifies a personalistic agent as a cause of affliction" (1997:23), which "means that causes have to be considered and dealt with" (26). The Papel use both of these "idioms," sometimes simultaneously and sometimes one following the other. "The white man's medicines" and a number of herbal medicines are often used for symptomatic treatment, but not always with success. The next step is then to move to the explanatory idiom, and when a cause is identified it can be treated.[36] For the Papel, all diseases need explanatory treatment to become cured; symptomatic treatment is preferred to ease pain and gain time.

The category of disease and appropriate care is most likely established through divination, that is, as described by Peek, "a trusted means of decision making, a basic source of vital knowledge" (1991b:2). However, more practical life situations, such as access to needed resources and time available, may influence action. Within the limitations of economic constraints and a heavy workload Papel mothers are fairly "rational and value-maximizing" individuals when seeking health care for their children.[37] Indeed, before I started my fieldwork I thought respectful and friendly health personnel was a determining factor in Papel women's choice of health care services. I have since revised that assumption. Most, but not all, Papel mothers are willing to suffer insults and maltreatment from health workers to obtain the care they consider most likely to help their sick child. Children's diseases are most often interpreted as a warning for ritual failure or the work of a malicious human or a supernatural being. Thus, disease demands attention, and in most cases *uso* furnishes mothers and others engaged in seeking care with options and allows hope for a cure. That is why mothers find death following no symptoms of disease unfair, and they interpret it as castigation for a serious ritual misconduct.

Whyte's (1997) focus on pragmatic agency fits with my understanding of Papel mothers' reactions to their children's diseases. Whyte is concerned with the agency and actions of those who experience misfortune and suffering. She argues for a pragmatic view on uncertainty: "when Nyole speak of agents of misfortune, make sacrifices, carry out rituals, and manipulate medicines . . . they are dealing with agents in order to alleviate misfortune" (1997:21).[38] Whyte identifies four types of misfortune as the most common for a visit to the diviner. Diseases, presented typically as "at home a child is sick" or "the woman had pain in her stomach," are the most common misfortune and occur in more than 80 percent of all cases in the diviners' records (16). The other three were failures of prosperity; problems of marriage, reproduction, and sexuality; and conflicts and lack of personal safety. Whyte emphasizes, "the qualities of purpose, possibility, and hope are central in Nyole dealings with misfortune" (24). Similarly, Papel mothers' react to their children's diseases by seeking help, trying a range of available alternatives, and keeping up hope until death is a fact. In principle, all of the children's health problems are conceived of as curable if adequately diagnosed and treated.

Papel mothers do not accept their children's death "with equanimity and resignation as an unalterable fact of human existence" as Scheper-Hughes (1992:275) claims apply to poor mothers in low-income countries. For the Papel there are no fatal diseases as such; most children die because of the shortcomings of humans. Children's deaths are always bad deaths that should have been avoided. Maternal grief is obvious. I firmly argue that neglect (selective or general) and lack of grief at child death is not a cultural pattern, as appears to be the case in the Alto. I take Scheper-Hughes (1992) to be trustworthy when she argues that at least some of the Alto mothers neglect their children, in particular those who are labeled as having the "child sickness," which is a fatal diagnosis. I take her seriously when she maintains "Alto women generally face child death stoically, even with a kind of *belle indifference* that is a culturally appropriate response. No one on the Alto do Cruzeiro criticizes a mother for not grieving for the death of a baby" (429).[39] Thus, child death appears to be emotionally less painful for the mothers in the Alto than for Papel mothers.

It is not an easy task to assess neglect and grief. Marilyn Nations and Linda-Anne Rebhun (1988) disagree with Scheper-Hughes that impoverished mothers in northeast Brazil do not grieve the death of their children, but they support the view that some children may be neglected. However, Nations and Rebhun interpret neglect differently, arguing that among the poor in northeast Brazil an ethical system supported by healers has evolved to help in decisions to treat illness or withdraw from care, such as "cutting back on the purchase of costly medicines, the ritual removal of material items which symbolize life . . . and the beginning of the emotional withdrawal of anticipatory grief" (1988:72). People do not interpret this withdrawal of care as the cause of death, and Nations and Rebhun prefer to see the label "child sickness" as "a social recognition of the point of no return" rather than an indication of neglect (173–74). Furthermore, they argue that many cases of "child sickness" are diagnosed after the child's death, and Scheper-Hughes (1992:386) seems to agree.

Sarah Castle (1994), who has studied management of children's diseases among Fulani in rural Mali, maintains with Nations and Rebhun that certain fatal diagnoses are often postmortem diagnoses. In addition, she found that children given these fatal diagnoses before death received no less treatment than those who were not given that label. In her opinion fatal diagnoses do not necessarily result in selective neglect. In rural Mali, these diagnoses shift the responsibility for death from the mother to the community as a whole and as such they "allow psychological adaptation to the frequent experience of death and contribute to a sense of coherence in a world that would otherwise seem uncontrollable" (1994:330). According to Castle, these diagnoses enable mothers to maintain their "stoic and unemotional face" in public. Mothers and others are not supposed to weep for dead children; it would be to act against the will of Allah and it would also impede the child's chances in the afterlife. However, mothers admitted to crying in private.

The biocultural anthropologist Katherine A. Dettwyler is also concerned with child death in Mali and argues that diseases and death are normally "attributed to Allah rather than to organic causes, witchcraft or sorcery" (1994:22). Dettwyler affirms that Mali is "a land where early death was too commonplace to be considered a tragedy" (26).[40] However, she explains that the women speak about their dead children in a low voice and some of them cry: "in some cases, it's been twenty or thirty years since these children have died, and the mothers have other grown children, even grandchildren, but they still choke up when they talk about the ones who died" (157–58). Like Castle, Dettwyler notes that it isn't considered appropriate for parents to weep when their child dies, particularly when very young infants die.

Despite the custom among Muslims in Mali to not cry publicly when children die, scholars have noted that in private, practice appears to be different. Castle (1994) talks about secluded weeping and Dettwyler (1994) observes emotional stress related to child death, even decades after the actual event. According to the Muslim men with whom I discussed child death and mourning, it was impossible to face child death without weeping, despite belief in an attractive afterlife for children and the will of Allah. I suggest there is no automatic relation between a concept of a comfortable afterlife, a fatal diagnosis of a sick child, and the mother's decision to give up seeking health care. Mothers may give up hope for survival and seek solace in a good death and happy afterlife, as in the Alto, or keep up hope and continue to seek a solution, as in Mali and Guinea-Bissau. Mothers and fathers who argue their children died because of God's will and have entered a good afterlife may still weep over their children's death. Grief is not necessarily eliminated by an attractive afterlife and an unproblematic cause of death.

Among the Papel child death is not considered a "minor misfortune."[41] In Biombo child death is interpreted as a warning whose origin must be identified and acted upon to prevent additional deaths. The question is always why did that particular child die? There is no "naturalness" in child deaths. "A child is born to live, not to die," people say. There is always a particular explanation behind every child's death, and a mother finds it particularly difficult to end her reproductive life with a dead child.[42] While a child's death is never a good death, the afterlife can at best be acceptable with the child's grandmother or father taking care of it in the other world. Mothers surely grieve. But the cause of death and nature of afterlife of children are not the only concerns. There are other considerations, reflected in the reciprocal nature of mother love, something we explored in the second chapter. Mother love is not self-sacrificing and unconditional; mothers suffer for their children but they expect to be compensated. When child death occurs the rewards of motherhood are gone. Maternal affection is an important reason for grief but not the only one; social and economic considerations contribute to distress as well.

In this chapter I have argued that Papel mothers do not neglect their children's health care, nor do they fail to grieve over their children's deaths. For a Papel mother child death is always a tragedy and matter of concern; sometimes an unresolved problem that may take away still more of her children. The conceptions of afterlife and cause of death can influence a mother's distress at a child's death, but these do not preclude grief. A comfortable afterlife and relatively unproblematic cause of death, for instance God's will, may still leave mothers, and others as well, in grief.

The thesis that mother love is automatically destroyed in societies with extreme poverty, high fertility, and high rates of child death does not hold in the case of Papel mothers. Scheper-Hughes's (1992:430) suggestion that the "local culture" protects mothers from grief in northeast Brazil does not apply in Biombo.[44] The question is whether the neglect thesis, which holds that poverty and high child mortality produce maternal indifference and neglect, applies only to the "worst bets," those children who are "listless," and "wanting to die," as described by Scheper-Hughes, or "lowered-viability" or "poor quality" infants, to use the terminology of sociobiology. It might be unfair to make a comparison between the Alto mothers' lack of dedication to their most sickly and unwanted infants and the Papel mothers' devotion to their most promising and adored children like Kodé.

In the next chapter I will continue my study of mother love and child death by looking at the Papel mothers' concerns for the survival of their "worst bets," that is those infants who are born abnormally, have an unusual appearance, or a dysfunctional body.

5

Nonhuman Children

After eight months in Biombo I notice a comment about a particular child who is said to be an *iran*. The concept of *iran* is not new to me as it is so frequently used by Guinean people. Indeed, I have already spent a lot of time trying to understand what *iran* means. Referring to a particular child as *iran* is, however, something new.

I am chatting with Margareta, an elderly woman. During our conversation a boy about twelve years old comes and exchanges a few words with Margareta before he leaves.

"He is my grandchild," she explains. Then she tells me that when her daughter-in-law gave birth to the boy, some people said that he was not a human child, he was an *iran*.

"*Iran?*" I ask.

"Yeah, that is what they said. Some people said he was dangerous and he had to die *(ten ke muri)*."

"Why?"

"He was born with a big head."

Margareta tells me that her husband, who is a Catholic, had reacted harshly against the idea that the boy is an *iran* and should therefore die. He proclaimed that the boy is welcome in this world, as are all children, and proposed that he and Margareta should foster him. So they did. "He is such a nice boy," Margareta says warmly. I am a little confused, but before I have time to ask for more details, another person comes and interrupts our conversation. It is late and already dark. I walk home and write my field notes that a child can somehow be an *iran,* nonhuman and dangerous, and had to die. I also note that being *iran* has something to do with being born with a big head. For the first time, the thought of infanticide enters my field notes.

Infanticide refers to the killing of a child, though the term is used differently in different disciplines (Barfield 1997). Within criminology, infanticide is frequently limited to mean the killing of a child less than one year of age. It also sometimes refers to the killing of a child by one of the parents, or only by the mother.

Various authors concerned with the killing of infants have classified infanticide as outright, direct, or violent in contrast to indirect or passive (Harris 1977, Miller 1987, Scrimshaw 1984). An outright, direct, or violent infanticide is committed when someone consciously causes the death of a child. On the other hand, an indirect or passive infanticide occurs through inaction, for instance by the withholding of food or the failure to seek care. Miller, who studied discrimination against females in India, argues that infanticide should be placed at "one extreme of the continuum effects of child abuse and neglect" (1987:96). In contrast, Scheper-Hughes (1992:357) distinguishes between child abuse in the United States and selective neglect as practiced in northeast Brazil because the latter is not motivated by anger, hate, and aggression toward the child. Howell (1979:62), who describes outright infanticide among the !Kung in South Africa, also emphasizes that feelings such as aggression and anger do not provoke the killing.

Whether the direct or indirect killing of children is rational, irrational, or pathological is a debated issue. Evolutionary approaches within biology, psychology, and anthropology have in the last few decades increasingly come to regard infanticide as an adaptive strategy among most species, including humans (Bartlett, Sussman, and Cheverud 1993, Hausfater and Hrdy 1984, Parmigiani and vom Saal 1994). Within these approaches infanticide is explained as an adaptive behavior that contributes to population control (Birdsell 1993, Harris 1977), or encourages reproductive success through a kind of postnatal abortion in which "poor offspring quality" or untimely births are eliminated (Ball and Hill 1996; Daly and Wilson 1984, 1988; Hrdy 1994, 1999; Scrimshaw 1984).[1]

The sociobiologists Martin Daly and Margo Wilson argue that the "adaptive functions of parental solicitude towards offspring seem obvious" (1984:488). In a worldwide study of infanticide based on ethnographic data from the Human Relations Area Files (HRAF), Daly and Wilson find that most of sixty randomly selected societies where infanticide was practiced can be divided into three categories based on predefined "cost-benefit questions" (488–92). The first category includes societies in which infants with "wrong" fathers are the victims of infanticide. The second group includes societies in which infants born with a deformity or some illness are killed, and in the third group are societies with infant killing due to maternal incapacity to rear the infant. Daly and Wilson argue that infanticide is primarily based on rational decision making, and "whatever the expressed rationale, however, choosing not to raise a deformed child obviously serves the parent's fitness interests" (492).

Although infanticide is practiced worldwide, cross-cultural comparison of the custom is difficult. It is a controversial and problematic issue, and the contemporary criminalization of infanticide has further contributed to its concealment. Detailed descriptions of infanticide are rare and important information is often missing, which further hampers comparative study. Nonetheless, an examination of ethnographic descriptions indicates that motives for infanticide vary among those societies where it has been accepted. In contrast, ethical considerations about killing reveal similarities since a distinction is made between the killing of an infant and a murder. In that context, the status of newborns, for example, humanness, personhood, and social membership, appears to be crucial for understanding the practice.

There is cross-cultural variation as to whether or not a newborn is considered to be a human being, a person, or a member of the community.[2] There is also great variation among societies concerning what criteria determine these statuses. The human nature of infants is not always related to the presence of a human soul (see chapter 3). The possession of human nature maybe related to a particular event after birth (Nicolaisen 1995),[3] or as a gradual process that culminates after death (Howell 1989).[4] Sometimes, the achievement of human nature and personhood are taken to be interdependent or to occur simultaneously. Scheper-Hughes (1992) emphasizes individual personality and human characteristics as important for an Alto infant's gradual achievement of humanness and that only first when an infant has a personal name is it considered fully human.[5] In some societies, naming is the very event that gives an infant a social membership (Alford 1987). Correct fatherhood may also be important for social membership (Legesse 1973, Oboler 1985).

Before addressing the issue of nonhuman children in Biombo I examine some ethnographic descriptions of infanticide with focus on motives and ethical considerations given by those committing the killing. An important question is whether or not those involved see the elimination of the infant as distinct from murder. As far as information is available, I also pay attention to how decisions to kill infants are taken, who commits the act, and the emotions expressed. Let's begin this examination with a summary of historical studies of infanticide in Europe and North America.

Infanticide

Most historians concerned with childhood history agree that infanticide was common in early Europe. Lloyd de Mause proposes that from antiquity to the fourth century, parents "routinely resolved their anxieties about taking care of children by killing them" (1974a:51). However, with the spread of Christianity in the fourth century, parents began to acknowledge children as human beings with a soul and consequently killing them became ethically more difficult. According to Mause, this resulted in abandonment and other passive forms of infanticide. Commonly, parents left their children to wet nurses, monasteries, nunneries, and foster families. Mause, like many scholars, takes infanticide and child abandonment to be characteristic of contemporary childrearing practices and indicative of a lack of emotional concern for all children. These authors emphasize the cruelty of selfish, ignorant, or superstitious parents. Hugh Cunningham (1995) maintains that attempts to measure the extent of infanticide are always fraught with difficulties. He argues that until the fourth century, undoubtedly many children were killed or abandoned, and that girls were more likely victims. According to Cunningham, infanticide still existed after the fourth century but had become a crime equivalent to murder and punishable by death, while abandonment was judged less harshly. Cunningham argues further that abandonment of one child does not mean indifference to all children.

A few historical studies focus on individual cases of infanticide. Regina Schulte's (1984) historical study of court records of infanticide in Bavaria, Germany, during the period 1878–1910 indicates a rather homogenous pattern for the killing of infants. Schulte demonstrates that mothers committed the killings, and they normally came from the lowest stratum of the rural community. Because of their work, none of the mothers would have been able to keep the child herself if it had been allowed to live. Yet Schulte concludes that the reasons given for infanticide did not reveal particularly extreme conditions. Rather, mothers expressed their lack of interest in the child. Mothers took the decision to kill the infant early during pregnancy, and seemingly they thought of the killing as a kind of late abortion. They killed the infant without looking at it and with minimal physical contact. Grief or guilt was seldom expressed before the judge. After their time in prison, between two to seven years, the mothers were likely to be accepted again in their community. Schulte argues that a mother's killing of one child clearly did not preclude her affection for her other children.

Peter C. Hoffer and N. E. H. Hull (1981) combine quantitative and qualitative approaches in their study of infanticide in England and New England between 1558 and 1803. They argue that infanticide is an ineffective method of population control and that the relationship between economic need and infanticide is not obvious. Hoffer and Hull offer more varied explanations of infant killing than Schulte (1984), including mothers' temporary or chronic mental disturbances, mothers' personalities, jealous fathers, and parents who kill their infants as a postnatal abortion. External pressure like exclusion, shame, loss of employment and reputation, and rape were also reasons given for infant killing. Finally, Hoffer and Hull maintain that infanticide has not been abolished, and "the underlying emotional causes" they identify in their study still exist (Hoffer and Hull 1981:xii). Hoffer and Hull's study indicates that the conditions into which the infant was born, however diverse, appear to have been the main reason for its elimination.[6]

Killing female infants is well documented among aboriginal populations in Australia, Eskimos in Canada and northern Alaska (Birdsell 1993, Savishinsky 1974, Smith and Smith 1994),[7] and groups in South Asia (Baker 1979, Croll 2000, Miller 1997, Wolf 1974). Barbara Miller (1987, 1997) argues that female infanticide is almost universal.[8] She maintains that in societies where few females are employed in agriculture and large dowries prevail, female infanticide is common.

According to Miller (1997), during the British colonial era infanticide was widely practiced in northwest India, and in certain higher caste villages all daughters were killed due to the practice of giving large dowries to secure a husband from a high status family. She notes that discrimination against daughters is spreading both regionally and among social groups. Miller points out the lack of documentation on "people's psychological motivations and emotions regarding intra-household discrimination" (208). Information is also missing about who makes the decision and who commits the killing. Elisabeth Croll maintains that in several recent field studies in India "parents remain quite open about discussing female infanticide and the circumstances in which they resort to such practices" (2000:101). Croll gives a few examples of poor parents in the southern state of Tamil Nadu who, due to economic considerations, decide to put their daughters "to sleep" rather than have a costly abortion. However, this is not done without emotional distress. Mothers-in-law are apparently involved, both in decision making and administration of the lethal drinks.

According to Margery Wolf (1974), the birth of a girl was often met with disappointment in China. Because a young woman would belong to the lineage of her husband, she could not contribute offspring to her father's lineage. Nor could a daughter contribute work to her father's family, since she would be given as a bride to another family when she became marriageable. Wolf argues that given the difficult economic situation of Chinese peasants "the high rate of female infanticide in traditional China should not be surprising" (158). Hugh D. R. Baker (1979) argues likewise that infanticide in China was an indirect result of poverty. Drowning was the method most frequently used, but smothering and burying alive were also common. Children were also sold or abandoned in the hope that they would be saved from death.

Killing infants for economic reasons, unwanted birth, or congenital deformities is commonly described. In such cases a mother is likely to kill her infant before it gains status as a human being or person, or acquires social membership. The Tarahumara in Mexico practice infanticide when the newborn infant has a severe birth impairment or when the mother's situation is extremely difficult (Mull and Mull 1987). Mothers, most of whom are Catholic, make the decision and then perform the killing directly after birth. Selective neglect of certain children occurs as well. Dorothy S. Mull and Dennis Mull (1987) propose that a delayed name-giving ceremony is crucial for the infant's identity as a person and late initiation of breastfeeding may contribute to delayed maternal attachment. They argue that "infanticide seems to be motivated by powerful human needs, including the survival instinct itself" (126).

Like the Tarahumara, Yanomanö mothers in South America sometimes choose to kill their newborns if they are born before the breastfeeding period of three years for a previous child is terminated (Chagnon 1968:48). A first-born female might also be killed, as mothers prefer the first child to be a boy. Selective passive neglect, which can be fatal, also occurs. According to Chagnon (1968), mothers strangle their infants with a vine, break their neck with a stick, do not stimulate them to breathe, or throw them against a tree or on the ground. Although an infant is not considered to have a complete soul, since that is only acquired through certain knowledge and experience, infanticide is emotionally difficult and some women prefer abortion.

Among the !Kung, a gatherer-hunter society in the Kalahari Desert, women are documented to have killed their infants for family planning purposes (Howell 1979). Killing an infant was not considered to be murder since an infant's life "begins with the giving of a name and the acceptance of the baby as a social person back in the village after birth. Before that time, infanticide was part of the mother's prerogatives and responsibilities, culturally prescribed for birth defects and for one of each set of twins born" (1979:120). A !Kung mother might also kill her child in case of the father's death, illegitimacy, or problematic fatherhood. Mothers were reluctant to report infanticide and "no doubt the custom of silence about birth spares the feelings of the mother" (120).[9]

In certain societies infants are killed or abandoned because their birth threatens the social order. These infants are thought to lack potential humanness, personhood, or social membership and sometimes they are considered to be dangerous to their community. The Girama of Kenya traditionally killed a child who was born feet first or whose first two top teeth erupted before the bottom ones, as such a child was believed to bring misfortune (Parkin 1985). An old woman, likely to be unrelated to the family, took the child to a tree-shaded area where it was drowned. The body was thrown into the surrounding bush and the place was called "the corpse of evil children." According to David Parkin, parents opposed the elimination of their own children, and "the Girama understand the conflict between parental love and the danger to the community that such children bring" (226).[10]

Attribution of nonhuman nature to certain infants has been documented among several West African populations (Allotey and Reidpath 2001, Dettwyler 1994, Gottlieb 1992, 2000a, Sargent 1988). Allotey (2001) proposes infanticide significantly contributes to the high rates of child mortality in Ghana while others describe the phenomenon as a rare event. Still, those infants being killed appear to already have a reduced chance of survival.[11] Carolyn F. Sargent (1988) suggests that infanticide or abandonment of an infant among the Bariba in Benin is a response to "atypical and aberrant events" such as breach presentations at birth or congenital abnormalities, which give rise to the suggestion that the child born is a witch child capable of harming its patrilineage. However, mothers may choose to give birth in solitude to hide eventual signs that suggest a child is a witch, or to dispose of an unwanted child. Katherine A. Dettwyler cites a village chief in Mali who tells her about children suspected to be evil spirits:

> These children never grow. They never reach out for things with their hands, they never sit up and walk, they never talk. Some begin to, but then stop. You keep praying and hoping and looking for medicine for them, but nothing helps. . . . Well, if they don't get better after a couple of years, then you know they are evil spirits, and you give up. . . . Well, you take them out into the bush and you leave them. . . . They turn into snakes and slither away. . . . You go back the next day, and they aren't there. Then you know for sure that they weren't really children at all, but evil spirits. When you see a snake, you wonder if it used to be your child. (1994:85–86).[12]

The village chief tells Dettwyler that in their village they had not had such a child for several years. Women have to be careful not to walk around at night while pregnant, he explains to her, because at that time evil spirits are looking for someone to take: "If that happens, your baby can be born dead, or deformed, or it may look all right at first, but then it becomes a child who never grows up" (86).

A pregnant Beng woman in the Ivory Coast who violates the taboo against eating on the path that connects the forest or fields with the village risks giving birth to a child that is a snake (Gottlieb 1992, 2000a). A snake, eager for human food, may invade her belly and take the fetus's place. At birth, the infant may look more or less human but with time people will recognize the child's behavior and movements as snakelike. Parents can take the child to a diviner who can test its real identity by taking the child to the forest. The diviner puts a plate with food favored by snakes on the ground, and if the child suddenly takes the plate and eats the food it is assumed to be a snake. However, parents often decide not to seek this diagnostic service because it is expensive and emotional. In such cases the child, referred to as a snake-person, is perceived as harmless and allowed to grow up. This child may be harassed and hit by stones; however, being boneless like a snake, the snake-person is thought to feel no pain. A snake-person never marries but may learn to perform some work, or just wander around in the village begging for food and sleeping anywhere (Gottlieb 1992:37, Gottlieb and Graham 1993:135–37).

The decisions to eliminate the infants described above are not motivated by the child's sex or a mother's disinterest in the child. Rather, the aim is to restore social order. Sometimes parents, who may not have the right to participate in decision making about the fate of their infants suspected to be evil, resist the elimination.

In previous chapters I argue that Papel mothers do not neglect their infants' daily care or illnesses. At the same time, as evidenced by Margareta's story, there are certain children who are thought to be dangerous and should thus be extinguished. This raises several questions. Why and how are they considered to be dangerous? What is the role of mothers in the eradication of these children? Do mothers grieve for these children as they grieve for other children?

Iran Children

Margareta is the first person to call my attention to *iran* children, these nonhuman, dangerous children who have to die. Later, I learn more about such children the hard way: I get to know a child who dies in procedure used to verify the child's human nature (see below). It is a disturbing experience, through which, however, I learn the necessary vocabulary to start a conversation.

During my fieldwork I have encountered seven children who are each suspected of being an *iran*. Three of them die in an identification process used to determine their nature. Of the four remaining children, one died, probably from malaria, but three are still alive when I leave Biombo. I also hear numerous stories about *iran* children from many people and understand early on that there are more ways a child can become a suspect *iran* than being born with a big head.

The suspected *iran* children I see with my own eyes have a wide range of physical anomalies or functional impairments. Some are minor, while others are more serious. Two of the children are severely paralyzed and cannot sit, walk, or reach for things. One child who is probably blind cannot sit or reach for things, but thrives physically and appears to be mentally sound. Another child is malnourished and cannot walk by two years of age. Still another child has a normal body, but was born prematurely and thus is very small. A girl has epileptic fits and her left arm and leg are partially paralyzed and atrophic. I hear still more stories of *iran* children from other people. One child is born with an abnormally long body; another has a deformed mouth and no nose (seemingly cleft lip and palate). One newborn has reddish skin and undetermined sex. Another has a complete, healthy body but a distorted face and stiff neck. Many people tell me about children who are severely paralyzed without deformities, evidently the most frequent impairment. Generally, without reference to a particular child, people describe *iran* children as having spineless bodies, pale skin, apathetic faces, bizarre eyes, and foaming mouths. In addition, some people say *iran* children can survive almost without food. Others stress that these children suckle their mothers' breast all the time and little by little they will eat up their mothers.

Albinos may belong to the group of children suspected to be *iran*. Among others, a middle-aged village woman points out to me that there were not so many albinos when she was a child.

"Today they are so many. Some say they are *iran*," she says.

"Why should albinos be *iran*? They have a normal body; only their color is a little different. In a way they are whites," I argue.

"Albinos are ugly, they are neither white nor black. There is something lacking in their skin and thus some say they are *iran*. At least, they are not normal," she maintains.

A normal birth is defined as one infant born headfirst. Only animals have multiple births, thus twins, triplets, or more are considered to be abnormal. Likewise a breach position at birth is seen as troublesome. Twins *(gemiu)* belong to a group of children with unclear status, but I have never heard a person say they are *iran*.

"Today women give birth to twins too often. Thanks to God, there were not so many twins born in the old days." Apili informs me. "They die easily." Apili argues that it is a problem to give birth to twins and she emphasizes all the practical problems they pose daily, but she also says "to give birth to twins is *mufunesa.*" A mother who has given birth to twins is not allowed to be present at funerals. A washing ceremony *(lava gemiu)* is performed. After the ceremony, the twins and their mother can participate in life as normal. If one of the twins dies at birth or later, the other twin has to go through the ceremonial twin washing.[13]

There are contradictory statements among people about whether or not the Papel destroyed their twins in the old days. A middle-aged Catholic woman states that the Papel never killed their twins; instead they always used to resolve the problem of twins with a washing ceremony, as do the Manjaco.[14] In contrast, Helena affirms, "all the ethnic groups in Guiné *(tudu rasa di Guiné)* used to throw away their twins." Helena does not believe it is bad to give birth to twins. She has given birth to twins, her mother gave birth to triplets, and her uncle's second wife gave birth to twins four times.

"Are twins considered human beings?" I ask.

"Twins are humans but people say it is *mufunesa* to give birth to many children at the same time like animals. Pigs have many offspring. Human beings give birth to only one each time. Therefore twins have to be thrown away. If not, the father, the mother, or somebody in the village may die," she explains.

Helena tells me many stories as a confirmation of her statement. She explains that many years ago a woman in the South gave birth to four children at the same time. The village chief took them all with the mother to Bissau to save their lives, and they were sent abroad where they grew up. Their father was so afraid that he ran into the bush. Further, it is important for a woman not to end her childbearing with twins.[15] Helena's last birth was twins; however, she will not give birth to more children, she insists. Helena is protestant and therefore sure she will not have any problems. "Black people do not like to have twins as a last birth. It is *mufunesa.*" Helena's maternal aunt wanted her to come to her village to perform the washing ceremony for her twins but she declined. She was afraid they would have been killed there in the bush, she tells me.

Mário, an elderly village man, asserts that twins were killed in the old days. "The Papel threw away one of their twins. A mother would choose to keep one of her twins and the other would be left to die, for example be burnt in an anthill. You understand, a mother has difficulties in breastfeeding two children at the same time," he explains to me. When I ask about other problems, he insists that it is only a question of practical problems: "It is hard work for a mother to take care of twins." He emphasizes that women who give birth to twins and do not have older daughters or other girls to help them have a particularly hard life because a mother can only carry one child at a time on her back. "For sure, twins are humans. They are not *iran,*" Mário adds.

The Papel agree about what causes some women to give birth to an *iran*. A pregnant woman should take care not to wash herself naked close to spring water well (manufactured wells are not dangerous). In such cases an *iran* with a sexual longing for that woman will penetrate her. Then the *iran* enters the child she has in her womb and prevents a human soul from entering the child or expels the human soul if one is already there. That *iran* will finally be born and have more or less the appearance of a child. Thus people say that pregnant women should always wash their laundry wearing underwear and they should wash their body quickly. Despite mothers' role in attracting an *iran,* I never heard a person blame mothers of *iran* children for their unlucky births. Rather, people feel pity for them.

When an *iran* child dies no funeral shrouds are wrapped around the body and no funeral rites are performed. In addition, no crying is allowed, though mothers are expected to grieve. The reason for these prescriptions is that the *iran* who occupied the child's body will become delighted with beautiful shrouds and aggrieved weeping and, consequently, be eager to repeat the whole event. It is important to extinguish the body; thus it is preferable to bury it in an ant heap and burn it. After the child's body has been destroyed the mother will be washed to prevent additional *iran* births. The mother walks to the rice fields where a washing ceremony is performed with the assistance of a *djambakus*. There she takes off all her clothes, which will be thrown away. She puts on a new *pano* (length of cloth) and walks to her house, passing crossroads without ever looking back. Once she enters her house and closes the door the mother stays there for several minutes before she can come out again. The *iran,* who lost her on the crossroads, is now unable to enter her again.

Obviously, an anomalous physical appearance at birth or a later deficient physical capacity instigate the questioning of a child's human nature. Considering the wide range of physical problems and anomalies described, the category *iran* child remains ambiguous. An infant is apparently not classified as an *iran* only with reference to its physical presentation, so more conclusive criteria are needed.[16]

Identification of *Iran* Children

The issue of *iran* children is not the first thing people discuss with a foreigner. However, once I learn the fundamentals about such children most people do not hesitate to tell me about *iran* children or what happened to them in the old days.

People agree that for whatever reason there were more *iran* children born in the old days. And they explain that these *iran* children were extinguished. Both men and women tell me that in the old days *iran* children were burnt in an ant heap. An elderly woman says that in her village, before she got married, there was a woman who gave birth to an *iran* child. The child was like a doll, it was *burmedju* (meaning "red," but the term is often used to describe the color of white people) and it was neither a boy nor a girl. "It was taken to an ant heap and burnt," she says. "Only in the old days, when people were stupid, did people burn these children like that."

People agree that suspected *iran* children were also "taken to the sea" *(levado mar)* to check their identity, an act that became prohibited by law during colonial times.[17] Several people describe to me how children were taken to the sea, and all the descriptions are similar. Mpone's version is as follows:

> You take an egg, you pound rice flour, and you take *kana* [distilled alcohol] and you put everything in a calabash. Then you put the child and the cala-bash on the beach, close to the sea. Then you withdraw behind the trees where you can observe the child. If the child is *iran* it will look around to discern whether anybody is observing, then it will drink the egg and disap-pear with the other items into the sea.

As the child belongs to its mother's lineage, the father and those of other lineages do not have much to say concerning the identification of suspected *iran* children, Mpone explains. Therefore, the child is taken to the sea only by elderly men and women of the child's lineage.[18] If the child disappears into the sea, people say that the *iran* has returned to where it came from, its true home. On the other hand, if the child feels uneasy on the beach and starts to cry when the sea comes in, it is not an *iran*. The child will be comforted and taken home to its mother. Mpone explains further that if an *iran* child is allowed to live it will harm the members of the mother's lin-eage. The mother is the person with the highest risk of suffering whatever misfortune—even death may befall her—especially if she does not stop breastfeeding the child. Nevertheless, Mpone maintains, mothers often re-fuse any suggestion that their own child is an *iran* and they will not easily agree to withhold the breast.

The only judicial case related to the identification of *iran* children I heard about happened under the Portuguese *(tempu di tuga)* some thirty years ago.[19] Augusta tells me about a couple who had a child that did not walk at the age of three years. Everybody said that this child was an *iran*. The parents, who lived in Bissau but came from Biombo, did not believe that. One morning when the father went to work and the mother to the market place, the child's maternal grandmother came for a visit. She took the child, put it into a sack and threw it into the sea. Somebody found the child in the sea, dead in the sack. The child's mother took her own mother to the police and she was put in prison for three years. "*Tuga* did not accept this," Augusta says. Augusta tells me that the old woman was so afraid of her grandchild that she did everything wrong: she did not take with her any of the items required for the diagnostic ceremony nor did she allow the child to decide to return to the sea or not.

The most sensitive issue regarding *iran* children is the identification procedure used to verify their true nature. Even though people say that *iran* children are less common today than in the old days, they claim that some women still give birth to an *iran*. They emphasize that it is necessary to verify the nature of such children and, if they are identified as *iran*, to do away with them. How can the true nature of a suspected *iran* child be determined today? Law prohibits "taking children to the sea." The discussion I have with Marta is revealing. One day when I visit her home village we find ourselves alone together. I use the opportunity to ask her about *iran* children.

"I don't know anything about *iran* children," she responds. "In my village we don't have any children like that."

"So you have never heard about such children?" I insist.

"Yeah, I have. A man and a woman who had moved to another village had a child that was *iran*. At two years of age the child could not sit or walk. It only suckled the breast all the time," Marta tells me.

"And what did they do?" I ask.

"The child was taken to the sea and disappeared into the water," she responds.

"When was that?"

"A year ago, more or less."

"Somebody could just throw the child into the sea, couldn't they?" I ask.

Marta sighs. "Who would do that? Nobody would throw a child into the sea. Jónína, there are people who are so stupid that they think other people are so stupid that they throw their children into the sea."

Marta tells me that many mothers know it is against the law to take suspected *iran* children to the sea, and that people are therefore not as willing to take children to the sea any more, or at least if they do, they try to do it secretly.

"Nevertheless, children are still taken to the sea, even without their mothers' consent," Marta affirms. "You understand, when the child is away and its mother has shaved off her hair everybody in the neighborhood knows that the family has taken the child to the sea."

"But somebody would go to the police, wouldn't they?"

"No. Who would do that? People don't go to the police. There is no other solution. The child is not human; it must be an *iran*. The mother has to accept it," Marta argues.

"But what about a visit to a *djambakus*?"

"Oh, yes. Of course, it is easier to specify a test period *(pui dias)*, then the mother waits to see if her child dies or not. That's better. To take a child to the sea is difficult, at least if the child can only lie on her or his back. It is much better to go to a *djambakus* than take the child to the sea."

"What exactly does it mean to go to a *djambakus*?"

"A knowledgeable *djambakus* will make an offering to his *iran* and ask for help, then the *djambakus* will specify a trial period. The *djambakus* gives the child water to drink and if it urinates, it is a sign that *iran* [the *iran* that works with that *djambakus*][20] agrees to do the work. If the child dies within the specified period of days it is an *iran,* if not it is not an *iran,*" Marta says. "But the mother is not allowed to breastfeed the child during that period. You have to feed the child with other food."

"Who is allowed to take the child to a *djambakus*?" I ask.

"Only maternal relatives. Nobody would dare to take a child who belongs to another lineage, neither to the sea nor to a *djambakus,*" Marta affirms. "It is a problem that when children are taken to the sea only those present know what happens."

Despite official condemnation of the practice, children suspected of being *iran* are still taken to the sea. Yet, a better accepted procedure among people today is to take such a child to a knowledgeable *djambakus* who will verify the true nature of the child through the child's survival of or death from the procedure.

Case-Stories of Suspected *Iran* Children

In the course of my fieldwork I hear many stories about *iran* children. In the following, descriptions of particular children have been modified to protect their identities. I will also retell Mpili's story about the two *iran* children she gave birth to.

My knowledge of the details in the following stories varies. Some of the children I meet many times and I have been much involved in discussions about their nature. Others I see only a few times or even just once. I will focus on the parents', especially the mothers', practical and emotional involvement in the identification process. I also want to pay attention to competing interpretations of the child's aberrant body or lack of functionality, which results in a variety of health-care-seeking alternatives. The ambiguity of the *iran* category is evident, and the identification procedure does not always give absolute answers. Even after the death of a child new interpretations of its nature may emerge.

Clara

Clara, who is three years old, was taken to a *djambakus* to verify her true nature because her mother's family demanded it. I don't know if Clara's mother accepted the decision or not. I happen to see her during the specified test period. Actually, when I come to her compound her mother sits with Clara in her arms and caresses her. The mother explains that Clara was born a healthy child but when the baby was three to four months of age she left her with another woman to go fishing. When she came back home her child was seriously ill and did not take the breast. The child was taken to the mission hospital and then to the national hospital in Bissau where she was admitted for twenty-five days. Since then she has never become healthy. I ask Clara's mother if she believes Clara is an *iran*.

"Yeah, it appears so . . ." she whispers, and starts to cry silently.

"But she was born healthy and became sick. You told me, right?" I ask.

Clara's mother does not respond but an elderly man explains that the child did not take the breast during all the twenty-five days in the hospital. She somehow survived only on intravenous fluid *(soru)*. "A normal child wouldn't do that," he argues. The man belongs to the mother's family and has been sent to see if the child would die, as it was the last day of the specified test period. Clara's maternal grandmother is *balobeiru*, which means that she collaborates with an ancestor spirit *(defuntu)*. Therefore it was not possible to have Clara at her home during the test period, which means that the girl stays the whole time with her mother, who has stopped breastfeeding as required.

I ask Clara's father if he believes his daughter is an *iran*.

"No, I don't know any *iran* children. Only old people say they exist," he responds. He tells me that the child had been taken to various *djambakus* for divination; one said she was an *iran*, another not. She has not been taken to the sea, he confirms.

Clara survives the appointed period of time, but she dies after a couple of weeks. Later, when I meet Clara's neighbors, two adult women, I ask them if they think Clara was an *iran*, or not. They are not sure but find it likely that she was an *iran*. They begin to question the identification procedure performed.

"It is no good to let the child stay with its mother during the test period," one of them explains. "But a person who owns *defuntu* can't be involved in *iran*. So there was no choice."

"It was somewhat mysterious how the girl survived in the hospital . . . only with *soru* for twenty-five days," the other argues. "Furthermore she was three years old and she could not sit or stand. That girl, she suckled the breast all night long."

"But she was born healthy," I emphasize.

"That's true," the other answers. "When Clara's mother left her with that woman somebody may have stolen her soul." They agree it is a possibility that she had had soul stolen *(alma furtadu)*.

Carlos

Carlos has problems similar to those of Clara. When I see him for the first time he is eight months old. He is a neatly dressed little boy, and obviously well cared for by his young mother. Carlos cannot sit or crawl, and his legs are extended and crossed. Carlos's mother tells me that he was probably born like that, without any control over his body. She has taken him several times to the mission hospital. Finally, the nun said she could not cure him. Carlos has already been treated for the cat and monkey diseases.

One day I meet a neighbor of Carlos. I have not seen Carlos for a couple of months and I ask about his health. She informs me that Carlos is gone.

"He was taken to the sea and disappeared into the water by his own force. You understand, he was already one year old, and he couldn't sit or do anything. It seems that he was born like that," she affirmed.

"Did Carlos's mother accept the fact that he was taken to the sea?" I asked.

The neighbor woman did not know, but remarked that mothers frequently refuse to allow their children to be taken to the sea. "Nevertheless, if the family insists, the mother has to accept it," she says.[21]

Marcelino

Marcelino is six months old and is a fat and well-formed boy at first glance. However, when I look closer at him I notice that his eyes whirl around and that he has no control over his body. Marcelino does not grasp for things or focus his eyes on anything. But I also notice that Marcelino looks like a happy boy as he sprawls on the ground and laughs to himself. The mother tells me that she has taken him many times to the mission hospital to seek care, but without results. Someone has proposed that Marcelino has the ant-bear disease (see chapter 4), and preparation for a washing ceremony is underway, she explains.

Marcelino's father, whom I never meet, has arranged for a consultation for his son at the rehabilitation center in Bissau. A physician who sees him proposes he might be blind but the aunt is frightened by the very idea that Marcelino might be blind. Children are not born blind, people say. Another woman tells me that she has never heard of a child being born blind: "You know, here we have never heard about such a child. Children who get measles or become sick in their eyes may become blind, and of course old people may lose their sight."

Marcelino's maternal great aunt demands that he be taken to the sea to see if he is an *iran* or not. Marcelino's mother refuses to allow him to be taken to the sea and his father's mother also dislikes the idea. Finally, they agree to take Marcelino to a *djambakus*. His father's mother is allowed to be present, but she is not allowed to say anything, as she does not belong to same lineage as Marcelino. On the other hand, Marcelino's mother is not permitted to be present. The *djambakus* makes his offer and specifies a test period of seven days. Marcelino stays with his great aunt during that period. She has arranged food for him, but his mother has to stop breastfeeding him. She is even forbidden to see her son during the trial period. Marcelino dies the last night of the appointed period without any indication of illness.

Marcelino's mother is filled with grief after the death of her son. "She cries and she cries and she cries," a family member tells me. People come to console her, but there is no funeral. "The body was just buried somewhere," she says. Then Marcelino's mother goes to stay with her father for a period of time to overcome her remorse. She is not happy with her situation; she has had no luck with childbearing. After five births she has no child who has survived. Marcelino's mother wants to take her aunt before the court for having killed Marcelino by withholding food. Her family members advise her to let it be. "She must understand that Marcelino was an *iran*. That's all. There was nothing else to do. Her aunt did the only right thing for the protection of her lineage," one of them tells me. Marcelino's mother never went to the police.

Three years later I hear from a neighbor that Marcelino's mother has given birth to a child that seems to thrive and has already learned to walk at one year of age. I ask my friend if everybody is still convinced that Marcelino was an *iran*. She tells me that finally, Marcelino's family has resolved the problem: Marcelino was not an *iran*. Marcelino's maternal grandmother, who died several years ago, killed him. Many years ago she became jealous of her younger co-wife and killed all her children with sorcery. The co-wife learned who had killed her children, and she responded with countersorcery. But God always punishes a person who practices counter-sorcery, and thus took the co-wife to the other world. From there the co-wife took vengeance on Marcelino's maternal grandmother and killed her. When the grandmother came to the other world, God punished her also for the killing of the co-wife's children: God obliged her to kill all her own grandchildren, that is, Marcelino and his siblings. The neighbor assures me the child Marcelino's mother has given birth to will not survive and that Marcelino was definitely not an *iran*.

Alfredo

When I see Alfredo for the first time he has not yet learned to walk, though he is two years old. He is small for his age, thin, a sorrowful-looking boy with big eyes and reddish hair. He never smiles at me when I try to get his attention.

"Alfredo was born small but clever and beautiful," his aunt informs me. However, he does not thrive and some people have suggested that he is an *iran*. An elderly woman who belongs to Alfredo's lineage made a divination and has concluded that he is an *iran*. However, Alfredo's maternal aunts refuse to take him to the sea. Somebody suggests that he has the sheep illness (see chapter 4). One of his aunts arranges money to get a washing ceremony performed by a knowledgeable Fulani man. The boy improves a little after the ceremony but still he does not walk. Finally, after nutritional rehabilitation he begins to walk and nobody speaks any more about him being an *iran*. A couple of months later he suddenly becomes sick and is taken to the mission hospital where he dies. "It was an illness that killed him. He got malaria. His body was all hot. He was not an *iran*. *Iran* children don't smile, whereas Alfredo smiled," his aunt affirms.

Alfredo's funeral is a normal one and there is a lot of crying.

Mpili's Iran *Children*

It is afternoon and already a little cooler after the hot midday sun. When I enter Mpili's compound a young mother breastfeeds her newborn, a two-year-old toddler sits with an extra meal in a calabash between his legs, and Mpili sits and chats with her younger co-wife, their common husband, and a female visitor.

I know from earlier that Mpili has given birth twice to *iran* children. I ask if she is willing to tell me about them. She is friendly and begins her story, as most mothers do, with her first-born child. She gave birth to four children who are all alive, she explains. Then she had a stillbirth and afterward she gave birth to two children who did not survive the first year. After that Mpili gave birth to a child she refers to as her last-born, *kodé*. When Mpili's ninth child was born some people immediately began to say that it was an *iran*. The newborn was normal but quite "long." Mpili and her husband did not believe the newborn was an *iran*. However, some ten days after birth she went to a local *djambakus* to identify its nature. The *djambakus* told her that if the infant was an *iran* it would die within a specified period of time, if not, it was not an *iran*. The very same evening her infant died without becoming sick. She had breastfed the infant all the time and it was buried in the normal way.

Mpili gave birth once more, this time at the health center in a nearby village. A woman who attended the birth ran away when she saw the infant; the upper lip and palate were missing. Mpili took her newborn home. Back home everybody agreed that the infant was an *iran* but Mpili and her husband rejected that idea. She breastfed the infant the best she could. The mouth was deformed, but by applying a special method Mpili managed reasonably well. However, after two to three months Mpili and her husband decided to go to a *djambakus,* this time in another village. The *djambakus* performed a ceremony and specified a period of time for trial. During that time the infant stayed with Mpili and she continued to breastfeed. The infant survived. A little later a female *balobeiru* who lived in the village came and had a serious talk with Mpili. She explained to Mpili that she had to stop breastfeeding the infant; otherwise it would kill her *kodé* and probably also herself. Mpili's husband also insisted that she stop breastfeeding the infant; he left the child behind the house where it died two days later. Nobody was courageous enough to touch its body. Mpili's husband sent for a maternal relative, who buried the body in an ant heap and set it on fire. Mpili herself did not perform any ceremony to clean herself; she did not want to give birth anymore.

Mpili speaks sorrowfully and in a low voice. Her husband and co-wife sit silently behind her and I notice that they occasionally nod their heads or utter something in agreement with her descriptions. When Mpili finishes her story we all sit silent for a while. The female visitor, who sits in front of Mpili, finally takes her hand and says full of consolation: "Mpili, thanks to God that the *balobeiru* came and helped you understand that you had to stop breastfeeding that infant. An *iran* child has to die, otherwise something terrible can happen."

Margareta's Grandson and Teresa

Not all mothers whose children are suspected of being *iran* must weep for the death of their children. Three such children I have known were to my knowledge never tested and they were still alive when I left Biombo.

Margareta's grandson's identity has never been tested because his paternal grandparents opposed the very idea of a child being an *iran* and decided to take care of him.[22] Luckily enough, his maternal family agreed. Today, the boy's appearance and ability are normal, and his grandmother praises his sweetness.

Teresa has not been tested either. I see her when she is four years old. Teresa is a nice little girl. She is short of stature and thin, but otherwise normal. She was born prematurely at seven months and she was extremely small at birth, thus, some people said she was an *iran,* Teresa's mother explains to me. Her mother-in-law prohibited her from breastfeeding the child. Then, Teresa's maternal grandmother decided to breastfeed the little girl in order to save her life, as she had passed childbearing age. Teresa's maternal grandmother took care of the child and when Teresa grew bigger everybody realized that she was just a normal child. She still lives with her grandmother. "They are used to each other," Teresa's mother explains and laughs. The whole story belongs to the past.

Celeste

When I see Celeste for the first time she is about ten years old. I do not pay much attention to her situation. I am told that she had convulsive attacks and she falls many times every day. Her left arm and leg are partially paralyzed and wasted, but she can drag herself along. Massive scars mark her thin body from having fallen into the fire many times. Celeste does not talk, but seems to understand a little.

Two years later I return to Celeste's compound. Celeste is in a miserable state: dirty, malnourished, and severely burnt. She fell into the fire a couple of weeks ago, I am told. When I propose to Celeste's parents to take her to the mission hospital for treatment, they gratefully accept. However, the next time I come to the village all the villagers are not so happy with my effort to improve Celeste's condition. In the first compound I visit a woman who remarks that it is a waste to give medicine to an *iran*. In the next compound there is a party. A group of people chatter and some are drunk.

"How is Celeste?" the senior wife asks.

"She is well, she is getting treatment for her burns," I respond.

"The nun will cure her?" she asks.

"That is how it is," I answer.

"You think she is a human being?" she asks me.

"Yes. Certainly," I said. "You should see Celeste washed in nice clothes. She is a nice girl."

"It would be better to give me some medicines than throw them away on an *iran*," another elderly woman argues and laughs.

Two more women ask about Celeste without commenting on her being an *iran*. At Celeste's compound people ask about her and they seem happy to hear that she is getting treatment. I later understand that not only the neighbors but also some of Celeste's relatives maintain that she is an *iran*. One day, a woman who belongs to Celeste's compound comments cynically that Celeste's mother not only spent all her time getting her *iran* cured, but she has also begun to arrange Celeste's hair in braids.

Even outside the village people ask me about Celeste. Once I stop my car to give a lift to a young woman who carries a child on her back. She asks me about Celeste.

"Celeste is well," I respond. "You know her?"

"Our fathers are kinsmen," she says.

"You think she is an *iran*?"

"Yeah, that is what we think," she answers.

"She takes white man's medicines that prevent her from falling. So if she is cured by the white man's medicine she can't be an *iran*? Isn't that the way it is?" I argue.

"That is how it is," she responds.

Later, I meet Fernando, a man in his fifties I have known for some time. What a surprise. He also asks me about Celeste.

"You know her?" I ask.

"I am a relative of her father," he explains.

"You think Celeste is an *iran*?"

"Yeah, that is what we think," he answers, and then he skillfully changes the subject.

Only one person with whom I discuss Celeste's nature argues that she is not an *iran*; Celeste was born healthy, and consequently it is more likely that her problems are caused by sorcery. This is consistent with what Celeste's parents say. They do not share the idea that their daughter is an *iran*. They say she was a chubby (*tene kurpu*, which means to "have body") and healthy child the first year of her life when she suddenly became sick. Celeste's mother remembers that day: there was a party and she was responsible for the arrangements. Celeste had started to walk and she sauntered around on her own. The pig had been just slaughtered and her mother was busy preparing the food. Suddenly Celeste screamed. She had severe convulsions. It started like that, suddenly.

Since then Celeste has been sick. Her parents took her to a *djambakus* who extracted a piece of pork from her body, an indication of sorcery. Nonetheless, Celeste did not become better. She continued to have convulsive attacks and she could not walk anymore. Celeste's parents took her to the health center and from there she was sent to the rehabilitation center in Bissau. She was trained to walk again with the help of some aids. In addition, a number of ceremonies have been performed, her father says, but he is not willing to explain them in further detail. He argues firmly that Celeste is not an *iran*. Celeste's mother is also sure that her daughter is not an *iran*; she knows Celeste was born healthy. Several people have tried to convince her to leave Celeste to die behind her house, but she has refused.

After weeks of treatment at the mission hospital Celeste returns to her village. Her burns are cured, she is well nourished, her hair is beautiful, and she has shoes on and a nice dress. However, most importantly, she takes medicines that prevent convulsive fits and falling. Celeste's mother stayed with her daughter most of the time at the hospital, but Celeste longed for her father. Celeste's affection for both of her parents is obvious, but they have a hard time protecting her. Celeste is stubborn and difficult to instruct. Still worse, some of the children like to tease her and she easily loses her self-control. Celeste is often the source of disturbance and dispute in her compound.

Before I leave Guinea-Bissau in April 1998 one of my last visits is to say good-bye to Celeste and her parents. When I arrive in the village I am told on my way to their compound that Celeste's mother is beating her. When I arrive her mother is quarrelling with another woman. They shout at each other for a while. Finally, they stop and Celeste's mother comes and greets me. What is the problem? I wonder. Celeste had hit a little child. The child's mother became upset and demanded that Celeste's mother should punish her daughter. She did, but not happily.

The struggle goes on *(luta continua)*.

Dealing with Deviations

In this chapter I situate the treatment of Papel children suspected of being nonhuman in the wider context of infanticide as a worldwide practice in past and present times. I present several ethnographic descriptions of infanticide and focus on motives for killing infants, as well as assumptions about their humanness, personhood, and social membership.

Despite the lack of details, an examination of the literature indicates that a variety of circumstances surround infant killing. Not always is the killing motivated by extreme poverty nor exclusively committed by mothers. I suggest that attribution of status to infants, such as humanness, personhood, and social membership in the respective society is essential to comprehend the wider circumstances of infanticide. I propose three categories of infanticide based on the motives given for the killing of infants by those involved.[23]

The first category includes infanticide directed specifically at girls, who are considered too expensive to rear. Female infanticide is not exclusively practiced among the poorest strata of a society, as demonstrated in India. Information about the ethical dilemma in killing these girls is largely missing; however, the influence of gender on the attribution of personhood and social membership is likely to be relevant. Information on who determines or commits the killing is mainly lacking. The second category includes infanticide performed for the eradication of surplus or unwanted infants, who are killed before they gain status as humans, persons, or members of society. Parents, most often mothers, kill the infant directly after birth.[24] The third group covers infanticide aimed at restoration of the social order. Here the infant is thought of as without potential for humanity, personhood, or social membership; often they are considered to be dangerous as well. The infant's parents may be opposed to the eradication of these children, which is normally committed by an outside person or professional specialist. The eradication of *iran* children in Biombo belongs to this category of infanticide.

The treatment described above for children suspected of being nonhumans resembles accounts from other West African societies. These children certainly are not some of their mothers' "best bets." Nonetheless, the mothers are likely to resist practical involvement in the identification procedure of their children. Papel mothers of suspected *iran* children invest a great deal of emotional and physical energy, limited resources, and reproductive time in keeping these children alive and finding them a cure, despite the fact that others consider these infants a threat to the safety of their own mother and lineage. Such maternal efforts contradict Hrdy's argument that "mothers evolved not to produce as many children as they could but to trade off quantity for quality, or to achieve a secure status, and in that way increase the chance that at least a few offspring will survive and prosper" (1999:10). The question is why do Papel mothers protect their aberrant children suspected of being nonhuman and dangerous?

Papel mothers fight for the survival of their children, even those who are disabled and deviant. Some mothers hinder the diagnostic process of identifying whether their infants are *iran,* while others resist but without success. Despite the assumption that mothers risk their own lives if they breastfeed an *iran,* in the histories I have collected the mothers are reluctant to stop breastfeeding a suspected child. Mpili, who herself takes the initiative to have her children's true human nature verified, breastfeeds throughout the trial period. Clara's young mother breastfeeds her "low-viability," "high-risk" daughter for three years, instead of "letting her go" to become pregnant again in hope of better luck with the next child.[25] Not only does Clara's mother waste her reproductive time on a fragile child, but also a potentially dangerous one. She is not the only mother to do this. How do we explain such irrational behavior?

There are some similarities between the "doomed" children of the Alto, in particular those who were suspected of having the "child sickness" and the suspected *iran* children in Biombo. The humanness of both *iran* children in Biombo and the "doomed" children of the Alto is questioned and they are stigmatized. Like the "child sickness," the definition of *iran* is "impossibly loose, fluid, elastic, and nonspecific" (Scheper-Hughes 1992:386). The wide range of physical impairments characteristic of suspected *iran* children demonstrates the ambiguity of the *iran* category. However, the reaction of the two groups of mothers of these stigmatized children is different. The dictum that a child is either born an *iran* or it is not an *iran* is a point Papel mothers tend to use when arguing that their own child is not an *iran.* When the child is obviously born with a disability, alternative explanations for its condition may be suggested. We see from the descriptions that there are many competing alternative interpretations of the child's anomalous body or impaired abilities. As a result, the suspected *iran* child is taken to a wide range of healers, diviners, and health personnel before the decision is made to perform the feared *iran* identification procedure. The hope for a cure is there and it encourages mothers and sometimes others to actively seek a solution.

The identification procedure is not faultless when it concerns the true nature of the child.[26] Sometimes the performance itself may be questioned, and then the child's death or survival is explained differently. A child's death may be attributed to the withholding of food or being thrown into the water. Survival may be explained by the mother's presence and breast-feeding of the child during the trial period. Despite a seemingly successful identification procedure, later, new evidence may give rise to new interpretations, as happened in the case of Marcelino.

Anxious maternal relatives may be more concerned with the extermination of an eventual *iran* child than a strictly performed verification of a suspected child. Marta recognizes this fact and admits it is a problem that only those present know what really happens. Marcelino's maternal great aunt is fearful because of the potential misfortune the child may cause her lineage. She demands an identification procedure and Marcelino dies. Marcelino's mother does not trust her aunt's impartiality. Augusta emphasizes that the frightened old woman who was put in prison for murder during colonial times did not follow the rules when she threw her suspected grandchild into the water in a sack.

Mpili's story demonstrates a combination of ambiguity and fear. She herself takes the initiative to identify her children suspected of being *iran* but does not stop breastfeeding. Her first suspected child appears to be almost normal, but despite being breastfed it dies suddenly after an identification ceremony is performed. Then the child is buried normally. At first Mpili and her husband do not accept the suggestion that their next born child is an *iran*, despite the fact that it was born with a visible deformity. Then an identification ceremony is performed with a continuation of breastfeeding and the child survives. Finally, after a respected person warns Mpili about the dangers of *iran* children for her and her lastborn, Mpili's husband acts against convention (the father does not share lineage with his child), he leaves the child behind the house, where it dies, probably from hunger. Later, full of fear, he calls on a maternal relative to cremate the body. Mpili performs no cleansing ceremony but decides not to give birth to more children.

Many of those with whom I discuss the issue of *iran* children emphasize that fear of them is an important factor that contributes to their destruction. It is the responsibility of elderly maternal kin to destroy *iran* children; otherwise they may bring *mufunesa* to their lineage members. Despite this, the mothers' devoted hope for a cure makes them reluctant to stop breastfeeding a weak child who clearly will not survive without the breast. Mothers and sometimes others (as did some of Alfredo's aunts), tend to argue for

other interpretations of their child's deviation, but still within the framework of the Papel *uso*. None of the mothers of suspected *iran* children I
talked to called into question the very existence of *iran* children. Another
alternative is to take a stance against and argue that *iran* children do not
exist, as did Clara's father and Margareta's Catholic husband. Many Christians take that position, but not all.

To dismiss the nonhuman, dangerous nature attributed to *iran* children
as a superstitious belief that contributes to natural selection and enhances
human survival, as is sometimes done within sociobiology, does not contribute to a better understanding of their fate. Furthermore, it is misleading
to classify the extermination of *iran* children as a rational reproductive
strategy, a killing of "lowered-viability infants." Some of the children suspected of being *iran* are healthy. At the same time there are still more disabled children who never become suspected of being an *iran* because their
impairment is interpreted differently and their humanness is never questioned. Truly human children are not killed despite severe physical deformity. To kill such children would be classified as murder and an immoral
and dangerous act. Strictly formulated, *iran* children are not killed either;
iran children are removed or allowed to return to their true home.

Infanticide is too often described as a straightforward routine act performed according to determined criteria with little controversy or repen-
tance. While attempting to understand Papel mothers' involvement in the
fate of their *iran* children, we are dealing with an anomaly and ambiguity
at the same time. According to Mary Douglas, "an anomaly is an element
which does not fit a given set of series; ambiguity is a character of statements capable of two interpretations" (1966:37). The question is whether
the *iran* children are best understood, in Douglas's terms, as "matter out of
place"? Douglas suggests, "we find in any culture worthy of the name various provisions for dealing with ambiguous or anomalous events" (39). The
Papel have their ways of acting: an *iran* should return to its true home or be
extinguished. However, the ambiguity of the *iran* category makes it difficult
to identify and deal with children who may or may not be *iran*. It is this ambiguity that gives mothers their chance to act in the case of individual children, but it does not necessarily allow mothers to challenge the very idea
that *iran* children are dangerous nonhumans and must be eliminated.

One cannot overlook the explanatory power of religion when it concerns *iran* children. Events are predicted if certain measures are not taken,
such as the mother's death if she does not stop breastfeeding a suspected
iran or she jeopardizes her lineage if an *iran* is allowed to live. Robert Horton (1993) argues that religions, like the modern sciences, are concerned
with explanations and the prediction and control of everyday events.[27] In
line with Horton's suggestion, the Papel religion or *uso* very much provides

a model for explanation, prediction, and control, but it is not a coherent, static, mechanical system with faultless solutions to any problem. The Papel recognize that there are alternative ways to explain and act upon misfortune, each way predicting still other potential events to come. When negotiating the fate of suspected *iran* children both mothers and their maternal relatives base their views on *uso*. Being able to construct clear and consistent arguments is important for those mothers who want their theory to guide action when it concerns the suspicion that their child is nonhuman.

In a similar way, as described in the previous chapter, mothers (and fathers) of suspected *iran* children maintain a hope for a cure in an unknown future, just as they do for their favorite and normal children. Thus, mothers resist the verification procedure of their suspected *iran* child. Mothers also often refuse to stop breastfeeding the child because they know it will not survive without the breast. And when the child dies the mother grieves, despite instructions to the contrary.

Conclusion

In this book I have examined what I refer to as the neglect thesis, which predicts that impoverished mothers in societies with high child mortality will as a survival strategy neglect their children, sometimes fatally, and fail to grieve their deaths. The neglect thesis is assumed to apply particularly to children who are unviable or unwanted. My argument is based on extensive fieldwork conducted among Papel women who experience high rates of fertility; a full one-third of their children born alive are likely to die before reaching five years of age.

I begin by locating Guinea-Bissau in an international context as one of the most disadvantaged countries in the world in terms of income, with a long history of warfare and exploitative relations with the colonial power, Portugal. Thereafter, through general descriptions and ethnographic accounts, I discuss the life of Papel women as wives and mothers. I attempt to emphasize the agency and voices of individual mothers, and to present their varied experiences, practices, and opinions. At the same time, I want to illuminate their common patterns of thinking and acting, as well as the constraints and structures that curtail their choices.

In the Biombo region, I situate Papel women within the matrilineal kinship system as wives and co-wives striving to make a living through horticulture, fishing, commerce, and collecting cashew nuts for the global market. I describe their motives for having children, as well as their experiences of menstruation, pregnancy, childbirth, and breastfeeding. I also present Papel women's conceptions about the nature of infants, their care of children and rearing practices, fosterage, and naming customs. I further discuss ideas related to disease, death, and the afterlife, together with mothers' interpretation of and reactions to their children's diseases and deaths. Finally, I examine the question of infanticide as a worldwide phenomenon, but also in relation to Papel conceptions of deviant and disabled children. Throughout the book, I am occupied with the question of whether Papel mothers neglect their children's daily care and illnesses or fail to mourn the death of a child. Thus, I focus on maternal dedication to and mourning for favorite children, such as the last-born and the normal child, but also those children who are born impaired or abnormal.

I conclude that Papel mothers' daily care of their infants and their active pursuit of health care for sick children is not characterized by indifference and neglect as predicted by the neglect thesis. Nor do mothers fail to mourn when their children die, regardless of the child's viability or favorite status. While individual cases of neglectful care are likely to occur, as elsewhere, I firmly argue that in the Biombo region this is not a cultural pattern. I draw this conclusion from a number of observations. First, mothers emphasize breastfeeding as essential for child survival, and undernourished and sickly children are consciously breastfed longer than healthy ones (chapter 2). Second, daily care of infants is characterized by physical closeness, rapid response to infant distress, and attention to the child's mental and physical development and well being (chapter 3). Third, children's diseases are recognized as a sign of danger to be treated in accordance with the interpretation of symptoms (chapter 4). The distance to preferred health care services, lack of necessary resources, and mother's limited time, sometimes in combination with little confidence in available health care instances, may, however, contribute to delay or even inhibit mothers from seeking health care. Finally, mothers mourn the deaths of their children, even those who are born impaired or deviant and suspected of being nonhuman and dangerous for the matrilineage (chapter 5). Immediate maternal reaction to a child's death is characterized by desperate weeping, while forgetting is a long-term bereavement strategy (chapters 4 and 5).

In this book I examine a number of assumptions frequently taken as evidence in support of the neglect thesis. First, according to maternal bonding theory, early mother-infant contact after birth, preferably within one or two hours, is essential to take advantage of the hormonally "sensitive period" for the establishment of maternal affection. Emotional support to mothers during childbirth and early initiation of lactation after birth, have also been identified as important for maternal affection and successful breastfeeding. My findings do not support any of these claims. Papel mothers become emotionally attached to their infants and breastfeeding is successful despite the lack of emotional support given to mothers during birth, despite the lack of early mother-infant contact after birth, and despite the delayed initiation of breastfeeding (chapter 2).

Second, delay or failure to attribute humanity, individual personality, personhood, or social membership to infants is assumed by the advocates of the neglect thesis to reflect maternal (parental) indifference to the well-being of infants and their survival. I maintain that this assumption is multifaceted. The very potential of infants to gain the desired status as human beings may give mothers (and others) enough motivation to care for them and grieve at their deaths (chapter 3 and 4). On the other hand, failure to attribute this status to newborns, or the categorization of an infant as being without such potential, is in many societies crucial in the decision to commit infanticide (chapter 5). Among the Papel, who believe in reincarnation, normal children are attributed with human nature, personality, and social membership at birth, and their demand for care is individual. However, nonhuman children, born without human souls and unable to get one, should be killed in order to prevent them from causing damage to their mother's lineage.

Three, the advocates of the neglect thesis sometimes take for granted that delayed naming of infants and the use of insulting, impersonal, or repetitious names in societies where child mortality is high reflects maternal (or parental) indifference to child survival caused by avoidance of attachment. Cross-cultural comparison of naming practices indicates that high child mortality influences name giving, both as to timing as well as the choice of names (chapter 3). Among other reasons given for delay in naming is fear of child death; a nameless child is said to be easier to forget. I maintain that such naming practices are not necessarily an indication of indifference. Forgetting is a bereavement strategy applied not only among the Papel but also in other societies, past and present. The common use of ugly, insulting, impersonal, or and repetitious names in many societies often originates in high child mortality but it does not necessarily indicate indifference to child survival. The use of unattractive or impersonal names among the Papel reflects maternal concerns for their child's survival.

Four, fosterage as a strategy for upbringing and education is practiced worldwide. Social historians who have studied child fostering in Europe often disapprove of the practice and ask why parents or mothers would allow other people to rear their children. Can they really love their children? Papel mothers frequently let their children grow up with others to live in better social conditions or have new opportunities, but rarely without sorrow (chapter 3). Women's obligations to give their own mothers a child and, less commonly, to give a daughter to a *baloba* as a return for ritual services to enhance child survival are additional reasons for fosterage. If these obligations are neglected, mothers run the risk that some of their children may die as punishment. Papel mothers' willingness to allow their children to enter into fosterage reflects maternal concern for children's survival, not indifference.

Five, advocates of the neglect thesis often take reluctance to seek health care for a sick child as an indicator of maternal indifference to child survival. Care-seeking is dependent on numerous factors, for example, interpretations of diseases, available options for health care, judgments of quality, time, and resources. I maintain that categorizations of diseases and access to resources are crucial for the type of care sought for Papel children. Thus, without taking these aspects into account, it is impossible to assess whether mothers are neglectful about seeking health care (chapter 4). Caution must be taken: a mother who believes her child has a fatal disease is frequently assumed to be reluctant to seek health care; however, studies have shown that this is not necessarily the case. Still, there seems to be a tendency to invoke a fatal disease after a child's death has occurred. The Papel conception of misfortune demands that action be taken to alleviate child illness. The inherent ambivalence of disease categories may give rise to various interpretations and actions (chapters 4 and 5). This ambivalence allows Papel mothers to maintain a spirit of hope of improvement, and thus, they can keep on seeking a solution.

Finally, I discuss the assumption that religious ideas about a comfortable afterlife and a relatively unproblematic or even positive cause of death will ease emotional distress of mothers and other mourners. For example, despite West African Muslim affirmation that child death is the will of Allah, the belief that children have a good afterlife, and mothers' apparent resignation, Muslim mothers still mourn their children. Absence of crying or apparent stoicism at child death does not necessarily imply lack of grief. For the non-Muslim Papel, child death is always considered to be bad and most likely caused by human failure, and the other world is not an appropriate place for children who are born to live, not die. Immediate grief is expressed with at times hysterical weeping, while the long-term strategy is to forget.

None of the assumptions discussed above seems to be universally valid; a wider social context is needed to understand maternal concern for child survival. With that in mind, let us make a final comparison between Papel

mothers and Brazilian Alto mothers as described by Scheper-Hughes
(1992). These two groups of mothers appear to differ fundamentally in
their child care practices and concern for the survival of their children.
However, they have some common experiences. Most importantly they
share the structural prerequisites of the neglect thesis: extreme poverty,
high rates of fertility, and frequent child death. In addition, their marriages
are unstable: fathers are absent in one way or another, sometimes they are
drunkards, and they commonly fail to share the burden of providing for
the livelihood of their children (see chapter 1).

Despite these similarities, not only is the Brazilian shantytown mother
more likely than the Papel mother to refrain from seeking health care or
remedies for her sick child; she is apparently also less emotionally disturbed
when her child dies. There are also differences regarding ideas about infants'
humanness, the nature of diseases and death, and ideas about the afterlife
of infants; all these differences are intertwined with considerations about
the individual, religion, and kinship. While Papel infants are thought of
as human at birth, Alto infants only gradually achieve their human status.
Alto mothers think of common childhood diseases as fatal, child death as
normal and even welcome, and the afterlife of children as attractive. In
contrast, Papel mothers interpret childhood diseases and child death as preventable and ultimately caused by human fault, and children do not have a
given place in the world of the dead. Evidently these differences are important for contrasting maternal concerns for child survival in the Alto and
Biombo. Nonetheless, in the case of Biombo I suggest that values attributed
to reproduction and motherhood are crucial to understanding Papel
mothers' eagerness to have many children, their dedication to child survival,
and their desperation when children die. Papel mothers are born into a kinship structure that allocates to them a fundamental role in reproduction
that gives them status and respect. Scheper-Hughes describes reproduction
in the Alto as a highly ambivalent and contradictory issue, and indeed, she
proposes that women's lack of control over their own fertility might contribute to maternal neglect, a suggestion worthy of more attention.

Scheper-Hughes's analysis of Alto mothers' neglect of their infants and
their lack of grief at their death is challenging. However, the suggestion that
the neglect thesis may be universally valid is problematic.[1] Nor do my findings (see chapter 5) support the thesis put forward by Hrdy (1999) that infanticide is a rational and adaptive reproductive strategy applied by mothers who have evolved "to trade off quantity for quality" (10). Hrdy treats
human biology as fundamental for maternal behavior. Accordingly, extreme poverty may trigger a predisposed behavior, while intellectual reasoning, religion, and moral conventions have a limited role to play.[2] Nevertheless, Hrdy recognizes certain exceptions that "innate responses" cannot

explain, such as "the many modern mothers" who, constrained by the tenets of "ethical behavior," act against nature and self-interest and "throw themselves utterly and wholeheartedly into care of babies unlikely to survive" (1999:459–60). Hrdy's line of reasoning suggests that only some modern Western mothers are guided by ethics, and in such cases social and cultural circumstances must be considered to explain their behavior. Consequently, other mothers appear to act in response to innate impulses in line with their evolved nature.[3]

As a continuation of my fieldwork in Biombo, a region with one of the highest child mortality rates in the world, I am currently conducting research in Iceland, a country with one of lowest child mortality rates in the world. The fieldwork setting is a neonatal intensive care unit.[4] My focus is on ethical questions concerning treatment and eventual life-and-death decisions of infants with birth weights under 1,000 grams and the implications of their births on the daily lives of the families involved. The fragile lives of these infants are sustained with the help of modern technology. As in Biombo, I am concerned with local conceptions about children and interpretations of their diseases and death. Interestingly, studies indicate that within the commonly assumed homogenous Western world there is a great variation in criteria and routines for life-and-death decisions for critically ill or disabled children whose lives are dependent on advanced technology.[5] The extent of parents' participation in these decisions likewise varies, as well as their willingness to take part (Munck et al. 1997, Vandvik and Førde 2000).

Indeed, the diverse views within bioethics and moral philosophy on parents' participation in decision making about the continuation of life-sustaining treatment for their severely ill or disabled children are illustrative of assumptions about human nature (Beauchamp and Childress 1994, Rachels 1993). Some argue that parents should not make life-and-death decisions for their children due to their emotional involvement; parents would never allow the child to die, irrespective of the severity of the child's situation and suffering. Others claim that the interests of the parents and the child are at odds, and parents, eager to have a healthy child, might let a disabled child die. Further, many emphasize parents' lack of professional knowledge to make an informed decision. Finally, a few maintain that the parents should exclusively make life-and-death decisions for their children, as they have to live with the outcome.

In Biombo, mothers do not make life-and-death decisions—they struggle for their children's survival. To understand that struggle it is essential to examine how history, economy, religion, and kinship shape gender relations and cultural values attributed to reproduction, motherhood, and the individual, and how these in turn inform maternal sentiments and practice.

Papel women want to have many children, both daughters and sons, for reasons related to practical existence, economic return, social esteem, and emotional well-being in the present life and a respectful entrance into the afterlife (chapter 2). Religious and kinship considerations are crucial in understanding the conceptions about children and interpretations of diseases and death. A serious child disease, and in particular sudden death without a disease, is interpreted as a sign of *mufunesa*, a misfortune resulting from an intentional agent. Hence, it must be acted on: neglect is not a valid option. Matrilineal descent and inheritance shape both gender and intra-familial relations. It sets the stage and delegates roles to the actors. The matrilineal kinship structure gives the mother and her lineage members a central role in seeking care and evaluating the consequences of death.

Maternal indifference is not an inevitable product of poverty and a high expectancy of child death. Poverty and a high expectancy of child deaths surely influence the Papel mothers' child rearing practices and their concerns for child survival. These conditions contribute to maternal anguish and distress. Mothers consciously recognize that poverty prevents them from adequately feeding their children and taking them to appropriate health care services. Without children who survive to adulthood their poverty becomes absolute and inescapable; the poorest of all poor are women without children. Thus, for a Papel woman of fertile age, pregnancy is likely to be wanted and planned, while child death is chaotic and frightful. Mother love in Biombo is bound up with notions of reciprocity, of give and take. Mother love is not unilaterally self-sacrificing and unconditional, nor is it simply a question of survival. Mothers suffer because they give birth to children, but they also expect to be rewarded for their suffering socially, economically, as well as emotionally. Child death erases that expectation.

In Biombo, child death is not an expected outcome of reproduction, nor is it confronted with indifference, of which mothers' weeping is an unmistakable sign. The Kriol phrase *no kansa tchora*, literally "we are tired of weeping," is a statement about an unbearable situation, a private or political one; it is a statement of pain, but also of protest. "There must be a solution"—*djitu ten ke ten*.

Notes

Introduction

1. For example, the Feminist Spiritual Movement in North America and Western Europe celebrates an essentialist view of womanhood (Sered 1994). According to their view, as mothers, women are assumed to "understand love, relationship, and spirituality in ways that men do not" (77). See Butler (1992) for a critique of Kristeva and Alsop, Fitzsimons, and Lennon (2002) for a summary of essentialist feminism.

2. The psychologists Keith Oatley and Jennifer M. Jenkins recognize Darwin as one of the founders of the psychology of emotions as he felt that "our emotions have a primitive quality. They are links to our past, both to the past of our species and to our own individual history. They are not fully under voluntary control" (1996:5).

3. In similar vein, Scheper-Hughes (1987c) argues, "maternal thinking and practices are socially produced rather than determined by a psychological script or innate and universal emotions" (188).

4. Scheper-Hughes borrows the concept of maternal thinking from Sara Ruddick (1980). Maternal thinking includes emotional, practical, and intellectual aspects of mothers' concerns for their children. While I recognize the utility of this concept, I don't use it for two reasons. First, it connotes an essentialist view of maternal emotional involvement. Secondly, I find it productive to treat the emotional, practical, and intellectual aspects of the concept separately.

5. The anthropologist Susan Greenhalgh argues that most demographic theories of fertility decline are expressions of "Eurocentric diffusionism," often with "an implicit belief in the historical superiority or priority of Europe over the rest of the world" (1995:10). Scheper-Hughes (1992:401–2) reminds the reader about similarities between contemporary Brazil and earlier periods in Europe and the United States. She refers to the "pre-demographic transition, reproductive strategy" of Alto mothers.

6. Linda Pollock (1983:22) shows how historians who use secondary sources, such as religious scripts, expert recommendations, paintings, fictional literature, travelers' accounts, newspaper reports, and legislation, describe the situation of

children in more negative terms than those who use primary sources such as diaries, memoirs, and letters. Pollock uses adult diaries, child diaries, and autobiographies in her study of parent-child relations from 1500 to 1900. She finds parent-child relationships to be less formal and more affective and stable over time than do historians who rely mainly on secondary sources (262–71).

7. In the 1980s and 1990s historians began to reevaluate the common assumption that historically parents were indifferent to their children's well-being and survival; parents, particularly mothers, are now seen as mainly loving toward their children, and if negligent care is identified it is explained in terms of lack of better alternatives for parents (Cunningham 1995, Pollock 1983).

8. The advocates of the neglect thesis are not unequivocal on the level of mothers' consciousness in neglecting their infants to death. Scheper-Hughes argues, "obviously these selective neglect practices are not fully conscious or intentional maneuvers. Consciousness constantly shifts back and forth between allowed and disallowed levels of awareness" (1992:390).

9. See also the writings of the anthropologists Claire Monod Cassidy (1987) and Susan C. Scrimshaw (1978, 1984) who argue that neglectful care is a survival strategy of the poor.

10. The Human Development Index (HDI) is a statistical manipulation of various indicators such as national income, health statistics, literacy rates, and so on. See UNDP (2001:239–40) for definitions of the Human Development Index.

11. Country Reports, http://www.countryreports.org/content/guineb.htm (accessed April 7, 2003).

12. According to the U.S. Department of State Annual Report on International Religious Freedom (1999), the Guinean constitution provides for freedom of religion. The varied religious communities have friendly relations and religious diversity is generally tolerated within the society.

13. The Kriol word *prassa* is derived from the Portuguese word *praça,* which means fortress, marketplace, or square. In INEP (National Institute of Studies and Research) (1991) a distinction between urbanized and rural population is emphasized.

14. The term *Biombo* is often used in daily language for the Ondame sector, which consists of the Biombo kingdom (see map 2, page 11).

15. To my knowledge there are no official statistics on the religious affiliation of Biombo's population. In the region, an estimated 8 percent of the inhabitants belong to ethnic groups other than the Papel and Balanta (Djatá 1998). Therefore, in terms of religion, those who adhere to African religions are by far the largest group, while Christians (Catholics and Protestants) and Muslims are found in low numbers.

16. See Cissoko (1987:32) and Moreira (1993:19).

17. According to the anthropologist Fernando Rogado Quintino (1964), each of the Papel lineages identifies with its totem in ceremonies, dances, dresses, masks, et cetera. All the lineage groups respect their totem and do not kill or eat it, and have a funeral for any that are found dead. *Djagra,* the lineage of the kings, has the lynx as their totem. The lynx is the superior animal of the forest. The lynx is capable of killing all the other animals, and all the other animals are afraid of it in the same way as

the Papel fear their king. *Bassutu* are as simple minded as the ant bear, *Bassafinte* are smart like the hare, *Basso* are dedicated to agriculture and fishing and therefore stay in water, as does the frog. *Bajoukumum* are fighters and they attack in the same way as the hyena. *Baíga* are as expeditious and quick as the forest goat, and *Batate* are the skilful extractors of the palm tree, climbing the trees like monkeys.

18. It is however not certain which of the sister's sons inherits from a man before the spirits have sanctioned the choice of an heir after the death of the maternal uncle. See Fortes (1950:271) for approval of an heir among the Ashanti.

19. I am told that blood still appears at ritual places in Quinara when an animal is offered in Biombo.

20. Cissoko (1987) and Moreira (1993) report similar stories about the origin of the Papel.

21. Moreira (1993) refers to Almada, André Alvares (1946 [1594]). "Tratado Breve dos Rios de Guiné," *Edição Nova de Luís Silveira,* Lisboa, p. 46.

22. If Almeida is right, the name Papel (or Pepel) has an African origin and it may be argued that the spelling *Papel* is more in line with the word's origins than *Pepel.* Pronunciation differs as some speakers use more of an [e] sound while others use more of an [a] sound, and still others (maybe most) use a sound typically in-between [e] and [a]. This variation is reflected in contemporary Guinean music. The renowned Papel musician Adriano Atchutchi, the leader of the legendary Orquestra Super Mama Djombo, uses the [a] sound as well as the spelling Papel (see *Homenagem a José Carlos Schwarz,* CD BAL 006/99) while Iva and Ichy (De Netos de N'Gumbé) use Pepel (*Canua ca na n'kadja,* NBV-001, 1998). The fact that the Portuguese word *papel* means paper has possibly contributed to some reluctance to use the spelling *Papel;* nonetheless I have found no evidence that supports the idea that there might be some connection between these two words. I have opted for the spelling *Papel.* At the same time I admit there are no unequivocal arguments for which spelling is more appropriate or correct.

23. Biombo refers here to the kingdom Biombo, not the entire region.

24. The power of the kings varies in both religious and political terms. For instance, there are significant differences in certain ceremonial practices between kingdoms, and caution must be taken not to generalize what is customary in one kingdom to be valid for all of them. See Lourenço-Lindell (2002:59–60) for discussion of the power relations of Papel kings in Bissau.

25. The slave trade, which contributed to interethnic and intraethnic raids, continued even after 1869 when the Portuguese officially abolished slavery (Rodney 1970). In the Cacheu region slave raids are reported to have occurred as late as 1915 (Crowley 1990:132).

26. As Crawly notes (Coelho 1953:40–41 [1669]) when a Papel king died in the early days of the Portuguese presence in Guinea-Bissau certain of his subjects were killed and buried with him (1990:81). When the king Mahana of Bissau died, 104 men, women, and children danced, drank, and sang for a year until they were slain to follow the king to the afterlife. Henrique Pinto Rema (1982) describes how Becompolo Có's funeral in 1696 was characterized by confusion because of his conversion to Catholicism; thus only nine girls and nine boys were buried with him.

27. See dos Santos (1971).

28. In the national census of 1950, 0.3 percent of the black population had the status of "civilized" (Lopes 1987).

29. See Carney (1988:60).

30. For instance, in 1945 the colonial administration commanded the population in Biombo to reclaim one thousand hectares of rice fields, but these were all abandoned several years later due to poor maintenance (Ribeiro 1987).

31. The cultivation of food crops was devastated during the war for independence. In 1953, the total area under cultivation was 480,000 hectares but only 250,000 hectares in 1974 (IRDC 1987). Rice production fell by 68 percent during the same period.

32. See Aguilar (1998), Aguilar and Stenman (1993, 1994), Aguilar and Zejan (1992), and Lourenço-Lindell (1993, 2002:68–91, 111–13).

33. In 1985 one U.S. dollar was approximately 120–40 pesos. At that time the monthly salary of a public health servant was about 3,000–5,000 pesos and the price of one sack of rice (50 kg) 900 pesos. In January 1992, the official exchange rate was 5,120 pesos *per* dollar and two years later, in 1994, it was 11,800 pesos *per* dollar (Aguilar and Stenman 1994:13). In 1994 a nurse could buy about a half sack of rice with the monthly salary.

34. See Rudebeck (1997).

35. See http://wwww.reliefweb.int/w/Rwb.nsf/ByCountry/0005B5E199FC1A7 AC12566B7006B5762?OpenDocument&StartKey=Guinea-Bissau&ExpandView (accessed February 4, 2004).

36. For a person living in Quinhamel, and in Guinea-Bissau, it is crucial to speak Kriol. Thus, I preferred to learn better Kriol than to split my energy between Kriol and Papel. In addition, I found no teaching material in Papel; the only printed matter I got were booklets from the Protestant mission, which according to my assistant were full of errors. Of course I learned some words and concepts in Papel, but I do not speak Papel.

37. See Pink (1998).

38. The Catholic mission hospital in Quinhamel has played a key role in health care delivery in Biombo for decades with its current share of about one quarter of all services directed at children and mothers in the region. Its services are also attractive for many who live in the capital Bissau. In 1997, for example, the hospital attended to more than 13,000 children and administered almost 6,000 vaccine doses to children less than five years of age. Prenatal clinics were attended by 1,475 pregnant women who came on average four to five times during their pregnancy, and 542 of them were assisted during delivery in the hospital. The hospital offers a popular ambulance service at a modest cost, reserved for seriously ill children and women in labor. The hospital is well known for its cleanliness, and its premises are well maintained.

39. The idea that it is not worthwhile to save the life of a destitute child because survival would only prolong its suffering never crossed my mind. The pediatrician Maurice King argues, "reduced childhood mortality must no longer be promoted as a necessary and sufficient condition for reduced fertility" (1990:666). Instead, family planning programs must be promoted, and in ecologically unsustainable

communities "such desustaining measures as oral rehydration should not be introduced on a public health scale, since they increase the man-years of human misery,
ultimately from starvation" (666). A number of female anthropologists express
similar views. Barbara Miller (1987:106) expresses her concern about the quality of
lives saved through public health intervention. The anthropologist Claire Monod
Cassidy (1987), influenced by evolutionary and ecologically informed approaches,
criticizes a project in India that succeeded "at getting mothers to feed more and better food to unwanted children, who therefore often survived." She asks about these
girls: "Have they been saved any suffering?" (312). Scheper-Hughes is "troubled by
an analysis based on a free market model of population demography predicated on
the assumption that childhood mortality is a bio-ecological mechanism for en-
hancing group survival through 'pruning'" (1987b:22), and she argues "there are
also moral limits to radical non-intervention as well" (22). Scheper-Hughes (1992)
asks, however, whether it is better to be rescued from one illness only "to be killed
later of another more prolonged and painful one?" She emphasizes that these unlucky, saved children "have no say. They cannot protest the international child survival programs and campaigns that can cruelly (although unintentionally) prolong
their suffering and death" (285 –86).

    40. An ethnographer's family situation surely matters for access to a community
(Cassell 1987, Flinn, Marshall, and Armstrong 1998). See also Gottlieb, Graham, and
Gottlieb-Graham (1998) for discussion of how the presence of the ethnographer's
son contributed to new insights about respect for children. Considering the main
theme of my research it was inevitably favorable for me to be a married woman and
breastfeeding at my arrival in Biombo. However, a researcher's common life experiences with the study group are not a requisite for effective communication.

    41. In comparison to other ethnic groups in Guinea-Bissau, literature on the
Papel is lacking, both by colonial and postcolonial anthropologists. Some have suggested that the academic qualifications and political motives of the colonial authors
explain their reluctance to study the Papel, but others also suggest that the Papel
may have intentionally distorted their portrayal of their lives (Cissoko 1987). The
unwillingness of postcolonial anthropologists to study Papel life has been explained by their geographical closeness to the capital Bissau, and thus they have
been assumed not to be exotic enough (Moreira 1993).

    42. See Gunnlaugsson (1997b). Cholera is a new disease in Guinea-Bissau, and
none in my family was vaccinated against the disease until autumn 1997; actually,
protection through vaccination is short lived. The transmission of cholera is in theory simple: the contagion enters the body through the mouth with food and water.
Thus my family and I were observant of what we ate and drank and practiced good
hygiene. Malaria was always a greater threat to my family despite rigorously applied
prophylaxis. My first-born son and I became seriously ill with malaria, and other
family members had symptoms of malaria but their contraction of the disease was
never confirmed by laboratory tests.

    43. In the 1980s many development aid organizations established "gender offi-
cers" to improve gender equality.

    44. Reflexivity in anthropological texts has become a convention as a response to
a postmodern call for a more experimental reflexive ethnographic writing (Clifford

and Marcus 1986, Marcus and Fisher 1986). The pitfalls and promises of postmodernist thinking are summarized in Mascia-Lees, Sharpe, and Cohen (1989). In this book I have taken a position described by Charlotte Aull Davies (1999). Davies emphasizes that "critical reflexivity is not an end in itself—research is not about the ethnographer; rather it is a means—in fact the only means—of coming to know, however imperfectly, other aspects of social reality" (213).

1. Marriage Relations

1. See Leacock (1981), Sacks (1979), and Sanday (1981) for arguments against the universal subordination of women.

2. The recent interest in kinship has emerged within studies concerned with the new reproductive technologies, gay and lesbian studies, and within studies on genetic research and the social construction of science in Western societies (Carsten 2000a, Finkler 2000, Franklin 1997, Franklin and McKinnon 2001, Stone 1997, Weston 1991).

3. Interestingly, Sarah Franklin (1997) notes that the European history of genealogy is more complex and varied than the critiques of kinship theory have suggested. She emphasizes the "'genealogical grid' that is argued to have been such a stable and rigid 'scale' for measuring other cultures' definitions of kinship can be argued itself to be destabilized and denaturalized by new technology" (1997:8). While recognizing the ethnocentric roots of kinship theory, Franklin finds it "an essential tool" to understand the anxiety in Euro-American societies about scientists 'playing God' with 'the facts of life'" (Franklin 1997:8). See also Finkler (2000: 14–43).

4. In contrast, Stone argues, "male/female difference in reproduction is universal (however varied the cultural construction of this difference might be) and that on the basis of this 'fact' we can begin to make meaningful cross-cultural comparison" (1997:4).

5. For discussion of the origin and use of the term *structural violence* see Maas Weight (1999).

6. Farmer (1996) identifies gender, ethnicity, and socioeconomic status as the most important factors that put individuals or groups of people at increased risk for experiencing extreme suffering, although wealth and power have at times protected individual women, gays, and ethnic minorities.

7. Connell proposes a practice-based theory for analysis of gender relations. What is needed, he maintains, is "a form of social theory that gives some grip on the interweaving of personal life and social structure without collapsing towards voluntarism and pluralism on one side, or categoricalism and biological determinism on the other" (1987:61). Connell points out that earlier studies on women's subordination have already identified two important structures for the relationship between men and women. The first has to do with division of labor and the second with power. Connell suggests an additional structure, for example, "the structure of cathexis," to understand the ways people create emotional links between each other (96–97). See also Thurén (1993, 1996).

8. The cashew tree produces fruits with each one attached to a cashew nut. The juice from the fruit is fermented to make an alcoholic drink, the highly valued cashew wine.

9. Joop de Jong (1987), a Dutch psychiatrist who worked in Guinea-Bissau for many years, maintains that failure to *torna boka* is one of the most important reasons behind anguish and anxieties among the Guineans.

10. In Kriol, nouns are not inflected according to number (Scantamburlo 1981). One uses a modifier like "many" *(manga di)* before a noun to indicate plurality. Hence the plural of *fidju* (son, child) is *manga di fidju*. When using Kriol words in my English text, however, the plural is indicated by context.

11. See Peek (1991a).

12. Each of the Papel kings has the mightiest *balobeiru* of his lineage serve as the main adviser and leader in community ceremonies.

13. The kapok tree is often central for ritual practice in West Africa (see Gottlieb [1992]).

14. The Papel say they got *kansaré* from the Manjaco, who taught them how to use it. See Carvalho (1998:260–63) and Crowley (1990:390–95, 602–17) for more details about *kansaré*, which has its origins in a revivalist movement following a retaliatory attack by the Portuguese against the Manjaco in 1897 (Crowley 1990:138–40). See Callewaert (2000) for an analysis of Kiyang-yang, a revivalist movement of the Balanta in Guinea-Bissau that started in 1986.

15. There are many *iran* living in the forest, fresh water, or the sea. Most are invisible but others are concealed, for example, in a serpent *(kobra)* or a python ("blind spirit" or *iran seku*), which are both attributed with strong supernatural powers. According to Crowley (1990:335), usually the python is believed to want human flesh for its services.

16. See Einarsdóttir, Passa, and Gunnlaugsson (2001) for a description of Papel women's religious role in fighting cholera in Biombo.

17. According Susan Starr Sered, women's religions, defined in terms of female domination of leadership and membership and awareness that it is a women's religion, is centralized around the issue of responsibility for the health and well-being of children. Sered argues that "women's religions teach that individuals have a great deal of control over their own and their children's destinies . . . they provide many different rituals designed to ensure children's well-being" (1994:83). Vibeke Christie (1997) argues that the Bijagós women in Guinea-Bissau have their strong position because of their religious knowledge about and control over death and destructive forces.

18. António Carreira (1962) maintains that a bride price is given, but usually of reduced worth, or only of symbolic value, for example, some domestic animal, cloth, or alcoholic drink and food eaten together without any large ceremony. According to Mário Cissoko (1987:29), a normal bride price requires the husband to bring with him the following items at the day of marriage: one goat, ten liters of distilled alcohol *(kana)* for the father-in-law, five liters of red wine for the mother-in-law, ten liters red of wine for the bride and her friends, six *bocado* (unit of measurement) of flour, one *pano* (length of cloth) for the wife to wear the first days she has sexual relations with her husband, two *pano* of everyday cloth in different colors,

one packet of needles and thread, one bottle of brandy, fifty to one hundred loaves of bread, 20,000 pesos for the mother-in-law, 30,000 pesos for the father-in-law, one cow (at the moment of marriage, but sometimes later), and wine and food for celebration for two days for his peers.

19. Physical disability may be compensated for through education and access to a white-collar job. People sometimes emphasize the importance for physically disabled boys to go to school and thereby secure survival.

20. In December 1995 I identified only three girls who attended school in their village, which has 694 inhabitants. Three girls (thirteen to fifteen years old) attended school compared with thirty-nine boys or young men. Eleven of the males who attended school were older than twenty (ranging eight to twenty-five years old). One man in the village had attended school for seven years while all the other villagers had spent less time in school. The school, situated in a nearby village five kilometers away, taught grades 1–4.

21. See Smith (2001) for discussion of romantic love and marriage arrangements in West Africa.

22. All women have a cord around their waist from infancy, which is said to make their bottom more beautiful.

23. In collaboration with male elders, each king organizes initiation ceremonies for males in the kingdom every four to twenty years. A ceremony for boys or men is performed before and after circumcision. Before the first ceremony, authorized men take the boys to the circumcision hut in the forest where they stay for at least one month after the circumcision to learn about the traditions of the Papel from the elders. Men and women participate in the ceremonies, but only circumcised men are involved in the act of circumcision and allowed to enter the circumcision hut. In the past men were not allowed to marry without circumcision, but this tradition is not always respected today.

24. The Papel use the Kriol word *mandjuandade* to refer to age groups of men and women of more or less the same age. According to Carreira (1962:665) the word *mandjuandade* is likely to be of Manjaco origin and it signifies "of the same age," or "belonging to the same generation." People belong to their group all their lives and thus do not pass from one age group to the next. These age groups are important during certain ceremonies such as funerals and at weddings.

25. See Breger and Hill (1998).

26. Levirate, which means that upon the death of a man his widow must marry one of his brothers, is commonly practiced in Africa (see Luke [2002] and Potash [1986]). Susan Reynolds Whyte (1997:89) describes how Nyole widows in Uganda often declined to be inherited, as widowhood was one of the few opportunities women had for an independent life. See also Fortes (1950:271). According to E. E. Evans-Pritchard, Nuer widows often lived together with Dinka men who had decided to reside in Nuerland, and "even if the children she may bear him do not count as his descendants he can gain their affection" (1969:224).

27. Papel women do not plant rice. A story tells how once upon a time the women lost their genitals when they were planting rice. Thereafter, men forbade women to plant any more. When men walk around in the rice fields with their hand in the water they are said to be looking for the private parts of their wives.

28. See Blazejewicz et al. (1981) for details of house construction in Guinea-Bissau.

29. See Bull (1994).

30. *Kana* is a term used for distilled alcohol from sugar cane, cashew wine, or in rare cases from palm wine. *Kana* is indispensable for offerings and all major ceremonies and parties.

31. Polygyny is prevalent among the Papel. In the region of Biombo 29 percent of the chiefs have four or more wives compared to less than 7 percent for all the other regions (Ministry for Rural Development and Agriculture 1990). In my village census about one fourth of all married men have more than one wife they have married themselves, and most of them also have inherited wives.

32. For a description of how polygyny economically favors women in fishing villages in Sierra Leone see Steady (1987). See also Shaw (2002:160–61) for descriptions of the advantages and disadvantages of polygyny for women in Sierra Leone.

33. According to Lifton (1991) the senior wife has the authority to interfere in the economic and practical matters of her co-wives; she also has the right to order them to sleep with the husband. In my view the authority of the senior wife is declining, partly because of an increased tendency for co-wives not to share a stove.

34. See Parkin and Nyamwaya (1987:12) for discussion of serial monogamy or having one wife and one or more mistresses as "modern manifestations of polygyny." John C. Caldwell, Pat Caldwell, and Pat Quiggin (1989) introduce the concept "African sexuality" with reference to free female sexuality as an explanation for the devastating AIDS epidemic in the region. While Caldwell, Caldwell, and Quiggin argue for "a distinct and internally coherent African system embracing sexuality, marriage, and much more" (1989:187), others have rejected that position (Ahlbeth 1994, Dover 2001:13, Einarsdóttir 2001, Heald 1995, Setel 1999:14 –18). Still, Caldwell (2000) argues that governments and foreign agencies "misinterpret the failure of the educational effort to curb the epidemic as a sign that the effort was not good enough or was not understood, rather than that it met with deliberate resistance from people satisfied with their sexual system and unprepared to change" (2000:130).

35. Papel women may also emphasize their repeated pregnancies and births as a cause of aging more quickly than their male age mates. See Bledsoe (2002:230–34, 351–53) and Levin (2001:161–62) for discussions of depletion related to reproduction and loss of family members among Mandinga women in Guinea and Muslim women in the Gambia.

36. See Mølsted (1995:23).

37. I have never spontaneously heard about homosexual relations during my fieldwork in Biombo. When I ask a middle-aged woman about such relationships she answers she does not know what young men do when they have fun together. Two women tell me that there is a young man in the village who is "used by other men like a woman." They say that the young man is indeed very much like a woman; they laugh and imitate his feminine movements and voice. When I ask about such relations between women the idea seems unthinkable to them; they say they do not understand my question.

38. An elderly man in Biombo, whose mother was Balanta and father Papel, told me that the Papel sometimes adopt the age group system of the Balanta, and all the

age group names given by Carreira (1962:666) as Papel age groups, correspond to those he named as Balanta age groups.

39. See Vaz (1987) for discussion of age groups for mobilization of work.

40. See Rodney (1970:177–81) on the influence of imported alcohol during colonial time. While fermented beverages of low alcoholic content were widely consumed in the area before Europeans arrived, strong alcoholic beverages were not.

41. One must remember that the son only comes to stay in the compound of his mother's brother after his death. Among matrilineal groups in Africa fathers have varied authority over their children, and children's residence in case of divorce also varies (Fortes 1950, Richards 1950:217). According to Bronislaw Malinowski, among the matrilineal, patrilocal Trobriands "it goes without saying that the children, in case of divorce, always follow their mother" (1929:147).

42. The king has the right to confiscate some of the animals offered as well as funeral shrouds brought by family members of the deceased and neighbors. These shrouds are wrapped around the body of the deceased, who takes them to family members in the other world.

43. See Christie (1997:106–8) for discussion of how *djongagu* may be interpreted as a rite of passage among the Bijagós in Guinea-Bissau.

44. This ceremony is performed for all adults and children in case of subsequent deaths within the family.

45. Ilda Lourenço-Lindell (2002) emphasizes the varied degree of success among women traders in Bissau. According to her, "the majority of them continue to operate at survival levels or have seen their conditions deteriorate" (158). See also Achinger (1990) and Havik (1995).

46. See Silberschmidt (1999) for an examination of conflicting relations between women and men facing changed roles, values, and norms in Kenya.

47. Wendy James finds "the notion of 'domination' far too crude to enable us to understand the relative authority of the sexes in any society" (1993:131). She argues that the position of women is not only a matter of status, wealth, and rights; it is also a moral question. James notes that in African matrilineal societies, but also in some of the patrilineal societies, the respect and honor attributed to motherhood is characteristic and "we can discern a common cluster of ideas about the wider importance of women's child-bearing capacity, their creative role in bringing up a new generation, and even a recurring notion about the natural line of birth being handed on through women" (139).

48. See Harkness and Super (2002) for discussion on the importance of non-kin relationships in Kenya. There is a general agreement that anthropologists have ignored or undervalued friendship in societies where kinship has been assumed to structure social relationships (Bell and Coleman 1999b). The concept of relatedness, as proposed by Carsten (2000b), may contribute to greater attention being paid to non-kin social relationships such as friendship. Holy (1996:168) and Stone (2001:690–92) find it problematic, however, that it is unclear what constitutes relatedness. To define friendship appears to be no easier (Bell and Coleman 1999a).

49. Cissoko (1987) maintains that the Papel are increasingly abandoning matrilineal inheritance, in particular in Bissau. Mary Douglas (1969) pays attention to scholars' generally pessimistic prospects for survival of matrilineal societies in a

modern world. She comes to the conclusion that a high demand for labor in a market economy is favorable to matriliny. Holy (1996:102–15) notes that the commonly observed breakdown of matrilineal inheritance is likely to depend on whether or not fathers and sons have cooperated to produce the wealth transmitted. Holy maintains, on the other hand, that there is "no logical reason to assume that a change in the system of inheritance has invariably to be accompanied by a change in conceptualization of descent" (109).

2. Burdens of Birth

1. See Freedman and Ferguson (1950) and Melzack (1984) for a critique of the idea of natural birth as painless.

2. Roger Jeffery and Patricia M. Jeffery (1993), who discuss the high maternal mortality in many low-income countries due to inadequate obstetric assistance, warn against a romanticization of "natural" childbirth and the assumption that midwifery is always respectable work, characterized by sisterhood and emotional support. They argue that in the Bijnor District in the state of Uttar Pradesh in north India, views on childbirth and pregnancy are shaped by concerns about "shame, pollution, and issues of vulnerability and danger" (12). See also Allen (2002). Robbie Davis-Floyd (2000) argues that inadequate birth assistance given by community midwives is most likely to be found in countries such as India and Bangladesh where women's status is low; where women's status is higher, the local midwives often develop lasting systems of knowledge about giving birth.

3. See Klaus et al. (1972) and Klaus and Kennel (1976).

4. The psychologist Diane E. Eyer (1992) critically traces the history of maternal bonding theory, which is still a widely accepted and influential doctrine, despite lack of valid evidence. See Riesman (1992) for a critique of the common notion within Freudian psychoanalytic theory that childcare practices determine the formation of adult personality.

5. I was myself brought up on a sheep farm in Iceland, and during my childhood I was often involved in taking care of the ewes during the lambing season. In order for a ewe to accept a lamb the most important behavior was for her to lick the lamb—her own or another's—immediately after birth. A few ewes would even eat the afterbirth.

6. See Crouch and Manderson (1995) for the enormous influence of the bonding theory both in popular and scientific literature and the changes it brought to maternity ward routines. The Baby Friendly Hospital Initiative identifies "ten steps to successful breastfeeding" (Murray 1994, WHO 1998). Two of the steps are influenced by the bonding theory, that is to assist mothers initiate breastfeeding within a half-hour of birth and rooming-in, which allows mothers and infants to remain together twenty-four hours a day.

7. Hrdy (1999:115–16) maintains that, in contrast to many other animals, primates find all babies lovely; consequently primates easily adopt and rear unrelated offspring. In addition, the social organization of primates lowers the risk of mixing up babies; thus instinctual bonding did not evolve among humans.

8. Hrdy (1999) suggests that infants with a particular appearance such as a fat body, big head, and rounded eyes are likely to gain their mother's affection. She proposes that there are "thresholds" for these maternal responses that "would be endocrinologically and neurologically set, possibly during pregnancy and prior to birth, rendering a mother more or less likely to become engaged in infantile cues as she makes decisions about how much of herself to invest in her infant" (1999:316).

9. For instance, Paulo, whose wife gave birth to their sixth child several years ago, still owes his father-in-law a cow. His father-in-law warns Paulo that if he does not pay that cow soon, he will be taken to court.

10. My own situation was repeatedly lamented. For a white woman to have three children is not too bad, but the fact that all three are boys is a problem. Is my youngest son *kodé* (the last born) or not? When I insist he is *kodé* my female friends emphasize I should not give up so easily as I am still young enough to have more children. They consider it essential to have at least one daughter to wash my body after my death.

11. Many Western feminists have rejected biological 'facts' of procreation as the cause for women's universal subordination (see for instance Chadorow [1974], Ortner [1974] and Rosaldo [1974]). Instead, they identified the social construction of the very same 'facts' as the culprit. According to Yanagisako and Collier, this contributed to the commonly held conclusion that "biological motherhood 'explains' the universal devaluation of women" (1987:19). Gwendolyn Mikell maintains that African feminism is primarily heterosexual and she argues, "Western feminists have been troubled that African women take their reproductive tasks seriously, celebrate their ability to give birth, and refuse to subordinate their biological roles to other roles within society" (1997:8).

12. The idea that sexual relations can corrupt breast milk and cause harm for the breastfeeding child is found in many cultures, present and past (Einarsdóttir 1988, Gunnlaugsson and Einarsdóttir 1993, Morse, Jehle and Gamble 1990). See also Adeokun (1983) and Caldwell, Orubuloye and Caldwell (1992:217–18) for discussion on postpartum sexual abstinence in sub-Saharan Africa.

13. See Levin (2001:163) and Madhavan and Diarra (2001:175–76) for similar expressions among Mandinga women in Guinea and Bamana women in Mali.

14. See Knight (1991) for discussion on menstrual synchrony.

15. Earlier anthropological studies of menstruation tended to be concerned with symbolic views on eventual powers, pollution, and taboos related to menstrual blood and menstruating women. Lately scholars have focused on positive aspects attributed to menstruation, women's experiences and interpretations of menstruation, as well as practices in managing menstruation (See Buckley and Gottlieb [1988], Choi [1995], Gottlieb [1995], Richardson [1995] and van de Walle and Renne [2001]).

16. Once, to my surprise I meet a woman who tells me that she has never experienced menstruation. She is about forty-years old, a mother of five living children and an additional four children had died. She tells me that she had never menstruated in her entire life. "Before I was married I never menstruated, nor between pregnancies. I have never understood what women mean when they say they have moon. When I give birth I bleed a lot, but I am not sure if that is what is called to have moon," she wonders.

17. Dettwyler discusses how village women in Mali see night blindness as a normal part of pregnancy but they also have problems with morning sickness (1994: 148).

18. See Caplan (1995) and Peacock (1991) for discussion of how childbearing affects women's productive work.

19. See Høj (2002) for a discussion on maternal mortality in Guinea-Bissau and the contributing factors. See also Obermeyer (2002) for a discussion on how the concept of risk related to childbirth in Morocco reflects women's real alternatives for controlling these risks.

20. See Leonard (2002).

21. This idea is documented among other peoples in West Africa (Fortes 1987: 228). Also, in China, after becoming a grandmother it is considered shameful for a woman to have more children (Baker 1979:5).

22. This is similar to ideas in Vanatinai, a small island southeast of New Guinea where intercourse with many men is considered to have a contraceptive effect, while conception is thought to occur only through repeated sexual relations with the same man (Lepowsky 1993:85).

23. See DeLoache and Gottlieb (2000).

24. See Gunnlaugsson (1997a) for regional statistics on prenatal consultations.

25. Routinely, women who attended prenatal consultation received chloroquine for malaria prophylaxis and iron tablets for anemia.

26. Among the Beng in Ivory Coast, pregnant women dance naked at the funeral of a woman who has died in childbirth, although they are not supposed to show their breasts for fear that another jealous woman might bewitch them and spoil their milk, thus causing the death of the newborn (Gottlieb and Graham 1993:151).

27. In a village situated ten kilometers from the mission hospital, about 30 of the 120 children under five years of age, born of 87 mothers, were born in the hospital or at the health center; of those, approximately 90 percent were born at the mission hospital. Two mothers were transferred to the National Hospital in Bissau because of complications. Most births (72 percent) occurred at the husband's home with an elderly woman in the compound, or alone. At the health centers, the nurses, most often males, assist mothers. The health center in the region with the highest number of assisted births is in Dorse where the head male nurse, a Mandinga and Muslim, assists all births. Female midwives work at three health centers in the region but all these have considerably fewer deliveries than the one in Dorse.

28. I have not attended a birth in Biombo. My presentation on birth is based on discussions with numerous women.

29. Some women in Guinea-Bissau, in particular Balanta, say they give birth alone to be able to cry out and whine without disturbing other people (Oosterbaan and da Costa 1990).

30. In a few cultures women give birth alone; it is interpreted as women's opportunity to demonstrate their courage and spirituality (Biesele 1997), or as an opportunity for mothers to commit infanticide in case of an unwanted pregnancy or deformity of the newborn (Howell 1979, Sargent 1982:89–93, Sargent 1988).

31. See Merrett-Balkos (1998) for an account of Anganen women in Papua New Guinea who demanded that the Catholic nuns return their placenta, or at least the umbilical cord, after birth. Prior to the establishment of a local aid post by the

Catholic mission Anganen women gave birth alone. See Davis-Floyd and Sargent (1997a) and Ram and Jolly (1998) for discussion about influences of Western bio-medicine on birth practices worldwide.

32. This new routine is in line with WHO's Baby Friendly Hospital Initiative (see WHO 1998b).

33. According to Anderson Mencagli (1992) *sapaté* leaves are used for the same purpose among other ethnic groups in Guinea-Bissau as well. See also Scarpa (1959).

34. I have only once during nearly eight years in Guinea-Bissau met a woman who did not have any milk at all. It was in 1984 when I was participating in a vacci-nation campaign in the eastern part of the country with my husband. We were introduced to a middle-aged woman who told us she never got milk in her breasts after delivery. This woman, who was one of the wives of the village chief and showed no sign of disease or undernourishment, did not give any explanation for this, but told us that her children had survived thanks to other women who breast-fed them.

35. It is possible that these mothers assume my question might be tied to re-wards, and expect an offer of a bottle and powdered milk. Mothers are aware that the nuns until recently offered bottles to mothers of twins.

36. Mariama's emphasis on mothers possessing a certain degree of intelligence as necessary for treating their breastfeeding problems is in contrast to the view pre-sented in an article published in 1958. The author's derogatory argument is that "so-phistication and ability to breastfeed are apparently becoming incompatible. In all the African mothers seen during the work that has been described . . . [e]ven partial failures were rare, and mostly occurred amongst the most wealthy and more intelli-gent" (Geber 1958:195).

37. See Gunnlaugsson and Einarsdóttir (1993).

38. A range of 5–15 percent of mothers said they had bad milk in the two sur-veys I carried out. Women in more rural villages are clearly less likely than urban women to say that they have bad milk. Urban women are also more likely to test their milk.

39. According to my informants in Biombo, a woman who has never given birth or a male will never produce milk. Relactation and induced lactation, that is, when women who have never given birth produce milk, is well documented (Einarsdóttir 1988, Helsing and King 1982:103–11, WHO 1998a). António Scarpa (1959), professor of ethnomedicine at the University of Milan, describes relactation in Guinea-Bissau, which at that time was considered by Western scientists only to be possible among primitive and uneducated races. Scarpa explains the capacity of Guinean women to relactate as a part of their genetic inheritance. See Hausman (2003:123–50) for description of how breastfeeding is advocated in the United States through use of evolutionary theory, and contemporary foraging peoples in Africa represent those who practice the "natural feeding." Male lactation is documented in some cultures, past and present (Einarsdóttir 1988). The Icelandic *Flóamanna Saga,* writ-ten about 1300, tells about a man of high standing in Iceland who breastfed his child for one year because the mother died (Flóamanna Saga 1947:42). See also http://www.unassistedchildbirth.com/milkmen.htm (accessed February 2, 2004).

40. About one-quarter of seventy-seven children in a more urbanized village had tried a bottle at least once, but no child was exclusively bottle-fed.

41. An account of Elina's story is also given in chapters 3 and 4.

42. See Armstrong (1991) and Labbok and Krasovec (1990) for breastfeeding definitions.

43. In the village survey I did in 1995–96, only 5 children of 120 were breastfed for a period shorter than eighteen months. Two of these children are siblings and their mother does not want to give any explanation for why she stopped breastfeeding them at seventeen months. One mother says she wants to stop breastfeeding at thirteen months, as she wants more children. She has given birth to three children but the first died directly after birth. Two mothers say they were forced by their husbands to stop breastfeeding, but they are not the fathers of the respective children. One is a young widow with three children who was obliged to stop breastfeeding the seventeen-month-old child of her dead husband by her new husband, who is more than thirty years older than she and has inherited her. The other mother is a forty-year-old woman who left her husband for several years for a lover in Bissau. She returned to her husband with a child of her lover, which she breastfed for fifteen months or until her husband demanded that she terminate breastfeeding.

44. See Høgsborg and Aaby (1990) for discussion about Bissau women's thoughts about sexual abstinence during the breastfeeding period. Some women said they were content not to have sexual relations with their husband during the breastfeeding period while others were afraid that their husbands would seek other women.

45. A study on the initiation of breastfeeding in suburban Bissau found that approximately 75 percent of Papel mothers did not put the newborn to breast within twelve hours after birth, and still 50 percent had not initiated breastfeeding twenty-four hours after birth (Gunnlaugsson, Silva, and Smedman 1992). Mothers who gave birth late in the afternoon or in the evening tended to wait until next morning for the first feeding, while mothers who gave birth in the morning tended to initiate breastfeeding before they went to sleep in the evening. See also Morse, Jehle, and Gamble (1990).

46. According to Scheper-Hughes, breastfeeding is an ambivalent issue and has almost disappeared in the Alto. Colostrum is rejected as a "dirty" substance; most mothers offer the breast to their newborn by the third or fourth day postpartum and always with gruel. In case of early infant death, mothers may take comfort that a baby not yet baptized and never breastfed could go to heaven free of the original sin passed into the infant through breast milk. After a week or two from birth breastfeeding is stopped, mothers say, because they lack milk. In addition, many mothers maintain they have "bad" milk, or that the child refused to take the breast. According to Scheper-Hughes, because of Alto mothers' harsh working conditions "bottle-feeding is really the only possible 'choice'" (1992:323).

47. Reasons given for or against breastfeeding a child vary over time and between cultures. The doctrine of Western medicine since the early 1970s is that "breast is best" (Hanson et al. 2002, Kramer and Kakuma 2002). However, Western mothers are documented as refraining from breastfeeding since they wish not to lose their maidenly shape; perceive breastfeeding as unhygienic, beastly, or sexual; want to share the care of the infant with the father; or want to enhance their individuality

(Earle 2002, Helsing and King 1982, Jelliffe and Jelliffe 1978, Oakley 1979). According to the Koran breastfeeding a child for two years is considered ideal, thus Muslim populations often consider it a religious obligation for mothers to breastfeed (Creyghton 1992, Delaney 2000:133, 136, Johnson 2001:68–72, Khatib-Chahidi 1992: 109, Simpson 1985:113). In addition, Islamic law recognizes milk kinship, which implies that persons who have suckled from the same woman are prohibited to marry. Vanessa Maher (1992:23–25) suggests that breastfeeding is sometimes prohibited by fathers in highly stratified societies to prevent the alignment of the child's loyalties with the mother and her relatives. Rural mothers in Mexico and Thailand argue that breastfeeding creates reciprocal relations and thus makes children indebted to take care of their mothers in old age (Millard and Graham 1985:58–59, van Esterik 1985:157).

48. See Klaus, Kennell, and Klaus (1995:86).

49. In *Death without Weeping* the issue of menstruation is not treated, and the only mother who clearly expresses her individual experience of pregnancy appreciates being pregnant (Scheper-Hughes 1992:467). We learn that in the last few years Alto women have increasingly begun to give birth in hospitals, but birth in general, is described as "hardly a time for rejoicing" (359).

50. Scheper-Hughes presents child neglect in this context in terms of "defiance" in response to coerced pregnancy (1992:428). She suggests that mothers' lack of control over reproduction may be an explanation for fatal maternal neglect: "Given the often 'coerced' nature of pregnancy on the Alto do Cruzeiro . . . it is also possible that refusal to grieve for the death of their infants is at times a gesture of defiance. It could be a way of saying, 'you can make me pregnant, but you cannot make me love all of them . . . or keep all of them either'" (428). Recall in chapter 1, the story of a young woman who committed suicide because she could not live with her forced marriage. I interpret her action as desperate, not as a heroic revolt or a brave challenge. To do that would simply to romanticize her suffering.

3. Conceptualization of Children

1. See Allotey and Reidpath (2001) and Leis (1982) for a description on reincarnated infants in the Kassena-Nankana district in Ghana and among the Ijaw in Nigeria. See also http://childpastlives.org/stevenson.htm, accessed February 2, 2004.

2. Interestingly, Gottlieb (2000b) has been able to identify only two full-length ethnographies on infants in a particular society, one of which focuses on paternal infant care (see Hewlett [1991]). Gottlieb (2000b) suggests that the observed disinterest in studying infants may be related to the ethnographers' own memories and parental status, the assumed lack of agency attributed to infants in the Western world, infants' dependency on others, particularly women, infants' inability to communicate verbally, infants' engagement in bodily processes, as well as ethnographers' Western understanding of rationality.

3. Don Kulick (1992) argues that Gapun conceptions of children were an important factor contributing to a rapid shift in language use from Taiap to Tok Pisin.

4. Scheper-Hughes stresses here the importance of social relationships in a society where such relationships appear to be weak and fragmented and where, for instance, spouses do not always even remember "the full family names of their spouses" (1992:414).

5. Scheper-Hughes emphasizes that she is dealing with maternal indifference toward infants but not abuse. Malignant child abuse and physical punishment are extremely rare in the Alto; infants and young children are seen as "innocent and irrational little creatures" and should not be physically disciplined (1992:357).

6. See Goody (1977) for a cross-cultural perspective of adoption and foster care. Some scholars have treated fosterage as identical to infanticide (Badinter 1980, de Mause 1974b, Hunt 1972, Piers 1978, Shorter 1975, Stone 1977). Anthropologists who have studied fosterage, for instance, in West Africa, have given a less condemnatory and more balanced picture of the custom (Bledsoe 1993, 1995; Bledsoe, Ewbank, and Isiugo-Abanihe 1988; Bledsoe and Isiugo-Abanihe 1989; Goody 1984).

7. Scheper-Hughes (1992) does not emphasize the influence of maternal indifference on naming practices as she does in earlier publications (Scheper-Hughes 1984, 1985). She contrasts the Alto name-giving practices with the present individualized American way of naming infants, stating that "certainly few of us would tolerate having been given the same name as a sibling (dead or alive), which would be viewed as an assault on the unalienable right to an individualized 'self'" (1992:415). However, Scheper-Hughes maintains that this individualized naming "has a recent social history that corresponds to the decline in family firms, especially the family farm" (415). Before that, Scheper-Hughes says, customs in the United States and Western Europe were similar to those observed in the Alto. According to Alford the first name of an American tends to "symbolize personal identity" and "express an individual's separateness and individuality" (1988:141). Nonetheless, Alford maintains, Americans prefer to use common, conventional names, particularly for boys.

8. The notion that an infant had to learn to see, hear, memorize, and categorize was common in earlier Western thought (see Mehler and Emmanuel [1994:4]).

9 Among the Beng, who believe in reincarnation, a name given to an infant may accidentally indicate who the reincarnated person is, or the infant may through persistent crying express discontent with a wrong name (Gottlieb 1998). Infants born after two sibling deaths have special names but they are seen as a reincarnation of one of the dead siblings. According to Gottlieb, the personalities of these infants is marked by their former experiences; they tend to be depressed and are able to predict deaths. The Bemba in Central Africa also use the infant's cry as an indication of an appropriate name; a shaman will repeat some ancestors' names until the infant stops crying as an acceptance of that name (Alford 1988).

10. My informants do not know how to explain the logic of this custom. A Balanta woman tells me that when a tooth comes out in the upper jaw the Balanta used to pull it out. She does not know why, but says that today people are more intelligent than in the old days and thus this is not done any more. A Papel woman has told me how the child of a Papel family she knew got the first teeth wrong and they followed with the Balanta tradition. Thus, the baby tooth was pulled out, but after ten years the child still had not gotten adult teeth. *Dinti di riba* is a Kriol saying

that refers to a person who carries bad omens. Carreira (1971) explains how the Mandinga, another ethnic group in Guinea-Bissau, believe persons with *dinti di riba* have difficulty in marrying (1971:193). Their solution is to marry each other, as the combination of two bad things neutralizes the problem. Another alternative is to marry someone of another ethnic group and thus be immune to the dangers following such persons. In particular, girls who cut their first teeth in the upper jaw live unmarried and without children, as it is assumed they and their child would die in childbirth. According to Johnson (2001:112), it is considered a misfortune if a Mandinga infant gets a top tooth before a bottom tooth. For prevention, the infant must wear an amulet with tiny seeds that sprout in sand that has settled on the leaves at the very top of trees during the Harmattan. This amulet must be carried for the child's whole life.

11. The ability of my sons to speak proper Kriol was often explained as a result of their youth in comparison to their parents, who never acquired the same fluency. However, once my husband Geir was praised for his excellence in Kriol only after having said two words. He entered a gas station to buy some diesel fuel. The assistant addressed him with *"Kuma?"* (How is life?). Geir responded *"Kansera só"* (Only fatigue). The assistant was apparently very pleased with that answer and said: *"Abo, bo ta papia Kriol diritu. Bo tarda li?"* (You speak excellent Kriol. You have been here for a long time?).

12. Among the Beng, babbling is valued and encouraged, and people purposefully teach infants to speak by both speaking for them and with them (Gottlieb 1998). See Ochs (1993) and Ochs and Schieffelin (1984) for interesting discussions about communicative styles of mothers.

13. Similar give and take games are described in Morton (1996) and Schieffelin (1990). The custom among many Guineans to ask for things has been interpreted as a way of greeting or to keep a conversation going (Pink 1998).

14. There are several similarities between the uses of physical punishment of Papel children and Tonga children (Morton 1996). In both cases mothers state that men are more inclined to beat children and they claim they find it emotionally difficult to hit children, while mothers appear to beat their own children more frequently than their fathers. The stated motives for physical punishment and the gradual playful introduction of smacking infants are also points of convergence. However, the beating of Tongan children appears more violent, more frequent, and less regulated than among the Papel.

15. See Layne (1999).

16. I asked eighty-three mothers or caregivers of children younger than five years of age if they took care of all of their own children. I also asked for the ages of children staying elsewhere, with whom they stayed and the reason for not staying with their own mothers.

17. Infertile Borana women (East Africa) or women whose children left home or have died can ask a relative for a child to secure their own subsistence and respect (Dahl 1990). It is difficult to reject such a request since people fear the evil eye of a woman without a child.

18. In addition to these three reasons for fosterage, two mothers in the study

referred to access to formal school education as a reason for fosterage, and one mother had given a child to a barren female relative.

19. Similar considerations have been documented among Mende parents in Sierra Leone; however, among the Mende the magnitude of fostered children is higher, and children are fostered at younger ages than among the Papel (Bledsoe 1995, Bledsoe and Isiugo-Abanihe 1989).

20. See similar considerations in Bledsoe and Isiugo-Abanihe (1989).

21. The mother in my second village survey who has given away most children to be fostered is herself a *katandeira*. She has left two of her children with her ex-husband and his second wife and three children with her own mother.

22. For accounts of a series of descriptive names used through a lifetime by the Punan Bah of central Borneo see Nicolaisen (1998), and for the Shona-speaking Manyika of eastern Zimbabwe see Jacobson-Widding (2000).

23. The name Impors is not always replaced later by another name. In the village survey three females (six months, two years, and fourteen years old) and four males (seven, fourteen, twenty-eight, and fifty years old) were registered with the name Impors.

24. Use of derogatory names to avoid tempting fate is common in West Africa. For discussion about the custom of using ugly names, dressing infants in rags, and rolling children in cow dung to protect them from greedy spirits among the Fulani and Mandinga in West Africa, see Johnson (1998, 2000:186–87) and Riesman (1992).

25. Geber describes "an all-round advance of development" of African children over European standards "which was greater the younger the child" (1958:186). For instance, among African children up to five months of age "the motor precocity was remarkable" (186). Geber explains the difference in terms of mothers' varied responsiveness to their infants. Before weaning, the African mother never leaves her child, as she carries it on her back. The mother breastfeeds her child on demand, and she "forbids him nothing, and never chides him. He lives in complete satisfaction and security, always under her protection" (1958:194). See also Trevarrthen (1989)

26. Linda L. Layne (2003:239–41) maintains that feminists are often reluctant to acknowledge pregnancy loss as a cause of grief, as it would imply an acceptance of anti-abortionist arguments about the personhood of embryos and fetuses. She argues that the recognition of personhood as culturally constructed concept, thus allowing differences both within and between cultures would give an understanding of how "the process of constructing personhood may be undertaken with some embryos and not others" (240).

27. Marilyn Nations and Linda-Anne Rebhun (1988), who have studied child health in northeast Brazil, convincingly criticize Scheper-Hughes's earlier writings (Scheper-Hughes 1984, 1985) about fosterage and the relationship between maternal indifference and naming in the Alto. Nations and Rebhun argue that naming of infants has to be understood in relation to religion and practical life. They argue that shantytown infants do not go unnamed because of maternal detachment, as suggested by Scheper-Hughes; rather "access to the Church is limited by economic,

geographic, and institutional barriers" (1988:165–66). There are, for example, churches that refuse to baptize children to unmarried mothers, even though marriage is an expensive luxury. Nations and Rebhun argue further that the practice of using ugly names and dressing children in rags (practice found in many cultures) cannot be explained as maternal detachment, as Scheper-Hughes does. Instead, according to Alford, these practices and others are intended for protection (1988:166–67). Nations and Rebhun argue still further that the frequent use of names such as Maria and Zé (diminutive for José, or Joseph) does not come from lack of individual concern for infants. In fact, by having such names, children are placed under the protection of powerful saints. See also Johnson (1998, 2000).

28. See Einarsdóttir (1999). An Icelandic woman told me that in earlier times the custom in Iceland to give children within a group of siblings the same name was due to a strong tradition to name children after a person important to the family, and probably also because of the relatively few names in use. Brothers could thus have the same name but were named after different persons; one was named after grandfather Jón, the second after uncle Jón, the third after a dead brother Jón, and the fourth after a helpful neighbor, also with the name Jón. For Icelandic naming traditions see Garðarsdóttir (1999).

29. Alford concludes that "naming systems both reflect and help create the conceptions of personal identity that are perpetuated within any society" (1988:167). Naming is accomplished through ritual because of the need to make a person a member of a society; it will "confer socialness rather than selfhood" (29).

30. Alford groups all the reasons he identified for late naming as the "supernatural" rationale. In his summary, he equates parents' wish "to reduce grief" and the "supernatural" rationale for delayed naming with avoidance of attachment (1988:49). Thus he contradicts his own conclusion that only rarely does ethnographic evidence support the assumption that "risks of attachment" cause delayed naming.

4. Diseases and Death

1. My home country Iceland has one of the lowest child mortality rates in the world: 5 per 1,000 live births in 1999 (UNDP 2001).

2. The decline in child mortality in Africa was, however, considerably lower, or 42 percent (Ahmad, Lopez, and Inoue 2000). Recently there has been increase in child mortality in Botswana, Namibia, Niger, Zambia, Zimbabwe, North Korea, and Papua New Guinea. Many explain the reversals and stagnation in child mortality rates, particularly in Africa, with the HIV/AIDS epidemic. Jacob Adetunji (2000) finds that the effect of the HIV/AIDS epidemic on child mortality has been overestimated, and the epidemic alone can only explain reversals in countries with a high HIV prevalence and relatively low child mortality. See also Schoepf, Schoepf, and Millen (2000).

3. Historians concerned with the explanations of the varied levels of child mortality in the past in Europe and North America stress similar factors as crucial to child survival; that is, standards of sanitation, social and economic welfare, the importance of modern medicine, the role of the state, infant feeding practices, and

cultural aspects (Bengtsson 1996; Garðarsdóttir 2000, 2002; Lithell 1999; Rollet 1997). The historian Ulla-Britt Lithell (1999) emphasizes better nursing practices (i.e., mainly increased breastfeeding but also use of pasteurized milk) as the main cause of decline in child mortality in Sweden from 1800 onwards. Lithell argues that this decrease in mortality continued even under declining economic conditions. In the 1940s, the introduction of penicillin led to a drop in deaths from pneumonia, a common cause of deaths among younger infants.

4. See Brockerhoff and Hewlett (1998:28) and LeVine and LeVine (2002).

5. See Castle (1994), Dettwyler (1994), Gottlieb (2004), and Scheper-Hughes (1987a, 1992).

6. In the 1960s, when Scheper-Hughes (1992) was working as a Peace Corps volunteer in the Alto, what surprised her most was the mothers' indifference to the death of their infants (270). Scheper-Hughes learned that it was easier to save a dehydrated child from death than "to enlist mothers themselves in the rescue of a child they perceived as ill-fated for life or as better off dead" (342). This was the experience that compelled her return to the Alto in the 1980s for a further study of mother love and child death.

7. Lynn M. Morgan (1998) describes similar ways of thinking among Ecuadorian mothers who relate their grief for dead children to how well they got to know their children before they died.

8. Whyte (1997:28) points out that in many African languages the term used for medicine may also be used to describe all sorts of things; in Lunyole, "almost any substance that has power to change something can be called a medicine, including shoe polish. " See also Pool (1994).

9. Hanne Overgaard Mogensen (1998), who examines how biomedicine enters the life of people in eastern Uganda, focuses on women's agency in seeking care for their children. She argues that biomedicine provides new opportunities for mothers that prompt others to deal with their problems.

10. I have not done any systematic survey to find out if women or men, old or young are more likely to take their children to a diviner. However, my impression is that women's health and fertility as well as the children's disease are often a reason for such a visit; commonly men and grandmothers consult diviners on behalf of women and children. See also Whyte (1991:168).

11. A female villager explains that if a person wants to bewitch an enemy a dog or a goat is needed. Its eyes will be drawn out and the animal will be buried alive. By night, the person goes to the sorcerer with *kana* and a chicken. The chicken will be killed, and the presentation of white testicles is an indication that the *iran* is willing to do the work. The necessary medicines will be prepared and put in a horn, and by night it is buried in the house of the enemy. With time somebody belonging to that house will become sick. *Balobeiru* or *djambakus* will come and examine if the house is dirty with hidden medicines. If the house is dirty most likely another more knowledgeable diviner will be recommended to neutralize the sorcery. The house will be investigated and finally she or he will turn up the item, likely to be a horn, that caused the problem. Sometimes the owner of the house is present and observes everything, sometimes not.

12. In-group accusations of witchcraft or sorcery, such as within the matrilineage

or among co-wives, are typical for ethnographic descriptions from Africa, which differs from Melanesian societies where accusations of witchcraft or sorcery are likely to be directed at outsiders. See Child and Child (1993) for a brief overview of studies on wizardry. See also Marwick (1982 [1970]) for selected works on witchcraft and sorcery.

13. See, for instance, description of such situations in Cameroon (Njikam Savage 1996).

14. See Leis (1982:156–60) for descriptions of Ijaw parents in southern Nigeria who have lost many children and begin to suspect that the same child is coming and going.

15. See Allotey and Reidpath (2001), Gottlieb (1998, 2004), and Leis (1982) for similar descriptions.

16. There are many animal diseases. The "forest goat" disease attacks newborns and kills rapidly. In the first days of life the infant gets sick with convulsions and its mouth becomes fixed and foamy. The similarities with neonatal tetanus are obvious. The disease can also attack adults, primarily hunters, but it does not kill adults as easily as it kills infants. The forest goat disease is thought to be less common today than in the old days. See Mølsted (1995:101).

17. *Pontada* (sudden pain) and *alma furtadu* (soul stolen) are other kinds of problems of ritual art that can cause a child's death. The knowledge about both of these diseases comes from the Balanta. A mother who gives a woven cloth in uneven numbers for a funeral may cause a child born later by that woman to die from *pontada*. Typically the child will die after one year of age. Only Balanta know how to diagnose that disease and perform the necessary ceremony. Women whose children die one after the other begin to suspect that *pontada* is the problem. The ceremony made will prevent her from losing additional children. Adult women may also die from *pontada*. *Alma furtadu* is also a disease the Papel have learned about from the Balanta. It may attack both adults and children. A person who is clairvoyant *(pauteiru)*, "has the head" *(tene kabessa)* and can see things normal people do not see may steal a soul from some person and install it in another one. For instance, a man who sees a pretty girl may steal her soul and install it into his wife. The person whose soul has been stolen will become mad and finally die if the disease is not diagnosed and the soul not reinstalled. Two persons I have seen were suspected to be victims of a stolen soul; however, one was finally found to have died from sorcery.

18. According to Eric Gable (1995:244–45), his Manjaco interlocutors emphasize their own role as agents and enforcers of spirits. Nonetheless, the spirits could be tricky, unpredictable, and even evil. Gable (1997) describes how a Manjaco informant claims whites are better witches than Manjaco, and he emphasizes the general weaknesses of the Manjaco, who fight among themselves instead of being unified as are the whites. During my fieldwork I encounter similar views among the Papel who, however, describe the spirits of the Manjaco as more fierce and uncompromising than their own. An elderly man argues that the whites are cleverer in their collaboration with spirits than the blacks, the latter having mainly used the spirits to "destroy their country and kill each others' children *[dana terra e mata fidju di utru]*." He refers to the effective cholera treatment at the health centers in Biombo as an example of a fruitful collaboration of whites with spirits. See Shaw (2002:210)

for a similar comparison made between European and African witches in Sierra Leone.

19. The diagnostic procedure is based on a test period, normally seven days. If the child is better after that time it is an indication that the problem was the cat disease, and a washing ceremony must be performed within a specified period of time. If the child is still sick after the test period some other problem has caused the child's ailment.

20. However, in a Biombo village chicken pox was mistakenly reported to the regional health board in Quinhamel as measles.

21. This ceremony is also performed in the case of all major disasters such as war, drought, and epidemics such as cholera (see Einarsdóttir, Passa, and Gunnlaugsson [2001]).

22. This assumption probably reflects the health authorities' primary emphasis on health care for children and pregnant women. Elderly, and sometimes adult, men complain that there is no help for them at the health centers. Further, at the nearest mission hospital only children and pregnant women are attended and women in birth are assisted.

23. This may contribute to the erratic use of drugs. A mother living in a village some forty kilometers outside Bissau explains how she sent someone to buy a capsule of antibiotics when her child got a severe ear infection causing pus to drain from the ears. The mother opened up the capsule and poured the content into the child's ear. See Whyte, van der Geest and Hardon (2003).

24. Explanations of undernourishment vary within the literature on child nutrition, but poverty, ignorance, mothers' indifference, and child illnesses are commonly named causes. The physical anthropologist Katherine Dettwyler argues that the main cause of child malnutrition and mortality in the world is caused by "ignorance and inappropriate cultural beliefs and practices. Ignorance in the sense of simple lack of knowledge, such as not understanding the relationship between food and health, or not understanding the critical importance of good nutrition during the first few years of a child's life" (1994:144–45). Scheper-Hughes (1992) relates undernourishment to a lack of adequate food due to poverty. However, she argues that in certain cases mothers withhold food.

25. Helle Mølsted describes how Balanta mothers negotiate with nurses in the Oio region in Guinea-Bissau during vaccination campaigns with "a mixture of seriousness and humour" (1995:101). Her description nicely reflects similar situations I have experienced in Biombo.

26. Until recently, Biombo was one of the most unpopular places for a nurse to work. Outsiders tend to talk about the population in the region as somewhat stubborn and "uncivilized." Health professionals consider Papel hygienic practices problematic, such as the stated lack of interest in using latrines, prolonged funeral feasts, and delayed burials. In addition, the Papel are not considered to be particularly generous in comparison to other ethnic groups. A Guinean scholar emphasized that the Papel were individualistic, a characteristic he regarded as un-African. The Papel men's reluctance to work and their excessive consumption of alcohol is frequently highlighted by the nurses, other educated Guineans, and some Papel women as one of the main reasons for Biombo's economically difficult situation, in

particular the low local output of agricultural products. One nurse argued that "the Papel are poor because they bury their wealth" referring to all the funeral shrouds in which corpses are wrapped before burial.

27. Some people refer to the Protestant spirit as an agent very much as they talk about *iran,* or other supernatural forces. An American miracle man came occasionally to Bissau on behalf of some Protestant groups. For months after these visits numerous stories flourished about how people got mysterious help for whatever misfortune had befallen them. See Gausset (1999) for an interesting discussion on choice of religion.

28. See also discussion of mixed marriages in chapter 1.

29. According to Sered (1994:92–93) women in the nineteenth-century United States converted to religions that offered consolation to mothers grieving over the death of a child. Such religions, she argues, tended to give meaning to the death, to emphasize that the child would have a pleasant life in another world, and to encourage communication between worlds. Sered does not mention, however, whether these women converted to protect their other children from death, which is often the case when Papel mothers convert to Protestantism.

30. See Rosenblatt (1993) and Rosenblatt, Walsh, and Jackson (1976) for discussion of cross-cultural similarity and diversity in grieving.

31. See Layne (2003) and Cecil (1996).

32. Scheper-Hughes's discussion (1992) of how she recorded the Alto women's reproductive histories is interesting. She maintains, "the events of pregnancy, birth, and child death were a vital part of women's culture" (306). When she asked about how many children they had given birth to, the mothers answered "X children, Y living" or "Y living, Z angels" (286). Mothers counted their children in birth order from the first born child using the expression that one child came leaning against the other. Only a few elderly women had difficulties in recalling names, ages, and circumstances of death for some of their children. According to Scheper-Hughes, one of the older women clearly confirmed their gratefulness when some of the "late-born and supernumerary children" died, but the last born to survive was "loved and indulged by all" (310).

33. A few foreigners in Guinea-Bissau defend their conviction that mothers' are indifferent to their children's survival by saying, "If they can't remember they don't care." A Guinean friend argues that some mothers do not cry when their children die, and thus their grief is internal only. This is because they have no tears and thus are unable to cry, because they have become too distressed, or because they are totally shocked.

34. During the cholera epidemics in Biombo in 1994 and 1996–97 the mortality rate for cholera was similar among children and adults. Six children aged two to four years were registered to have died from cholera in the whole region.

35. *Gloria* is the Kriol word for heaven, also used here by Muslims to refer to the better place in the afterlife. The Papel refer to the afterlife as the other world.

36. Whyte (1997) recognizes that her distinction between symptomatic and explanatory idioms overlaps with Horton's dichotomy between two ways of knowing, that is, common sense and theory, but also with the distinction between natural and supernatural disease categories. Robert Pool (1993, 1994) opposes colleagues who criticize earlier ethnographies of illness and misfortune in Africa for placing

too much emphasis on supernatural causation of diseases. Pool argues that "the emphasis on naturalistic causation and practical activity in the definitions of African medical systems does not make them broader, as the protagonists claim but, rather, narrower, and that descriptions of 'medical systems' are not more accurate representations of how Africans interpret and cope with illness but biomedically determined constructs which are imposed on African culture in medical ethnography" (1994:1). I tend to agree with Pool's view.

37. See the use of the term "rational and value-maximizing" individuals in Handwerker (1986), Lesthaeghe (1989), and Adepoju (1997).

38. Whyte (1997:18–21) develops her argument from John Dewey's pragmatic view of uncertainty.

39. Scheper-Hughes argues that she has "found no evidence of 'delayed' or displaced grief in the days, weeks, and months following the death of an infant, unless, perhaps, a new pregnancy can be seen as a symptom of displaced grief " (1992:425).

40. Dettwyler is also concerned with women's lack of control over reproduction and whom they marry when she writes that "if part of the problem [child neglect] is women's lack of control over their own bodies, rooted in the position of women within the traditional social organization, then the solution becomes much more elusive" (1994:159–60).

41. See Scheper-Hughes (1992:275).

42. Explaining a child's death and having a new child after having lost one appears to be important for mothers to cope with grief. A national study in Sweden on stillbirth and maternal well-being demonstrates the importance to know the cause of death for the women's psychological health (Rådestad 1998:80–81). The women who lost a child had a lower self-esteem than women who had given birth to a live child, as they felt less valued outside home and experienced a challenge to their reproductive capacity. Most of the women felt support from the child's father and giving birth to a new child were the most important factors for recovering from grief (78). A phenomenological study of the experiences of a sudden child death in North American families also reveals the importance to be able to find a meaning in and to explain a child's death (Gudmundsdottir 2000). In addition, the parents included in the study "tried to rebuild their sense of themselves as parents either by becoming pregnant as soon as possible after the death and/or by refocusing on their living children" (267). See also Cecil (1996).

43. Scheper-Hughes (1992) argues that culture is organized to help mothers psychologically cope with child death (which contributes to additional deaths of children). In contrast, but still in a functionalist tradition, LeVine, Dixon, and LeVine (1994:50–52) argue that African child care practices have adapted to save the lives of children. See also Leiderman, Tulkin, and Rosenfeldt (1992 [1977]). Both Scheper-Hughes (1992) and LeVine et al. (1994) maintain that the cultures are successful in achieving their respective goals.

5. Nonhuman Children

1. See Dagg (1999) for a critique.

2. Still, comparison is difficult because various authors use these terms without

always defining them. The anthropological literature on personhood, self and identity is extensive. See Cohen (1994), Fortes (1987), Jackson and Karp (1990), and Riesman (1992).

3. For the Punan Bah of central Borneo an infant acquires human status when an ancestor spirit has taken a permanent residence in its body, which occurs when the infant is able to turn its body or has got its first teeth (Nicolaisen 1995). Shortly thereafter an infant will be given a name and considered a person.

4. For the Chewong (Malay Peninsula) conceptions of humanity and personhood are seen as fused but their achievement is related to acquisition of knowledge (Howell 1989).

5. Morgan (1998), who describes conceptions about the nature of fetuses and infants in Ecuador, argues in a similar way. According to Morgan, for her Ecuadorian informants acquisition of personhood is a gradual process for which baptism is an important demarcation. Morgan contrasts these ambiguous and unclear categories with the clear-cut definition of the U.S. National Right to Life members on fetuses as not only human beings but also persons from the moment of conception. The controversial philosopher Peter Singer argues that a human being does not automatically have an individual right to live. What matters is "characteristics like rationality, autonomy, and self-consciousness" (1993:182). Singer assumes that newborns lack these characteristics and argues, "killing them, therefore, cannot be equated with killing normal human beings, or any other self-conscious beings" (182). Singer emphasizes that to kill a healthy or a disabled infant is equally acceptable; what matters is the parents' will, as only they should decide if an infant is to live or die.

6. The pediatricians Chris J. Hobbs and Jane M. Wynne (1996) maintain that infanticide still occurs in the United States and Western Europe. They argue deaths that result from both child abuse and neglect are likely to be concealed within the diagnosis of sudden infant death syndrome (SIDS). See Meyer, Oberman, and White (2001) for a discussion about infanticide in the contemporary United States, and Jónsson (2000) and Tillhagen (1983) for discussions about the history of infanticide in Iceland and Sweden.

7. Sons' ability to repay the cost of their upbringing through material and labor contributions has been proposed as an explanation for female infanticide among the Inuit (Smith and Smith 1994). Joseph Birdsell maintains that preferential female infanticide was common throughout the Australian continent: 25–45 percent of newborn girls were killed for child spacing and population control. The reasons, according to Birdsell, were "very simple and culturally adaptive" (1993:4). The killing did not cause any psychological injuries, as people believed that the spirit of the child murdered returned to the totem spot where it came from, where it might then reenter the mother later.

8. See also Scrimshaw (1984).

9. In Shostak's book, *Nisa,* more details are given on the practice of infanticide among the !Kung (1981:54–56, 76–77).

10. Also in Kenya, a Nandi child born to an unmarried woman fell outside social categories; therefore such a child was to be killed by the midwife directly after birth (Oboler 1985). Since a child's first cry was believed to signal the entry of an ancestral spirit into the body, the infant would be suffocated by stuffing dung into the

mouth and nose of the newborn. If the newborn was suffocated before it cried, it was considered to have never lived.

11. See Håkansson for a critical view of missionaries describing African peoples as "continuously busy practicing infanticide" (1998:1767). Nancy Howell (1979) argues that the rate of infanticide among the !Kung in the Kalahari Desert did not exceed a small percentage of all live births, and killing of the deformed, twins, and unplanned births had little effect on the population size, since they would probably die anyway.

12. For instance, the Nuer referred to twins as birds and deformed children as hippopotami (Evans-Pritchard 1956:84–85, 128–33). When twins and deformed children died, which was common, the Nuer said that the twins would return to the air and the deformed returned to water or were laid in water where they belonged.

13. Carreira (1971:167) interprets the washing ceremony as a substitute for infanticide. He maintains that the Papel consider twins to be the work of the sorcerer, thus they were born with malicious instincts. Twins were assumed to kill each other or alternatively they would kill their parents (210–11).

14. Many of my informants agree that in earlier days the Balanta left to die one or both of the twins, some say they still do. A Balanta woman tells me that the Balanta threw away both of the twins directly after birth: they were put in a calabash and taken to the sea and it was allowed to float away. She says people are cleverer today and they do not get rid of twins anymore. See Renne (2001) for a discussion about the changed attitude toward twins among the Yoruba in Nigeria.

15. Elsa has two pairs of twins and her sister has one pair of twins. I was present at the washing ceremony of Elsa's twins, and she, despite being in her forties and having many children, gave birth to one more so as not to finish her births with twins.

16. See Furnes (1998) for discussion about the lives of disabled children in Biombo and Sætersdal (1998) for historic accounts of the situation of disabled children in Norway.

17. Many authors have described the procedure of taking a deformed child to the sea, even among other ethnic groups in Guinea-Bissau (Carreira 1971, Crowley 1990, Jao 1995b, Mølsted 1995, Person 1989). Those who live far away from the sea leave the child in the forest and check to see if it has disappeared the next day. Carreira (1971) mentions that as a response to the action of the colonial authorities most groups have stopped killing their deformed and twin children. Crowley (1990) writes that the Portuguese campaigned to stop infanticide in Guinea-Bissau in the 1940s. She describes the act of taking infants to the sea in the present tense, while Jao (1995a) treats the practice as belonging to the past. Jao emphasizes that the killing of anomalous infants does not have an economic rationale (to eradicate unproductive infants); rather it contributes to restoration of social security.

18. However, an elderly man insists that only women participate, often the maternal grandmother, and only those who belong to the child's lineage.

19. Today the Kriol word *tuga* refers to white people. However, initially it referred only to the Portuguese.

20. It is important to remember that each *djambakus* collaborates with a particular *iran* and that their work is specialized. While some *djambakus* can, for

instance, make a divination to determine whether or not a particular child is human, others can also cause its death.

21. It varies whether or not mothers are able to prevent their children from being put through identification procedures. A woman tells me about a child with a distorted face who was taken to the sea and disappeared into the water at six months of age. At that time the child was already sitting and crawling. I asked if its mother had accepted the decision. "She accepted. How could she refuse?" the woman responds. Another woman tells about a one-year-old child who could neither sit nor walk, but otherwise its body was normal. The mother refused to take her child to the sea or to a *djambakus* to check its identity. Finally the child died at home.

22. There is a difference between Papel people who adhere to their own religion and those who have converted to the Christian faith when it concerns interpretation of *iran*. Catholics view *iran* as the devil while Protestants claim there are no *iran* children and such abnormalities are caused by disease. Thus Papel who are Catholics may be still more afraid of *iran* than those adhering to the Papel religion, which attributes to an *iran* both positive and negative aspects.

23. These three categories of infanticide do not encompass all known cases of infanticide. One of the Icelandic Sagas, *Finnboga Saga Ramma,* for instance, tells about a wealthy man in Iceland who demands that his newborn should be left to die, something only considered to be appropriate for those who are poor (Finnboga saga ramma 1987). He does not want to have more children with his wife as she allowed their daughter to marry a man without his permission and knowledge. His wife arranges events in such a way that a neighbor couple finds and raises the infant. Another example that falls outside these categories is Shaw's (1994) interpretation that many black slave women chose to kill their children as a revolt against an oppressive system. She argues that when slave women "engaged directly or indirectly, in abortions and infanticide, they picked away at one of the bases of the system's life itself—reproduction" (1994:253). See also Reyes (2002:33–77).

24. Abortion would fall within this category of infanticide if we apply the line of reasoning of the U.S. National Right to Life movement (see Morgan 1998). See Rapp (2000) and Steinbock (1992) for discussion about the moral and legal status of embryos and fetuses and the use of amniocenteses for detecting defective fetuses for selective abortion.

25. Recall that the Papel practice sexual abstinence during the breastfeeding period, thus a new pregnancy will not occur until the child is weaned.

26. Even prenatal testing performed with modern advanced technology is uncertain and may contribute to ambiguity and anxiety. See Getz (2001) and Rapp (2000).

27. See Morris (1987), Peek (1991b), and Shaw (1991) for critical discussion of Horton's theory of religion.

Conclusion

1. As already discussed in introduction, Scheper-Hughes is ambivalent about the universality of her findings. On one hand, she argues for cultural construction of

maternal thinking (see Scheper-Hughes 1992: 341–42). On the other hand, she emphasizes that "throughout much of human history—as in a great deal of the impoverished Third World today" selective neglect and passive infanticide are expected maternal responses to hostile conditions and may be seen as survival strategies (Scheper-Hughes 1993:35). Scheper-Hughes (1993) emphasizes the commonalities in maternal responses to child death in impoverished communities with high rates of child mortality. She emphasized that selective neglect is a survival strategy in such communities, and she states, "infant death becomes routine in an environment in which death is anticipated and bets hedged" (35). See also Scheper-Hughes (1992:275, 401–2).

2. While discussing the infanticide in Europe, Hrdy argues that "historical and ecological context had important implications for how mothers assessed what their own, or this particular infant's, prospects were. Social and economic context had everything to do with the alternatives a mother had to choose from. But whereas these represent highly relevant circumstances, they are not explanations for *why* mothers were abandoning babies. . . . Indeed, understanding the biological basis of 'mother love' is essential for understanding what is going on here" (1999:311).

3. See Hrdy (1999:56–57, 114, 376–80). Hrdy argues that humans, in contrast to animals, "are able to consciously make choices counter to their self-interest" (1999: 460), and she presents choices based on ethical considerations or moral conventions as exceptional. She concludes that parents in the Western society of today "are respected and admired for caring for the same infants that in other societies mothers would be condemned by their neighbors for not disposing of" (460). In Hrdy's argument there is a notion of the "savage noble" mother who allows innate impulses to drive her to neglect or kill her "low-quality" infants, in contrast to the modern Western mother. Western culture with its ethical considerations appears as to have corrupted the inborn maternal instincts, thereby demanding of mothers that they dedicate their lives to unviable children, which should be eliminated to enhance human survival.

4. In contrast to the fieldwork in Biombo, I am spared much anxiety since my personal involvement does not influence chances of survival of the prematurely born infants (see Einarsdóttir 2002).

5. See Anspach (1987, 1993), Brichmann (1999, 2000a, 2000b), Cullini et al. (1999), and Wyatt (1999).

Glossary

almu furtadu	soul stolen, a disease the Papel learned about from the Balanta
badjuda	unmarried girl
baloba	kapok tree where an ancestral spirit has settled
balobeiru	a male or female diviner or religious specialist capable of communicating with God
bianda	boiled rice
bombolom	slit-gong drum
bota sorte	divination, perform a divination
defuntu	an ancestral spirit, a dead person
Deus	God
djakassi	mix up, a disease combined with sorcery
djambakus	a male or female diviner, healer, or a religious specialist who collaborates with a spirit, diviner, healer
djintis di prassa	comes from a town or city, urban
djintis di tabanka	from a village
djongagu	soul oracle, a ceremony performed as part of a funeral to identify the cause of death
djorson	lineage
doensa di limária di matu	animal diseases, a group of child diseases that all have their names derived from animals
dona	grandmother, mother-in-law, or any closely related elderly woman
dona kasa	senior wife, first wife
donu	owner, chief
es mundu	this world
fanadu	initiation ceremony for males
fetiseru	sorcerer
fidju di kasa	son of the house, son who has not inherited
iran	spirit that can heal or kill with sorcery

kana	distillate alcohol
kansaré	Godly ordeal, divination instrument
katandeira	girl who has been given to a *baloba* in return for ritual services to prevent child deaths
lava gemio	washing ceremony for twins
lava lua /olha lua	wash moon, see moon, menstruate
lei di prumedu	the original law
madrassa	mother's co-wife
mafé	sauce eaten with boiled rice
mal feitu	sorcery, bad work
mala	box
mandjuandade	age group
mesinhu di branku	white man's medicine
mesinhu di terra	local medicine
mufunesa	misfortune caused by an intentional agent, state of ritual danger
neto	daughter-in-law, son-in-law, grandchild
pano	textile, cloth, funeral shroud
passa prasu	to be passed fertile age, menopause
pauteiru	clairvoyant
pekadur	human being
pontada	disease that the Papel have learned about from the Balanta
ronia iran	ceremony a woman or a man must perform to become *djambakus*
semana sagradu	women's marriage ceremony, holy week
tabanka	village
tchon	land, territory
tchuru	funeral, weeping
tempu di fomi	famine time
toca tchur	beating-the-drum ceremony, which helps a deceased person enter the other world
tokadur	slit-gong drummer
torna boka	to pay back what is promised in a ritual contract
uso	tradition, custom
utru mundu	the other world, afterlife
visti mindjer	to marry a woman

References

Aaby, Peter, Joaquim Gomes, Lars Høj, and Anita Sandström. 1997. *Estudo de Saúde de Mulheres em Idade Fertil e os Seus Filhos. Dados de 1990–1995.* UNICEF/Projecto de Saúde de Bandim, Bissau.

Abu-Lughod, Lila. 1993. *Writing women's worlds: Bedouin stories.* Berkeley: University of California Press.

Achinger, Gertrud. 1990. Efeitos do Programa de Ajustamento Estructural sobre as condições económicas e socias das mulheres da zona rural. *SORONDA* 14:65–82.

Adeokun, Lawrence A. 1983. Marital sexuality and birth-spacing among Yoruba. In *Female and male in West Africa,* ed. Christine Oppong, 127–37. London: George Allen & Unwin.

Adepoju, Aderanti. 1997. *Family, population and development in Africa.* London: Zed Books.

Adetunji, Jacob. 2000. Trends in under-five mortality rates and the HIV/AIDS epidemic. *Bulletin of the World Health Organization* 78 (10):1200–6.

Aguilar, Renato. 1998. *Guinea-Bissau 1994: Going into high gear.* Country Economic Report, 6. Gothenburg: Gothenburg University.

Aguilar, Renato, and Åsa Stenman. 1993. *Guinea-Bissau: Facing new temptations and challenges.* Gothenburg University. Macroeconomic Studies, 43. Gothenburg: Gothenburg University.

———. 1994. *Guinea-Bissau 1994: On the eve of tomorrow.* Macroeconomic Studies, 56. Gothenburg: Gothenburg University.

Aguilar, Renato, and Mario Zejan. 1992. *Guinea-Bissau: Getting off the track.* Macroeconomic Studies, 25. Gothenburg: Gothenburg University.

Ahlbeth, Beth Maina. 1994. Is there a distinct African sexuality? A critical response to Caldwell. *Africa* 64 (2):220–42.

Ahmad, Omar B., Alan D. Lopez, and Mie Inoue. 2000. The decline in child mortality: A reappraisal. *Bulletin of the World Health Organization* 78 (10):1175–91.

Alford, Richard D. 1988. *Naming and identity: A cross-cultural study of personal naming practices.* New Haven: HRAF Press.

Allen, Diensen Roth. 2002. *Managing motherhood, managing risk: Fertility and danger in West Central Tanzania*. Michigan: University of Michigan Press.

Allotey, P., and D. Reidpath. 2001. Establishing the cause of childhood mortality in Ghana: the "spirit child." *Social Science and Medicine* 52 (7):1107–12.

Almeida, António de. 1963. Sobre a etnonímia das populações nativas da Guiné Portugueasa. *Estudos sobre a etnologia do ultramar Português. Estudos, ensinos e documentos* 3 (102):223–40.

Alsop, Rachel, Annette Fitzsimons, and Kathleen Lennon. 2002. *Theorizing Gender*. Cambridge: Polity Press.

Anderson Mencagli, Kirsen. 1992. *Medicina tradicional*. Secretariado para o Desenvolvimento e Promoção Humana, Bissau. Boletim número 4. Bissau: Secretariado para o Desenvolvimento e Promoção Humana.

Andersson, Sören. 1999. HIV-1 and HIV-2 infections in Guinea-Bissau, West Africa: Studies of immune responses, prevailing viruses and epidemiological trends. Ph.D. dissertation, Karolinska Institute, Stockholm.

Andrén, Ulla. 2000. The forgotten conflict in Guinea-Bissau. *News from the Nordic Africa Institute* 1:4–7.

Anspach, Renee. 1987. Prognostic conflict in life-and-death decisions: the organization as an ecology of knowledge. *Journal of Health and Social Behavior* 28:215–31.

———. 1993. *Deciding who lives: Fateful choices in the intensive-care nursery*. Berkeley: University of California Press.

Argenti, Nicolas. 2001. Kesum-body and the places of the gods: the politics of children's masking and the second-world realities in Oku (Cameroon). *Journal of the Royal Anthropological Institute* 7:67–94.

Ariès, Philippe. 1962. *Centuries of childhood*. New York: Vintage.

Armstrong, H. C. 1991. International recommendations for consistent breastfeeding definitions. *Journal of Human Lactation* 7 (2):514.

Badinter, Elisabeth. 1980. *Mother love: Myth and reality*. New York: Macmillan.

Baker, Hugh D. R. 1979. *Chinese family and kinship*. London: Macmillan.

Ball, Helen L., and Catherin M. Hill. 1996. Reevaluating "twin infanticide." *Current Anthropology* 37 (5):856–63.

Barfield, Thomas. 1997. *The dictionary of anthropology*. Oxford: Blackwell.

Bartlett, Thad Q., Robert W. Sussman, and James M. Cheverud. 1993. Infant killing in primates: a review of observed cases with specific reference to the sexual selection hypothesis. *American Anthropologist* 4:958–90.

Beauchamp, Tom L., and James F. Childress. 1994. *Principles of biomedical ethics*. 4th ed. Oxford: Oxford University Press.

Bell, Sandra, and Simon Coleman. 1999a. *The anthropology of friendship*. Oxford: Berg.

———. 1999b. The anthropology of friendship: Enduring themes and future possibilities. In *The anthropology of friendship*, ed. Sandra Bell and Simon Coleman, 1–19. Oxford: Berg.

Bengtsson, Magdalena. 1996. *Det hotade barnet. Tre generationers spädbarns- och barnadödlighet i 1800-talets Linköping*. Hälsa och samhälle. Linköping studies in arts and science 145. Linköping: Linköping universitet.

Berry, Jo de, and Jo Boyden. 2002. Children in adversity. *Forced Migration* 9:33–6.

Bideau, Alain, Bertrand Desjardins, and Héctor Pérez Brignoli. 1997. *Infant and child mortality in the past*. Oxford: Clarendon Press.

Biesele, Megan. 1997. An ideal of unassisted birth: Hunting, healing, and transformation among the Kalahari Ju/'hoansi. In *Childbirth and authoritative knowledge: Cross-cultural Perspectives*, ed. Robbie E. Davis-Floyd and Carolyn F. Sargent, 474–92. Berkeley: University of California Press.

Birdsell, Joseph B. 1993. *Microevolutionary patterns in aboriginal Australia: A gradient analysis of clines*. Oxford: Oxford University Press.

Blanchet, Thérèse. 1996. *Lost innocence, stolen childhoods*. Dhaka: University Press Limited/Rädda Barnen.

Blazejewicz, Dorota, Rolf Lund, Klas Schönning, and Silke Steincke. 1981. *Arquitectura tradicional—Guiné-Bissau*. Stockholm: SIDA.

Bledsoe, Caroline. 1993. The politics of polygyny in Mende education and child fosterage transactions. In *Sex and gender hierarchies*, ed. Barbara D. Miller, 170–92. Cambridge: Cambridge University Press.

———. 1995. Marginal members: children of previous unions in Mende households in Sierra Leone. In *Situating fertility: Anthropology and demographic inquiry*, ed. Susan Greenhalgh, 130–53. Cambridge: Cambridge University Press.

———. 2002. *Contingent lives. Fertility, time, and aging in West Africa*. Chicago: University of Chicago Press.

Bledsoe, Caroline, and Uche Isiugo-Abanihe. 1989. Strategies of child-fosterage in Sierra Leone. In *Reproduction and social organization in sub-Saharan Africa*, ed. Ron J. Lesthaeghe, 442–74. Berkeley: University of California Press.

Bledsoe, Caroline, Douglas C. Ewbank, and Uche C. Isiugo-Abanihe. 1988. The effect of child fostering on feeding practices and access to health services in rural Sierra Leone. *Social Science and Medicine* 27 (6):627–36.

Brantley, Cynthia. 1997. Through Ngoni eyes: Margaret Read's matrilineal interpretations from Nyasaland. *Critique of Anthropology* 17 (2):147–69.

Breger, Rosemary, and Rosanna Hill. 1998. *Cross-cultural marriage: Identity and choice*. Cross-Cultural Perspective on Women. Oxford: Berg.

Brichmann, Berit Støre. 1999. When the home becomes a prison: living with a severely disabled child. *Nursing Ethics* 6 (2):137–43.

———. 2000a. Ethical decision making in neonatal units—the normative significance of vitality. *Medicine, Health Care and Philosophy* 4:193–200.

———. 2000b. "They have to show that they can make it . . .": Vitality as a criterion for the prognosis of premature infants. *Nursing Ethics* 7 (2):141–47.

Brison, Karin J., and Stephen C. Leavitt. 1995. Coping with bereavement: Long-term perspectives on grief and mourning. *Ethos* 23 (4):395–400.

Brockerhoff, Martin, and Paul Hewlett. 1998. *Ethnicity and child mortality in sub-Saharan Africa*. Population Council. Policy Research Division Working Paper, 107. New York: Population Council.

Buckley, Thomas, and Alma Gottlieb, eds. 1988. *Blood magic: The anthropology of menstruation*. Berkeley: University of California Press.

Bull, Benjamin Pinto. 1988. *O Criolo da Guiné-Bissau: Filosofia e Sabedoria*. Lisboa/Bissau: ICALP/INEP.

Bull, Marianne. 1994. *A importância das mulheres para o sector da pesca. Um estudo da pesca em pequena escala sobre as mulheres e homens na Guiné-Bissau. Relatório preparado para Direcção das Pescas, República da Guiné-Bissau.* Göteborg: SWEDMAR.

Butler, Judith. 1992. The body politics of Julia Kristeva. In *Revaluing French feminism: Critical essays on difference, agency, and culture,* ed. Nancy Fraser and Sandra Lee Bartky, 162–76. Bloomington: Indiana University Press.

Cabral, Nelson E. 1984. Portuguese Creole dialects in West Africa. *Interaction through language. Sociolinguistic Research, Cases, and Applications* 36 (1):77–85.

Caldwell, John C. 2000. Rethinking the African AIDS epidemic. *Population & Development Review* 26 (1):117–35.

Caldwell, John C., I. O. Orubuloye, and Pat Caldwell. 1992. Fertility decline in Africa: A new type of transition. *Population and Development Review* 18 (2):211–42.

Caldwell, John C., Pat Caldwell, and Pat Quiggin. 1989. The social context of AIDS in sub-Saharan Africa. *Population and Development Review* 15 (2):185–233.

Callewaert, Inger. 2000. The birth of religion among the Balanta of Guinea-Bissau. Ph.D. dissertation. Department of History of Religions, University of Lund, Lund.

Caplan, Pat. 1995. "Children are our wealth and we want them": A difficult pregnancy on northern Mafia Island, Tanzania. In *Women wielding the hoe: Lessons from rural Africa for feminist and development practice,* ed. Fahy Deborah Bryceson, 131–49. Oxford: Berg.

Caputo, Virginia. 1995. Anthropology's silent "others": A consideration of some conceptual and methodological issues for the study of youth and children's cultures. In *Youth cultures: A Cross-cultural perspective,* ed. Vered Amit-Talai and Helena Wulff, 19–42. London: Routledge.

Carney, Judith A. 1988. Struggles over land and crops in an irrigated rice scheme: The Gambia. In *Agriculture, women, and land. The African experience,* ed. Jean Davison, 131–49. Boulder: Westview Press.

Carreira, António. 1962. Organização social e económia dos povos da Guiné Portuguesa. *Boletim Cultural da Guiné Portuguesa* 16 (64):641–732.

———. 1971. O infanticídio ritual em África. *Boletim Cultural da Guiné Portuguesa* 26 (101):149–216.

Carsten, Janet. 2000a. *Cultures of relatedness: New approaches to the study of kinship.* Cambridge: Cambridge University Press.

———. 2000b. Introduction: Cultures of relatedness. In *Cultures of relatedness: New approaches to the study of kinship,* ed. Janet Carsten, 1–36. Cambridge: Cambridge University Press.

Carvalho, Clara. 1998. Ritos de Poder e a Recriação da Tradição. Os Régalos Manjaco da Guiné-Bissau. Ph.D. dissertation. Instituto Superior de Ciências do Trabalho e da Empresa, Lisboa.

Cassell, Joan. 1987. *Children in field: Anthropological experiences.* Philadelphia: Temple University Press.

Cassidy, Claire Monod. 1987. World-view conflict and toddler malnutrition: Change agent dilemmas. In *Child survival: Anthropological perspectives on the treatment and maltreatment of children,* ed. Nancy Scheper-Hughes, 293–324. Dordrecht: D. Reidel Publishing Company.

Castle, Sarah. 1994. The (re)negotiation of illness diagnoses and responsibility for child death in rural Mali. *Medical Anthropology Quarterly* 8 (3):314–35.

Cecil, Rosanne, ed. 1996 *The anthropology of pregnancy loss: Comparative studies in miscarriage, stillbirth, and neonatal death.* Oxford: Berg.

Chagnon, Napoleon A. 1968. *Yanomanö: The fierce people.* New York: Holt, Rinehart and Winston.

Child, Alice B., and Irvin L. Child. 1993. *Religion and magic in the life of traditional peoples.* New Jersey: Prentice Hall.

Chodorow, Nancy. 1974. Family structure and feminine personality. In *Woman, culture, and society,* eds. Michelle Zimbalist Rosaldo and Louise Lamphere, 43–66. Stanford: Stanford University Press.

Choi, Precilla Y. L. 1995. The menstrual cycle and premenstrual syndrome. What is this news on the menstrual cycle and premenstrual syndrome? *Social Science and Medicine* 41 (6):759–68.

Christie, Vibeke. 1997. Når de døde dreper. Håndtering av død som forutsetning for liv på Bijagós i Guinea-Bissau. Cand. Polit. avhandling. Institut og museum for antropologi, Universitetet i Oslo, Oslo.

Cissoko, Mário. 1987. Bunau: Povo e cultura. In *A realidade social e o sistema educativo em Bunau,* ed. Mário Cissoko, Ibraima Diallo, Alexandrino A Gomes, Rui Correia Landim, and Virgolino A Vaz, 11–50. Bissau: Edições DEPOL/INDE.

Clifford, James, and George E. Marcus. 1986. *Writing culture: The poetics and politics of ethnography.* Berkeley: University of California Press.

Cohen, Anthony P. 1994. *Self-consciousness: An alternative anthropology of identity.* London: Routledge.

Connell, Robert William. 1987. *Gender and power: Society, the person and sexual politics.* Cambridge: Polity Press.

Corsini, Carlo A., and Pier Paolo Viazza. 1997. *The decline of infant and child mortality: The European experience 1750–1990.* The Hague: Martinus Nijhoff.

Cosslett, Tess. 1994. *Women writing childbirth: Modern discourses of motherhood.* Manchester: Manchester University Press.

Crehan, Kate. 1997. Of chickens and Guinea fowl: Living matriliny in northwestern Zambia in the 1980s. *Critique of Anthropology* 17 (2):211–27.

Creygton, Marie-Louise. 1992. Breast-feeding and baraka in northern Tunisia. In *The anthropology of breast-feeding: Natural law or social construct,* ed. Vanessa Maher, 37–58. Oxford: Berg.

Croll, Elisabeth. 2000. *Endangered daughters: Discrimination and development in Asia.* London: Routledge.

Crouch, Mira, and Lenore Manderson. 1995. The social life of bonding theory. *Social Science and Medicine* 41 (6):837–44.

Crowley, Eve Lakshmi. 1990. Contracts with the spirits: Religion, asylum, and ethnic identity in the Cacheu region of Guinea-Bissau. Ph.D. dissertation. Yale University.

Cunningham, Hugh. 1995. *Children and childhood in Western society since 1500.* London: Longman.

Cuttini, M., M. Rebagliato, P. Bortoli, G. Hansen, R. de Leeuw, S. Lenoir, J. Persson, M. Reid, M. Schroell, U. de Vonderweid, M. Kaminski, H. Lenard, M. Orzalesi, and R. Saracci. 1999. Parental visiting, communication, and participation in ethical decisions: A comparison of neonatal practice in Europe. *Archives of Disease in Childhood Fetal & Neonatal Edition* 81 (2):84–91.

Dagg, Anne Innis. 1999. Infanticide by male lions hypothesis: A fallacy influencing research into human behavior. *American Anthropologist* 100 (4):940–50.

Dahl, Gudrun. 1990. Mats and milk pots: The domain of Borana women. In *The creative communion: African folk models of fertility and the regeneration of life,* ed. Anita Jacobson-Widding and Walter van Beek, 129–36. Uppsala/Stockholm: Uppsala University/Almqvist & Wiksell International.

Daly, Martin, and Margo Wilson. 1984. A sociobiological analysis of human infanticide. In *Infanticide: Comparative and evolutionary perspectives,* ed. Glenn Hausfater and Sarah Blaffer Hrdy, 497–502. New York: Aldine Publishing Company.

———. 1988. Evolutionary social psychology and family homicide. *Science* 242: 519–24.

Davies, Charlotte Aull. 1999. *Reflexive ethnography. A guide to researching selves and others.* London: Routledge.

Davis-Floyd, Robbie. 2000. Mutual accommodation or biomedical hegemony. Anthropological perspectives on global issues in midwifery. *Midwifery Today* 53: 12–16, 68–69.

Davis-Floyd, Robbie E., and Carolyn F. Sargent, eds. 1997a. *Childbirth and authoritative knowledge: Cross-cultural perspectives.* Berkeley: University of California Press.

———. 1997b. Introduction to *Childbirth and authoritative knowledge: Cross-cultural perspectives,* ed. Robbie E. Davis-Floyd and Carolyn F. Sargent, 1–51. Berkeley: University of California Press.

Delaney, Carol. 2000. The view from the Wuro. A guide to child rearing for Fulani parents. In *A world of babies: Imagined childcare guides for seven societies,* ed. Judy S. DeLoache, and Alma Gottlieb, 117–44. Cambridge: Cambridge University Press.

DeLoache, Judy S., and Alma Gottlieb, eds. 2000. *A world of babies: Imagined childcare guides for seven societies.* Cambridge: Cambridge University Press.

Dettwyler, Katherine A. 1994. *Dancing skeletons: Life and death in West Africa.* Waveland: Prospect Heights, Ill.

Diallo, Ibrahim. 1987. Alguns aspectos da situação linguistica e sociolinguistica da tabanca de Bunau. In *A realidade social e o sistema educativo em Bunau,* ed. Mario Cissoko, Ibraima Diallo, Alexandrino A Gomes, Rui Correia Landim, and Virgolino A Vaz, 52–66. Bissau: Edições DEPOL/INDE.

Djatá, Paulo. 1998. *Perfil Sanitário.* Quinhamel/Bissau: Ministério da Saúde Pública, Guinea-Bissau.

dos Santos, N. Valdez. 1971. As fortalezas de Bissau. *Boletim Cultural da Guiné Portuguesa* 26 (103):481–519.

Douglas, Mary. 1966. *Purity and danger: An analysis of concepts of pollution and taboo.* London: Routledge and Kegan Paul.

———. 1969. *Is matriliny doomed in Africa?* In *Man in Africa,* ed. Mary Douglas and Phyllis M. Kaberry, 121–35. London: Tavistock Publications.

Dover, Paul. 2001. A man of power: Gender and HIV/AIDS in Zambia. Ph.D.

dissertation. Department of Cultural Anthropology and Ethnology, Uppsala University, Uppsala.

Earle, Sarah. 2002. Factors affecting the initiation of breastfeeding: Implications for breastfeeding promotion. *Health Promotion International* 17 (3):205–10

Einarsdóttir, Jónína. 1988. Breastfeeding in cross-cultural perspective. Guinea-Bissau: A case study. B.A. thesis, Department of Social Anthropology, Stockholm University, Stockholm.

————. 1999. Delayed naming, derogatory names, and maternal indifference. *Antropologiska Studier* 64–65, 56–63.

————. 2001. *In times of AIDS: Sexuality and death in Africa*. Paper presented at the Africa Days of the Africa Institute, Uppsala, February 21–24.

————. 2002. Fieldwork on child death: Mingling under a mango tree and in between incubators. Paper presented at *the American Anthropological Association Annual Meeting November 20–24, New Orleans*.

Einarsdóttir, Jónína, Alberto Passa, and Geir Gunnlaugsson. 2001. Health education and cholera in rural Guinea-Bissau. *International Journal of Infectious Diseases* 5:133–38.

Evans-Pritchard, Edward Evan. 1956. *Nuer religion*. Oxford: Oxford University Press.

————. 1969 [1949]. *The Nuer: A description of the modes of livelihood and political institutions of a Nilotic people*. New York: Oxford University Press.

Eyer, Diane E. 1992. *Mother infant bonding: A scientific fiction*. New Haven: Yale University Press.

Farmer, Paul. 1996. On suffering and structural violence: A view from below. *Dædalus* 125 (1):261–83.

————. 1999. *Infections and inequalities: The modern plagues*. Berkeley: University of California Press.

Field, Tiffany. 1996. Attachment and separation in young children. *Annual Review of Psychology* 47:541–61.

Finkler, Kaja. 2000. *Experiencing the new genetics: Family and kinship on the medical frontier*. Philadelphia: University of Pennsylvania Press.

Finnboga saga ramma. 1987. In *Íslendingasögur: Fyrra bindi,* ed. Bragi Halldórsson, Jón Torfason, Sverrir Tómasson, and Örnólfur Thorsson, 625–73. Reykjavík: Svart á hvítu.

Fisk, Karen. 1997. The transcendent quality of pain in childbirth. *Mothering: The Magazine of Natural Family Living* 82:57–60.

Flinn, Juliana, Leslie Marshall, and Jocelyn Armstrong, eds. 1998. *Fieldwork and families: constructing new models for ethnographic research*. Honolulu: University of Hawaii Press.

Flóamannasaga. Íslendingasögur, tólfta bindi: Árnesinga sögur og Kjalnesinga. 1947. Reykjavík: Íslendingasagnaútgáfan.

Fortes, Meyer. 1950. Kinship and marriage among the Ashanti. In *African systems of kinship and marriage,* ed. A. R. Radcliffe-Brown and Daryll Forde, 252–84. Oxford: Oxford University Press.

————. 1987. *Religion, morality and the person*. Cambridge: Cambridge University Press.

Foster, George M. 1965. Peasant society and the image of the limited good. *American Anthropologist* 67 (2):293 –66.

Franklin, Sarah. 1997. *Embodied Progress. A cultural account of assisted conception.* London: Routledge.

Franklin, Sarah, and Susan McKinnon, eds. 2001. *Relative values: Reconfiguring kinship studies.* Durham: Duke University Press.

Freedman, Lawrence Z., and Vera Masius Ferguson. 1950. The question of pain in primitive cultures. *American Journal of Anthropology* 20 (2):363 –72.

Furnes, Sylvi T. 1998. Funksjonshemmede og normale barns dagligliv i en landsby i Guinea-Bissau. Hovedfagsoppgave, Institut for Specialpedagogikk, Univeristet i Oslo, Oslo.

Gable, Edward Eric. 1992. *Modern Manjaco:* The ethos of power in a West African society. Ph.D. dissertation. University of Virginia.

————. 1995. The decolonization of consciousness: local skeptics and the "will to be modern" in a West African village. *American Ethnologist* 22 (2):242–57.

————. 1997. A secret shared: Fieldwork and the sinister in a West African village. *Cultural Anthropology* 12 (2):213 –33.

Galli, Rosemary E. 1990. *Guinea-Bissau.* World Bibliographic Series. Volume 121. Oxford: Clio Press.

Galli, Rosemary E., and Jocelyn Jones. 1987. *Guinea-Bissau: Politics, economics and society.* London: Frances Pinter and Lynne Rienner Publishers.

Garðarsdóttir, Ólöf. 1999. Naming practices and the importance of kinship networks in early nineteenth-century Iceland. *The History of the Family* 4 (3): 297 –314.

————. 2000. The implications of illegitimacy in late-nineteenth-century Iceland: The relationship between infant mortality and the household position of mothers giving birth to illegitimate children. *Continuity and Change* 15 (3):435 –61.

————. 2002. Saving the child: Regional, cultural and social aspects of the infant mortality decline in Iceland, 1770–1920. Ph.D. dissertation. The Demographic Data Base, 19, Umeå University, Umeå.

Gausset, Quentin. 1999. Islam or Christianity? The choices of the Wawa and the Kwanja of Cameroon. *Africa* 69 (2):257–78.

Geber, Marcelle. 1958. The psycho-motor development of African children in the first year, and the influence of maternal behavior. *The Journal of Social Psychology* 47:185 –95.

Getz, Linn. 2001. General practitioners and prenatal testing—follow the experts or scrutinise the issue? *Scandinavian Journal of Primary Health Care* 19:45 –47.

Glauser, Benno. 1990. Street children: Deconstructing a construct. In *Constructing and reconstructing childhood: Contemporary Issues in the sociological study of childhood,* ed. Allen Prout and Allison James, 138 –56. London: Falmer Press.

Goody, Esther. 1984. Parental strategies: Calculation or sentiment? Fostering practices among West Africans. In *Interest and emotion. Essays on the study of family and kinship,* ed. Hans Medick and David Warren Sabean, 266 –78. Cambridge: Cambridge University Press.

Goody, Jack. 1977. *Production and reproduction: A comparative study of the domestic domain.* Cambridge: Cambridge University Press.

References

Gottlieb, Alma. 1992. *Under the kapok tree: Identity and difference in Beng thought.* Bloomington: Indiana University Press.

―――. 1995. American premenstrual syndrome: A mute voice. *Anthropology Today* 4 (6):10–13.

―――. 1998. Do infants have religion? The spiritual lives of Beng babies (Côte d'Ivoire). *American Anthropologist* 100 (1):122–35.

―――. 2000a. Luring your child into this life: A Beng path for infant care. In *A World of babies: Imagined childcare guides for seven societies,* ed. Judy S. DeLoache and Alma Gottlieb, 55–89. Cambridge: Cambridge University Press.

―――. 2000b. Where have all the babies gone? Toward an anthropology of infants (and their caretakers). *Anthropological Quarterly* 73 (3):121–32.

―――. 2004. *The afterlife is where we come from: The culture of infancy in West Africa.* Chicago: University of Chicago Press

Gottlieb, Alma, and Philip Graham. 1993. *Parallel worlds: An anthropologist and a writer encounter Africa.* New York: Crown/Random House.

Gottlieb, Alma, Philip Graham, and Nathaniel Gottlieb-Graham. 1998. Infants, ancestors, and the afterlife: Fieldwork's family values in rural West Africa. *Anthropology and Humanism* 23 (2):121–26.

Gove, S. 1997. Integrated management of childhood illness by outpatient health care workers: Technical basis and overview. *Bulletin of the World Health Organization* 75 (Supplement 1):7–24.

Greenhalgh, Susan. 1995. Anthropology theorizes reproduction: Integrating practice, political economy, and feminist perspectives. In *Situating fertility: Anthropology and demographic inquiry,* ed. Susan Greenhalgh, 3–28. Cambridge: Cambridge University Press.

Gudmundsdottir, Maria. 2000. When the world of the family is shattered: Narratives of loss and healing after the sudden death of a child. Ph.D. dissertation. University of California San Francisco.

Gunnlaugsson, Geir. 1993. Age at breastfeeding start and postneonatal growth and survival. *Archives of Disease in Childhood* 69:134–37.

―――. 1997a. *Biombo: Annual Report 1996.* Regional Health Board of Biombo, Ministério da Saúde Pública, Bissau and DanChurchAid, Copenhagen.

―――. 1997b. Regional health services and the 1994 epidemic cholera in rural Guinea-Bissau, West Africa. M.P.H thesis. Karolinska Institute, Stockholm.

Gunnlaugsson, Geir, and Jónína Einarsdóttir. 1993. Colostrum and ideas about bad milk: A case study from Guinea–Bissau. *Social Science and Medicine* 36:283–88.

―――. 1999. Corpses and the spread of cholera. *Lancet* 353:671.

Gunnlaugsson, Geir, Jónína Einarsdóttir, Frederick J. Angulo, Alberto Passa, and Robert V. Tauxe. 1998. Funerals as a risk factor for cholera transmission in Guinea-Bissau, West Africa. *Epidemiology and Infection* 120:7–15.

―――. 2000. Epidemic cholera in Guinea-Bissau: The challenge of preventing deaths in rural West Africa. *International Journal of Infectious Diseases* 4 (1):8–15.

Gunnlaugsson, Geir, Maria C. Silva, and Lars Smedman. 1992. Determinants of delayed initiation of breast-feeding: A community and hospital study from Guinea-Bissau. *International Journal of Epidemiology* 21:935–40.

Gupta, Akhil. 2002. Reliving childhood? The temporality of childhood and narratives of reincarnation. *Ethnos* 67 (1):33–57.

Håkansson, N. Thomas. 1998. Pagan practices and the death of children: German colonial missionaries and child health care in South Pare, Tanzania. *World Development* 26 (9):1763–72.

Handwerker, W. Penn. 1986. *Culture and reproduction: An anthropological critique of demographic transition*. Boulder, Colo.: Westview Press.

Hanson, Lars Åke, Marina Korotkova, Liljana Håversen, Mattsby-Inger Baltazar, Mirjana Hahn-Zoric, Sven-Arne Silverdal, Birgitta Strandvik, and Esbjörn Telemo. 2002. Breastfeeding, a complex support system for the offspring. *Pediatrics International* 44 (4):347–52.

Harkness, Sara, and Charles M. Super. 2002. The ties that bind: Social networks of men and women in a Kipsigis community of Kenya. *Ethos* 29 (3):357–70.

Harris, Marvin. 1977. *Cannibals and kings: The origins of cultures*. New York: Random House.

Hausfater, Glenn, and Sarah Blaffer Hrdy, eds. 1984. *Infanticide: Comparative and evolutionary perspectives*. New York: Aldine Publishing Company.

Havik, Philip. 1995. Relação de género e comércio: estratégias inovadoras de mulheres na Guiné-Bissau. *SORONDA* 19:25–36.

Heald, Suzette. 1995. The power of sex: Some reflections on the Caldwells' "African sexuality" thesis. *Africa* 65 (4):489–505.

Hecht, Tobias. 1998. *At home in the street: Street children of northeast Brazil*. Cambridge: Cambridge University Press.

Helsing, Elisabeth, and F. Savage King. 1982. *Breast-feeding in practice: A manual for health workers*. Oxford Medical Publications. Oxford: Oxford University Press.

Hewlett, Barry S. 1991. *Intimate fathers: The nature and context of Aka Pygmy paternal infant care*. Ann Arbor: University of Michigan Press.

Hobbs, Chris J., and Jane M. Wynne. 1996. Child abuse and sudden infant death. *Child Abuse Review* 5:155–69.

Hoffer, Peter C., and N. E. H. Hull. 1981. *Murdering mothers: Infanticide in England and New England 1558–1803*. New York: New York University Press.

Høgsborg, Marianne, and Peter Aaby. 1990. Sexual relations, use of condoms and perceptions of AIDS in an urban area of Guinea-Bissau with a high prevalence of HIV-2. In *Sexual behaviour and networking: Anthropological and socio-cultural studies on the transmission of HIV*, ed. Tim Dyson, 203–31. Liège: Derouaux-Ordina.

Høj, Lars. 2002. Mødredødeligheden i Guinea-Bissau. Størrelse, årsager og risikofaktorer. Ph.D. dissertation. Det Sundhedsvidenskabelige Fakultet, Aarhus universitet, Aarhus.

Holmgren, Birgitta Gabrielle. 2002. Age and gender patterns of HIV-1, HIV-2, and HTLV-I in Guinea-Bissau: Epidemiological and behavioural aspects. Ph.D. dissertation, Danish Epidemiology Science Centre, University of Copenhagen, Copenhagen.

Holmqvist, Tove. 2000. "The Hospital is a Uterus:" Western discourses of childbirth in late modernity—a case study from Northern Italy. Ph.D. dissertation. Stockholm Studies in Social Anthropology 45, Stockholm University, Stockholm.

Holy, Ladislav. 1996. *Anthropological perspectives on kinship*. London: Pluto Press.

Horton, Robert. 1993. *Patterns of thought in Africa and the West: Essays on magic, religion and science*. Cambridge: Cambridge University Press.

Howell, Nancy. 1979. *Demography of the Dobe !Kung*. New York: Academic Press.

Howell, Signe. 1989. From child to human: Chewong concepts of self. In *Acquiring culture: Cross-cultural studies in child development*, eds. Gustav Jahoda and I. M. Lewis, 147–68. London: Routledge.

Hrdy, Sarah Blaffer. 1994. Fitness tradeoffs in the history and evolution of delegated mothering with special reference to wet-nursing, abandonment, and infanticide. In *Infanticide and parental care*, ed. Stefano Parmigiani and Frederick S. vom Saal, 3–41. Chur, Switzerland: Harwood Academic Publishers.

———. 1999. *Mother nature: A history of mothers, infants, and natural selection*. New York: Pantheon Books.

Hunt, David. 1972. *Parents and children in history*. New York: Harper & Row.

INEP (National Institute of Studies and Research). 1991. *Sobre a integração da mulher no processo de desenvolvimento da Guiné-Bissau*. Bissau: Ministério de promoção feminina/PNUD.

IRDC. 1987. The Guinea-Bissau: A Study of the food and agricultural sector. Rural Development Studies, 23. Uppsala: Swedish University of Agricultural Sciences.

Jackson, Michael, and Ivan Karp. 1990. Introduction. In *Personhood and agency: The experience of self and other in African cultures*, ed. Michael Jackson and Ivan Karp, 15–30 Uppsala/Stockholm: Uppsala University/Almqvist & Wiksell International.

Jacobson-Widding, Anita. 2000. *Chapungu: The bird that never drops a feather: Male and female identities in an African society*. Uppsala: Acta Universitatis Upsaliensis.

Jahoda, Gustav, and I. M. Lewis, eds. 1989. *Acquiring culture: Cross cultural studies in child development*. London: Routledge.

James, Allison, Chris Jenks, and Alan Prout. 1998. *Theorizing childhood*. Cambridge: Polity Press.

James, Wendy. 1993. Matrifocus on African women. In *Defining females: The nature of women in society*, ed. Shirley Ardener, 123–45. Oxford/Providence: Berg.

Jao, Mamadú. 1995a. A questão da etnicidade e a origem étnica dos Mancanhas. *SORONDA* 20: 19–31.

———. 1995b. *Estudo sobre o infanticídio nas etnias mancanha, manjaco e pepel*. INEP, Bissau. Bissau: INEP.

Jeffery, Roger, and Patricia M. Jeffery. 1993. Traditional birth attendants in rural North India: The social organization of childbearing. In *Knowledge, power, and practice: The anthropology of medicine and everyday life*, ed. Shirley Lindenbaum and Margaret Lock, 7–31. Berkeley: University of California Press.

Jelliffe, D. B., and E. F. P. Jelliffe. 1978. *Human milk in the modern world: Psychosocial, nutritional, and economic significance*. 2d ed. Oxford: Oxford University Press.

Johannisson, Karin. 1996. *Kroppens tunna skal: Sex essäer om kropp, historia och kultur*. Stockholm: Bokförlaget Pan Nordstedts.

Johnson, Michelle C. 1998. *Fighting disease and fooling the spirits: Naming strategies and the crisis of infant death among the Mandinga of Guinea-Bissau.* Paper presented at the Annual Meeting of the African Studies Association, Chicago, October 29 –November 1.

_____. 2000. The view from the Wuro: A guide to child rearing for Fulani parents. In *A World of babies: Imagined childcare guides for seven societies,* eds. Judy S. DeLoache and Alma Gottlieb, 171–98. Cambridge: Cambridge University Press.

_____. 2001. Being Mandinga, being Muslim: Transnational debates on personhood and religious identity in Guinea-Bissau and Portugal. Ph.D. dissertation. Department of Anthropology, University of Illinois at Urbana-Champaign.

de Jong, Joop T. V. M. 1987. *A descent into African psychiatry.* Amsterdam: Royal Tropical Institute.

Jónsson, Már. 2000. *Dulsmál 1600–1900. Fjórtán dómar og skrá. Heimildasafn sagnfræðistofnunar.* Reyjavík: Háskólaútgáfan.

Jordan, Birgitte. 1983. *Birth in four cultures.* Montreal: Eden Press.

Khatib-Chahidi, Jane. 1992. Milk kinship in Shi'ite Islamic Iran. In *The anthropology of breast-feeding: Natural law or social construct,* ed. Vanessa Maher, 109 –32. Oxford: Berg.

King, Maurice. 1990. Health is a sustainable state. *Lancet* 336:664 –67.

Kitzinger, Jenny. 1990. Who are you kidding? Children, power and the struggle against sexual abuse. In *Constructing and reconstructing childhood: Contemporary issues in the sociological study of childhood,* ed. Allen Prout and Allison James, 157 –83. London: Falmer Press.

Klaus, M. H., P. Jerauld, N. Kreger, W. McAlpine, M. Steffa, and J. Kennell. 1972. Maternal attachment: Importance of the first postpartum days. *New England Journal of Medicine* 286:460 –63.

Klaus, Marshall H., and John H. Kennell. 1976. *Maternal-Infant bonding.* St. Louis: C.V. Mosby Co.

Klaus, Marshall H., John H. Kennell, and Phyllis H. Klaus. 1995. *Bonding: Building the foundations of secure attachment and independence.* New York: Merloyd Lawrence Book/Addison-Wesley Publishing Company.

Kleinman, Arthur, Paul E. Brodwin, Bryon J. Good, and Mary-Jo DelVecchio Good. 1992. Pain as human experience: An introduction. In *Pain as human experience: An anthropological perspective,* ed. Mary-Jo DelVecchio Good, Paul E. Brodwin, Bryon J. Good, and Arthur Kleinman, 1–28. Berkeley: University of California Press.

Kleinman, Arthur, Veena Das, and Margaret Lock, eds. 1997. *Social suffering.* Berkeley: University of California Press.

Knight, Chris. 1991. *Blood relations: Menstruation and the origins of culture.* New Haven: Yale University Press.

Koivula, Tuija. 1998. Mycobacterial sputum isolates from patients in Guinea-Bissau. Med. lic. thesis. Karolinska Institute, Stockholm.

Kramer, Michael S., and Ritsuko Kakuma. 2002. *The optimal duration of exclusive breastfeeding: A systematic review.* WHO/NHD/01.08. Geneva: World Health Organization.

Kristeva, Julia. 1980. Motherhood according to Giovanni Bellini. In *Desire in language: A semiotic approach to literature and art,* ed. Leon S. Roudiez, 237 –70. New York: Columbia University Press.

Kulick, Don. 1992. *Language shift and cultural reproduction: Socialization, self, and syncretism in a Papua New Guinean village.* New York: Cambridge University Press.

Labbok, M., and K. Krasovec. 1990. Towards consistency in breastfeeding definitions. *Studies in Family Planning* 21 (4):226–30.

Lamb, M. E., and C.- P. Hwang. 1982. Maternal attachment and mother-neonate bonding: A critical review. In *Advances in Developmental Psychology,* eds. M. E. Lamb and A. C. Brown, 1–39. Hillsdale, N.J.: Erlbaum.

Landim, Rui Correia. 1987. Política, ideologia, realidades e relações de poder en Bunau. In *A realidade social e o sistema educativo em Bunau,* ed. Mario Cissoko, Ibraima Diallo, Alexandrino A Gomes, Rui Correia Landim, and Virgolino A Vaz, 85–96. Bissau: Edições DEPOL/INDE.

Layne, Linda L., ed. 1999. Transformative motherhood: On giving and getting in a consumer culture. New York: New York University Press

———. 2003. *Motherhood lost: A feminist account of pregnancy loss in America.* New York: Routledge.

Leacock, Elinor. 1981. *Myths of dale dominance.* New York: Monthly Review Press.

Legesse, Asmaron. 1973. *Gada: Three approaches to the study of African society.* New York: Free Press.

Leiderman, P. Herbert, Steven R. Tulkin, and Anne Rosenfel, eds. 1977. *Culture and infancy: Variations in the human experience.* New York, San Francisco, London: Academic Press.

Leis, Nancy B. 1982. The not-so-supernatural power of Ijaw children. In *African religious groups and beliefs: Papers in honor of William R. Bascom,* ed. Simon Ottenberg, 151–69. Berekeley/Meerut, India: Folklore Institute/Archana Publications.

Leonard, Lori. 2002. "Looking for children:" The search for fertility among the Sara of Southern Chad. *Medical Anthropology* 21:79–112.

Lepowsky, Maria. 1993. *Fruit of the motherland: Gender in an egalitarian society.* New York: Columbia University Press.

Lesthaeghe, Ron J., ed. 1989. *Reproduction and social organization in sub-Saharan Africa.* Berkeley: University of California Press.

Levin, Elise. 2001. The meaning of menstrual management in a high-fertility society: Guinea, West Africa. In *Regulating menstruation: Beliefs, practices, interpretations,* ed. Etienne van de Walle and Elisha P. Renne, 157–71. Chicago: University of Chicago Press.

LeVine, Robert A., and Sarah E LeVine. 2002. The schooling of women: Maternal behavior and child environments. *Ethos* 29 (3):259–70.

LeVine, Robert A., Suzanne Dixon, Sarah LeVine, Amy Richman, P. Herbert Leiderman, Constance H. Keefer, and T. Berry Brazelton. 1994. *Child care and culture: Lessons from Africa.* Cambridge: Cambridge University Press.

Lewis, Oscar. 1966. The culture of poverty. *Scientific American* 215 (4):3–10.

Lifton, Carey. 1991. *Social soundness and WID analysis for USAID legal reform project paper.* USAID, Bissau. Bissau: USAID.

Lithell, Ulla-Britt. 1999. *Små barn under knappa villkår. En studie av bakgrunden till minskningen av dödligheten bland spädbarn under förra hälften av 1800-och 1900-talet i Sverige.* Torsby: Torsby Finnkulturcentrum.

Lopes, Carlos. 1987. *Guinea-Bissau: From liberation struggle to independent statehood.* Boulder: Westview Press/Zed Books.

Lourenço-Lindell, Ilda. 1993. Informal food production, distribution and consumption in a peripheral district of Bissau. M.A. thesis, Department of Human Geography, Stockholm University, Stockholm.

————. 2002. Walking the tight rope: Informal livelihoods and social networks in a West African city. Ph.D. dissertation. Stockholm Studies in Human Geography 9, Stockholm University, Stockholm.

Lovett, Margot L. 1997. From sisters to wives and "slaves": Redefining matriliny and the lives of Lakeside Tonga women 1885–1955. *Critique of Anthropology* 17(2): 171–87.

Luke, Nancy. 2002. *Widows and "professional inheritors": Understanding AIDS risk perceptions in Kenya*. Paper presented at Population Association of America Annual Meetings, Atlanta, May 8–11.

Lutz, Catherine. 1986. Emotions, thought, and estrangement: Emotions as a cultural category. *Cultural Anthropology* 1 (3):287–309.

————. 1988. *Unnatural emotions: Everyday sentiments on a Micronesian atoll & their challenge to Western theory*. Chicago: University of Chicago Press.

Lutz, Catherine, and Lila Abu-Lughod, eds. 1990. *Language and the politics of emotion*. Cambridge: Cambridge University Press.

Maas Weight, Kathleen. 1999. Structural Violence. In *Encyclopedia of violence, peace and conflict*, ed. Lester R. Kurtz, 431–40. San Diego: Academic Press.

MacCormack, Carol P, ed. 1982. *Ethnography of fertility and birth*. London: Academic Press.

MacCormack, Carol, and Marilyn Strathern, eds. 1980. *Nature, culture, and gender*. Cambridge: Cambridge University Press.

Madhavan, Sangeetha, and Aisse Diarra. 2001. Menstrual regulation among the Bamana of Mali. In *Regulating menstruation: Beliefs, practices, interpretations*, eds. Etienne van de Walle and Elisha P. Renne, 172–86. Chicago: University of Chicago Press.

Maher, Vanessa. 1992. Breast-feeding in cross-cultural perspective: paradoxes and proposals. In *The anthropology of breast-feeding: Natural law or social construct*, ed. Vanessa Maher, 1–36. Oxford: Berg.

Malinowski, Bronislaw. (1929). The sexual life of savages in north-western Melanesia: An ethnographic account of courtship, marriage and family life among the natives of the Trobriand Islands, British New Guinea. New York: Readers League of America.

Marcus, George E., and Michael M. J. Fisher. 1986. *Anthropology as a cultural critique: An experimental moment in the human science*. Chicago: University of Chicago Press.

Marwick, Max. 1982 [1970]. *Witchcraft and sorcery: Selected readings*. Middlesex: Penguin Books.

Mascia-Lees, Frances E., Patricia Sharpe, and Colleen Cohen. 1989. The postmodernist turn in anthropology: Cautions from a feminist perspective. *Sign* 15:7–33.

de Mause, Lloyd. 1974a. The evolution of childhood. In *The history of childhood*, ed. Lloyd de Mause, 1–73. New York: Harper Torchbooks.

————. 1974b. *The history of childhood*. New York: Harper Torchbooks.

Mehler, Jacques, and Dupoux Emmanuel. 1994. *What infants know: The new cognitive science of early development*. London: Basil Blackwell.

Melzack, Ronald. 1984. The myth of painless childbirth. *Pain* 19:321–37.

Mendy, Peter Karibe. 1994. *Colonialismo Português em África: A Tradição de Resistência na Guiné-Bissau (1879–1959)*. Bissau: INEP.

Merrett-Balkos, Leanne. 1998. Just add water: Remaking women through childbirth, Anganen, Southern Highlands, Papua New Guinea. In *Maternities and modernities: Colonial and postcolonial experiences in Asia and the Pacific*, ed. Kalpana Ram and Margaret Jolly, 213–38. Cambridge: Cambridge University Press.

Meyer, Cheryl L., Michelle Oberman, Kelly White, Michelle Rone, Priya Batra, and Tara C. Proano. 2001. *Mothers who kill their children: Understanding the acts of moms from Susan Smith to the "Prom Mom."* New York: New York University Press.

Mikell, Gwendolyn. 1997. Introduction to *African feminism: The politics of survival in sub-Saharan Africa*, ed. Gwendolyn Mikell, 1–50. Philadelphia: University of Pennsylvania Press.

Millard, Ann V., and Margaret A. Graham. 1985. Breastfeeding in two Mexican villages: Social and demographic perspectives. In *Breastfeeding and child spacing: Crosscultural perspectives*, ed. Valerine Hull and Mayling Simpson, 55–77. London: Croom Helm.

Miller, Barbara D. 1987. Female infanticide and child neglect in rural North India. In *Child survial: Anthropological perspectives on the treatment and maltreatment of children*, ed. Nancy Scheper-Hughes, 95–112. Dordrecht: D. Reidel Publishing Company.

———. 1997. *The endangered sex: Neglect of female children in rural North India*. 2d ed. Delhi: Oxford University Press.

Ministry for Rural Development and Agriculture. 1990. Guinea-Bissau: Agricultural census 1988/89, Vol. 2. Bissau: Ministry for Rural Development and Agriculture.

Mølsted, Helle. 1995. Contextualising vaccination: Balanta appropriation of preventive health measures in Guinea-Bissau. Speciale til Kandidateksamen, Institut for Antropologi, Institut for Antropologi, Københavns Universitet, København.

Moreira, Margarida Mira. 1993 *O casamento na etnia Papel da Guiné-Bissau*. Licenciatura, Departamento de Antropologia, Universidade Nova de Lisboa, Lisboa.

Morgan, Lynn M. 1998. Ambiguities lost: Fashioning the fetus into a child in Ecuador and the Unites States. In *Small wars: The cultural politics of childhood*, eds. Nancy Scheper-Hughes and Carolyn Sargent, 58–74. Berkeley: University of California Press.

Morris, Brian. 1987. *Anthropological studies of religion: An introductory text*. Cambridge: Cambridge University Press.

Morris, David B. 1991. *The Culture of Pain*. Berkeley: University of California Press.

Morse, J. M., C. Jehle, and D. Gamble. 1990. Initiating breastfeeding: A world survey of the timing of postpartum breastfeeding. *International Journal of Nursing Studies* 27 (3):303–13.

Morton, Helen. 1996. *Becoming Tongan. An ethnography of childhood*. Honolulu: University of Hawaii Press.

Mukhopadhyay, Carol C., and Patricia J. Higgins. 1988. Anthropological studies of women's status revisited. *Annual Review of Anthropology* 17: 461–95.

Mull, Dorothy S., and Dennis Mull. 1987. Infanticide among the Tarahumara of the

Mexican Sierra Madre. In *Child survival: Anthropological perspectives on the treatment and maltreatment of children*, ed. Nancy Scheper-Hughes, 113 –32. Dordrecht: D. Reidel Publishing Company.

Munck, S. S., L. Skov, A. Sylvest, W. Schmelling, L. Pedersen-Bjergaard, S. Jonassen, and B. Peitersen. 1997. Forældreholdninger til behandling af ekstremt tidligt fødte børn. *Ugeskrift for Læger* 159 (50):7488 –91.

Murdock, George Peter. 1959. *Africa: Its peoples and their culture history*. New York: McGraw-Hill.

Murray, Susan F. 1994. *Baby friendly, mother friendly*. London: Mosby.

Myers, P. 1984. Mother-infant bonding: The status of the critical period hypotheses. *Dev Rev.* 4:420.

Nassum, Manuel. 1994. Política linguística pós-colonial: ruptura ou continuidade? *SORONDA* 17:45 –78.

Nations, Marilyn, and Linda-Anne Rebhun. 1988. Angles with wet wings can't fly: Maternal sentiment in Brazil and the image of neglect. *Culture, Medicine and Psychiatry* 12:141–200.

Nicolaisen, Ida. 1995. Persons and nonpersons: Disability among the Punan Bah of Central Borneo. In *Disability and culture*, eds. Benedicte Ingstad and Susan. Reynolds Whyte, 38 –55. Berkeley: University of California Press.

———. 1998. Ancestral names and government names: Assessing self and social identity among the Punan Bah of Central Borneo. In *Personnamn och social identitet. Handlingar från ett Natur och Kultur-symposium i Sigtuna 19–22 september 1996*, eds. Thorsten Andersson, Eva Brylla, and Anita Jacobson-Widding, 361–82. Stockholm: Kungl. Vitterhets Historie och Antikvitets Akademien/ Almqvist & Wiksell International.

Nieuwenhuys, Olga. 1994. *Children´s lifeworlds: Gender, welfare and Labour in the developing world*. London: Routledge.

———. 1996. The paradox of child labor and anthropology. *Annual Review of Anthropology* 25:237 –51.

Njikam Savage, Olayinka M. 1996. "Children of the rope" and other aspects of pregnancy loss in Cameroon. In *The anthropology of pregnancy loss: Comparative studies in miscarriage, stillbirth and neonatal death*, Rosanne Cecil, 95 –109. Oxford: Berg.

Norrgren, Hans. 1998. HIV-2 infection in Guinea-Bissau, West Africa, with special reference to clinical, immunological and epidemiological aspects. Ph.D. dissertation. Department of Infectious Diseases and Medical Microbiology, Lund University, Lund.

Oakley, Ann. 1979. *Becoming a mother*. Oxford: Martin Robertson.

Oatley, Keith, and Jennifer M. Jenkins. 1996. *Understanding emotions*. Cambridge: Blackwell.

Obermeyer, Carla Makhlouf. 2002. Risk, uncertainty, and agency: Culture and safe motherhood in Morocco. *Medical Anthropology* 19:173 –201.

Oboler, Regina Smith. 1985. *Women, power, and economic change: The Nandi of Kenya*. Stanford: Stanford University Press.

Ochs, Elinor. 1993. Indexing gender. In *Sex and gender hierarchies*, ed. Barbara Diane Miller, 146 –69. Cambridge: Cambridge University Press.

Ochs, Elinor, and Bambi Schieffelin. 1984. Language acquisition and socialization: Three developmental stories. In *Culture theory: Essays in mind, self and emotion,* ed. Richard A. Shweder and Robert A. LeVine, 276–320. Cambridge: Cambridge University Press.

Oosterbaan, Margreet, and Maria Virginia Barreto da Costa. 1990. *A maternidade na Guiné-Bissau: "os conhecimentos das mulheres sobre os riscos." Um estudo antropologico.* Centro Materno-Infantil, Bissau. Bissau: Centro Materno-Infantil.

Ortner, Sherry B. 1974. Is female to male as nature is to culture? In *Woman, culture, and society,* ed. Michelle Zimbalist Rosaldo and Louise Lamphere, 67–87. Stanford: Stanford University Press.

———. 1996. *Making gender: The politics and erotics of culture.* Boston: Beacon Press.

Ortner, Sherry B., and Harriet Whitehead, eds. 1981. *Sexual meanings: The cultural construction of gender and sexuality.* Cambridge: Cambridge University Press.

Overgaard Mogensen, Hanne. 1998. Mothers' agency—others' responsibility: Striving for children's health in eastern Uganda. Ph.D. dissertation. Institute of Anthropology, University of Copenhagen.

Parkin, David. 1985. Entitling evil: Muslim and non-Muslim in coastal Kenya. In *The Anthropology of Evil,* ed. David Parkin, 224–43. Oxford: Basil Blackwell.

Parkin, David, and David Nyamwaya. 1987. Introduction to *Transformation of African Marriage,* ed. David Parkin and David Nyamwaya, 1–53. Manchester: Manchester University Press for the International African Institute.

Parmigiani, Stefano, and Frederick S. vom Saal. 1994. Preface. In *Infanticide and parental care,* ed. Stefano Parmigiani and Frederick S. vom Saal, xi–xvi. Chur, Switzerland: Harwood Academic Publishers.

Peacock, Nadine R. 1991. Rethinking the sexual division of labor: Reproduction and women's work among the Efe. In *Gender at the crossroads of knowledge: Feminist anthropology in the postmodern era,* ed. Micaela di Leonardo, 339–60. Berkeley: University of California Press.

Peek, Philip M. 1991a. *African divination systems: Ways of knowing.* Bloomington: Indiana University Press.

———. 1991b. Introduction: The study of divination, present and past. In *African divination systems: Ways of knowing,* ed. Philip M. Peek, 91–100. Bloomington: Indiana University Press.

Pélissier, René. 1989a. *História da Guiné: Portugueses e africanos na Senegâmbia (1841–1936).* Vol 1. Translated by Franco de Sousa. Lisboa: Editorial Estampa.

———. 1989b. *História da Guiné: Portugueses e africanos na Senegâmbia (1841–1936).* Vol 2. Translated by Franco de Sousa. Lisboa: Editorial Estampa.

Person, Ulla. 1989. Handikappade barns sociala nätverk och skolgång i Guinea-Bissau. En fallstudie av två byar. Stockholm/Bissau: Institutionen för internationell pedagogik/INDE.

Peters, Krijn, and Paul Richards. 1998. "Why we fight": Voices of youth combatants in Sierra Leone. *Africa* 68 (2):183–210.

Peters, Pauline E. 1997a. Against the odds: Matriliny, land and gender in the Shire Highlands of Malawi. *Critique of Anthropology* 17 (2):189–210.

————. 1997b. Revisiting the puzzle of matriliny in South-Central Africa: Introduction. *Critique of Anthropology* 17 (2):125 –46.

Piers, Maria. 1978. *Infanticide*. New York: W. W. Norton & Company.

Pink, Sarah. 1998. The white "helpers": Anthropologists, development workers and
local imaginations. *Anthropology Today* 14 (6):9 –14.

Pollock, Linda A. 1983. *Forgotten children: Parent-child relations from 1500 to 1900*.
Cambridge: Cambridge University Press.

Pool, Robert. 1993. *Dialogue and the interpretation of illness: Conversations in a
cameroon village*. Oxford: Berg.

————. 1994. On the creation and dissolution of ethnomedical systems in the
medical ethnography of Africa. *Africa* 64 (1):1–20.

Poovey, Mary. 1987. "Scenes of an indelicate character:" The medical "treatment" of
Victorian women. In *The meanings of the modern body: Sexuality and the society
in the nineteenth century*, ed. Cathereine Gallager and Thomas Laqueur, 137 –68.
Berkeley: University of California Press.

Potash, Betty. 1986. *Widows in Africa*. Stanford: Stanford University Press

Poulsen A. G., B. Kvinesdal, P. Aaby, K. Mølbak, K. Fredericksen, F. Dias, and E.
Lauritzen. 1989. Prevalence of and mortality from human immunodeficiency
virus type 2 in Bissau, West-Africa. *Lancet* i:827 –31.

Prout, Allen, and Allison James, eds. 1990a. *Constructing and reconstructing childhood: Contemporary issues in the sociological study of childhood*. London: Falmer
Press.

————. 1990b. A new paradigm for the sociology of childhood? Provenance,
promise and problems. In *Constructing and reconstructing childhood: Contemporary issues in the sociological study of childhood*, eds. Allen Prout and Allison
James, 7 –34. London: Falmer Press.

Quinn, Naomi. 1977. Anthropological studies on women's status. *Annual Review of
Anthropology* 6:181–225.

Rachels, James. 1993. *The elements of moral philosophy*. New York: McGraw-Hill.

Rådestad, Ingela. 1998. Att föda ett dött barn. Vården vid förlossningen och
kvinnans situation tre år efter barnets död. Ph.D. dissertation, Karolinska Institute, Stockholm.

Ram, Kalpana, and Margaret Jolly, eds. 1998. *Maternities and modernities: Colonial
and postcolonial experiences in Asia and the Pacific*. Cambridge: Cambridge University Press.

Rapp, Rayna. 2000. *Testing women, testing the fetus: The social impact of amniocen-
tesis in America*. London: Routledge.

Reddy, William M. 1997. Against constructionism: The historical ethnography of
emotions. *Current Anthropology* 38 (3):327 –40.

————. 1999. Emotional liberty: Politics and history in the anthropology of
emotions. *Cultural Anthropology* 14 (2):256 –88.

Reiter, Rayna R. 1975. *Toward an anthropology of women*. Monthly Review Press:
New York.

Rema, Henrique Pinto. 1982. *História das Missões Católicas da Guiné*. Braga: Editorial Franciscana.

Renne, Elisha P. 2001. Twinship in an Ekiti Yoruba town. *Ethnology* 40 (1):63 –78.

Reyes, Angelita. 2002. Mothering across cultures. Postcolonial representations. Minnesota: University of Minnesota Press.

Ribeiro, Rui. 1987. Barragens em bolanhas de água salgada. *SORONDA* 4:38–57.

Richards, Audry. 1950. Some types of family structure amongst the Central Bantu. In *African systems of kinship and marriage*, ed. A. R. Radcliffe-Brown and Daryll Forde, 207–51. Oxford: Oxford University Press.

Richards, Paul. 1996. *Fighting for the rain forest: War, youth & resources in Sierra Leone*. Oxford: The International African Institute in association with James Currey and Heineman.

Richardson, John T. E. 1995. The premenstrual syndrome: A brief history. *Social Science and Medicine* 41 (6):761–77.

Riesman, Paul. 1992. *First find yourself a good mother*. New Brunswick: Rutgers University Press.

Rodney, Walter. 1970. *A history of the Upper Guinea coast 1545–1800*. Oxford: Clarendon Press.

Rogado Quintino, Fernando. 1964. O totemismo na Guiné Portuguesa. *Boletim Cultural da Guiné Portuguesa* 74:115–30.

Rollet, Catherine. 1997. The fight against infant mortality in the past: An international comparison. In *Infant and child mortality in the past*, ed. Alain Bideau, Bertrand Desjardins, and Héctor Pérez Brignoli, 38–60. Oxford: Clarendon Press.

Rosaldo, Michelle Zimbalist. 1974. Woman, culture, and society: A theoretical overview. In *Woman, culture, and society*, eds. Michelle Zimbalist Rosaldo and Louise Lamphere, 17–42. Stanford: Stanford University Press.

Rosaldo, Michelle Zimbalist, and Louise Lamphere, eds. 1974. *Women, culture, and society*. Stanford: Stanford University Press.

Rosaldo, Renato. 1989. *Culture and truth: The remaking of social analysis*. Boston: Beacon Press.

Rose, Lionel. 1986. *The massacre of the innocents*. London: Routledge & Kegan Paul.

Rosenblatt, Paul C. 1993. Grief: The social context of private feelings. In *Handbook of bereavement: Theory, research, and intervention*, ed. Margaret S. Stroebe, Wolfgang Stroebe, and Robert O. Hansson, 102–11. Cambridge. Cambridge University Press.

Rosenblatt, P. C., R. P. Walsh, and D. A. Jackson. 1976. *Grief and mourning in cross-cultural perspective*. New Haven: Human Relations Area File Press.

Rougé, Jean-Louis. 1986. Uma hipótese sobre a formação do crioulo da Guiné-Bissau e da Casamansa. *SORONDA* 2:28–49.

———. 1995. A propósito da formação dos crioulos de Cabo Verde e da Guiné. *SORONDA* 20:81–97.

Ruddick, Sara. 1980. Maternal thinking. *Feminist Studies* 6 (2):342–67.

Rudebeck, Lars. 1974. *Guinea-Bissau: A study of political mobilization*. Uppsala: Scandinavian Institute of African Studies.

———. 1997. *"Buscar a Felicidade": Democratização na Guiné-Bissau*. Bissau: INEP.

———. 1998. Guinea-Bissau: Military fighting breaks out. *Review of African Political Economy* 25 (77):484–86.

————. 2000. Multiparty elections in Guinea-Bissau: viewed against late-colonial non-party and post-colonial single-party elections. In *Elections in Africa*, eds. Michael Cowen and Liisa Laakso, 104–27. London: James Currey.

————. 2001. *On democracy's sustainability: Transition in Guinea-Bissau*. Sidastudies no. 4. Stockholm: Sida.

Rutstein, Shea O. 2000. Factors associated with trends in infant and child mortality in developing countries during the 1990s. *Bulletin of the World Health Organization* 78 (10):1256–70.

Sacks, Karen. 1979. *Sisters and wives: The past and future of sexual equality*. Westport, Conn.: Greenwood.

Sætersdal, Barbro. 1998. *Tullinger, Skrullinger og Skumlinger—Fra Fattigdom til Velferdsstat*. Oslo: Universitetsforlaget.

Sanday, Peggy R. 1981. *Female power and male dominance: On the origins of sexual inequality*. Cambridge: Cambridge University Press.

Santos, Mário. 1987. Alguns considerações sobre a nossa situação sociolinguística. *SORONDA* 4:3–14.

Sargent, Carolyn F. 1982. *The cultural context of therapeutic choice: Obstetrical care decisions among the Bariba of Benin*. Dordrecht: D. Reidel Publishing Company.

————. 1988. Born to die: witchcraft and infanticide in Bariba culture. *Ethnology* 27 (1):79–95.

Savishinsky, Joel S. 1974. *The trial of the hare: Life and stress in an Arctic community*. New York: Gordon and Breach Science Publishers.

Scantamburlo, Luigi. 1981. *Grámatica e Dictionário da Língua Criol da Guiné-Bissau (GCr)*. Bolonga: Cooperativa "Servizio Missionario."

Scarpa, António. 1959. Novos conhecimentos provenientes de casos recentes de "lactatio agravidica" ou "serotina" na Guiné Portuguesa. *Boletim Cultural da Guiné Portuguesa* 14 (54):167–91.

Scheper-Hughes, Nancy. 1984. Infant mortality and infant care: Cultural and economic constraints on nurturing in Northeast Brazil. *Social Science and Medicine* 19:535–46.

————. 1985. Culture, scarcity, and maternal thinking: Mother love and child death in Northeast Brazil. *Ethos* 3 (4):291–317.

————, ed. 1987a. *Child survival: Anthropological perspectives on the treatment and maltreatment of children*. Dordrecht: D. Reidel Publishing Company.

————. 1987b. Introduction: The cultural politics of child survival. In *Child Survival: Anthropological Perspectives on the Treatment and Maltreatment of Children*, ed. Nancy Scheper-Hughes, 1–29. Dordrecht: D. Reidel Publishing Company.

————. 1987c. Culture, scarcity, and maternal thinking: Mother love and child death in Northeast Brazil. In *Child survial: Anthropological perspectives on the treatment and maltreatment of children*, ed. Nancy Scheper-Hughes, 187–208. Dordrecht: D. Reidel Publishing Company.

————. 1992. *Death without weeping: The violence of everyday life in Brazil*. Berkeley: University of California Press.

————. 1993. Lifeboat ethics: Mother love and child death in Northeast Brazil. In *Gender in cross-cultural perspective*, ed. Caroline B. Brettell and Carolyn F. Sargent, 31–37. New Jersey: Prentice Hall.

Scheper-Hughes, Nancy, and Carolyn Sargent, eds. 1998. *Small wars: The cultural politics of childhood*. Berkeley: University of California Press.

Schieffelin, Bambi. 1990. *The give and take of everyday life: Language socialization of Kaluli children*. Cambridge: Cambridge University Press.

Schlegel, Alice. 1972. *Male dominance and female autonomy: Domestic authority in matrilineal societies*. New Haven: HRAF Press.

Schneider, David Murray. 1984. *A critique of the study of kinship*. Ann Arbor: University of Michigan Press.

Schoepf, Brooke G., Claude Schoepf, and Joyce Millen. 2000. Theoretical therapies, remote remedies: SAPs and the political ecology of poverty and health in Africa. In *Dying for growth: Global inequality and the health of the poor*, eds. Jim Young Kim, Joyce V. Millen, Alec Irwin, and John Gershman, 91–125. Monroe, Maine: Common Courage Press.

Schulte, Regina. 1984. Infanticide in rural Bavaria in the nineteenth century. In *Interest and emotion: Essays on the study of family and kinship*, ed. Hans Medick and David Warren Sabean, 77–102. Cambridge: Cambridge University Press.

Scrimshaw, Susan C. M. 1978. Infant mortality and behavior in the regulation of family size. *Population and Development Review* 4:383–403.

———. 1984. Infanticide in human populations: Societal and individual concerns. In *Infanticide: Comparative and evolutionary perspective*, eds. Glenn Hausfater and Sara Blaffer Hrdy, 439–62. New York: Aldine Publishing Company.

Sered, Susan Starr. 1994. *Priestess mother sacred sister: Religions dominated by woman*. Oxford: Oxford University Press.

Setel, Philip W. 1999. *A plague of paradoxes: AIDS, culture, and demography in Northern Tansania*. Chicago: University of Chicago Press.

Shaw, Rosalind. 1991. Splitting truths from darkness: Epistemological aspects of Temne divination. In *African divination systems: Ways of knowing*, ed. Philip M. Peek, 91–100. Bloomington: Indiana University Press.

———. 2002. Memories from the slave trade. Ritual and the historical imagination in Sierra Leone. Chicago: University of Chicago Press.

Shorter, Edward. 1975. *The making of the modern family*. New York: Basic Books.

Shostak, Marjorie. 1981. *Nisa: The life and words of a !Kung woman*. Middlesex: Penguin Books

SIDA (Swedish International Development Agency). 1989. *Guinea-Bissau: Economic difficulties and prospects for structural adjustment*. Stockholm: Studies in Macroeconomic Management, SIDA.

———. 1994. *Landöversikt: Guinea-Bissau*. Sveriges Ambassad, Bissau. Bissau: Sveriges Ambassad.

Silberschmidt, Margrethe. 1999. *"Women forget that men are the masters": Gender antagonism and socio-economic change in Kisii District, Kenya*. Uppsala: Nordiska Afrikainstitutet.

Simpson, Mayling. 1985. Breast-feeding, infant growth, and return to fertility in an Iranian city. In *Breast-feeding, child health, and child spacing: Cross-cultural perspectives*, ed. Valerine Hull and Mayling Simpson, 109–38. London: Croom Helm.

Singer, Peter. 1993. *Practical ethics*. 2d ed. Cambridge: Cambridge University Press.

Smedman, Lars. 1999. Pediatrik i u-länder. In *Barnmedicin,* ed. Tor Lindberg and Hugo Lagerkrantz, 359 –80. Lund: Studentlitteratur.

Smith, Daniel Jordan. 2001. Romance, parenthood, and gender in a modern African society. *Ethnology* 40 (2):129 –51.

Smith, Eric Alden, and S. Abigial Smith. 1994. Inuit sex-ratio variation: Population control, ethnographic error, or parental manipulation? *Current Anthropology* 35 (5):595 –624.

Steady, Filomina Chioma. 1987. Polygamy and the household economy in a fishing village in Sierra Leone. In *Transformation of African marriage,* ed. David Parkin and David Nyamwaya, 211–29. Manchester: Manchester University Press for the International African Institute.

Steinbock, Bonnie. 1992. *Life before birth: The moral and legal status of embryos and fetuses.* New York: Oxford University Press.

Stephens, Sharon, ed. 1995. *Children and the politics of culture.* Princeton: Princeton University Press.

Stone, Laurence. 1977. *The family, sexuality and marriage in England 1500–1800.* London: Weidenfeld & Nicolson.

Stone, Linda. 1997. *Kinship and gender: An introduction.* Boulder: Westview Press.

————. 2001. Book Review of *Cultures of relatedness: New approaches to the study of kinship. American Ethnologist* 28 (3):690–92.

Thurén, Britt–Marie. 1993. *El Poder Generizado. El Desarrollo de la Antropología Feminista.* Madrid: Instituto de Investigaciones Feministas, Universidad Complutense de Madrid.

————. 1996. Om styrka, räckvidd och hierarki, samt andra genusteoretiska begrepp. *Kvinnovetenskaplig Tidskrift* 17 (3 –4):69 –85.

Tillhagen, Carl-Herman. 1983. *Barnet i folktron. Tillblivelse, födsel och fostran.* Stockholm: LTs förlag.

Trevarrthen, Colwyn. 1989. Universal co-operative motives: How infants begin to know the language and culture of their parents. In *Acquiring culture: Cross-cultural studies in child development,* eds. Gustav Jahoda and I. M. Lewis, 37 –90. London: Routledge.

Trevathan, Wenda R. 1997. An evolutionary perspective on authoritative knowledge about birth. In *Childbirth and authoritative knowledge: Cross-cultural perspectives,* ed. Robbie E. Davis-Floyd and Carolyn F. Sargent, 80–88. Berkeley: University of California Press.

Turner, Victor. 1996 [1957]. *Schism and continuaity in an African society: A study of Ndembu village life.* Oxford: Berg.

UNDP (United Nations Development Programme). 1998. *Human development report 1998.* New York: UNDP.

————. 2003. *Human Development Report 2003 Millennium Development Goals: A compact among nations to end human poverty.* New York and Oxford: United Nations Development/Programme Oxford University Press.

UNICEF (The United Nations Children's Fund). 1999. *The State of the world's children.* New York: UNICEF.

U.S. Department of State. 1999. *U.S. Department of State annual report on international religious freedom for 1999: Guinea-Bissau*. Washington, D.C.: The Bureau for Democracy, Human Rights, and Labor.

van de Walle, Etienne, and Elisha P. Renne. 2001. *Regulating menstruation: Beliefs, practices, interpretations*. Chicago: University of Chicago Press.

van Esterik, Penny. 1985. The cultural context of breast-feeding in rural Thailand. In *Breast-feeding, child health and child spacing: Cross-cultural perspectives*, eds. Valerine Hull and Mayling Simpson, 139–61. London: Croom Helm.

Vandvik, I. H., and R. Førde. 2000. Ethical issues in parental decision-making: An interview study of mothers of children with hypoplastic left heart syndrome. *Acta Paediatrica* 89 (9):1129–33.

Vaz, Virgolino A. 1987. A influência das actividades sócio-económicas e sócio-culturais na situação escolar das crianças. In *A realidade social e o sistema educativo em Bunau*, ed. Mario Cissoko, Ibraima Diallo, Alexandrino A Gomes, Rui Correia Landim, and Virgolino A Vaz, 67–84. Bissau: Edições DEPOL/INDE.

Weston, Kath. 1991. *Families we choose. Lesbians, gays, kinship*. New York: Columbia University Press.

WHO (World Health Organization). 1998a. Relactation: Review of experience and recommendations for practice. Geneve: WHO.

———. 1998b. *Evidence for the ten steps to successful breastfeeding*. Geneva: WHO.

Whyte, Susan Reynolds. 1991. Knowledge and power in Nyole divination. In *African divination systems: Ways of knowing*, ed. Philip M. Peek, 91–100. Bloomington: Indiana University Press.

———. 1997. *Questioning misfortune: The pragmatism of uncertainty in Eastern Uganda*. Cambridge: Cambridge University Press.

Whyte, Susan Reynolds, Sjaak van der Geest, and Anita Hardon, 2003. *Social lives of medicines*. Cambridge Studies in Medical Anthropology. Cambridge: Cambridge University Press

Wolf, Margery. 1974. Chinese women: Old skills in a new context. In *Woman, culture, and society*, eds. M. Rosaldo and L. Lamphere, 155–72. Stanford: Stanford University Press.

Wulff, Helena. 1995. Introducing youth culture in its own right: The state of the art and new possibilities. In *Youth cultures: A cross-cultural perspective*, ed. Vered Amit-Talai and Helena Wulff, 1–18. London: Routledge.

Wyatt, John S. 1999. Neonatal care: Withholding or withdrawal of treatment in the newborn infant. *Baillière's Clinical Obstetrics and Gynaecology* 13 (4):503–11.

Yanagisako, Sylvia Jane, and Jane Collier. 1987. Toward a unified analysis of gender and kinship. In *Gender and kinship: Essays toward a unified analysis*, ed. Jane Collier and Sylvia Yanagisako, 14–50. Stanford: Stanford University Press.

Index

abortion, 106–7, 189n26, 198n24

abstinence, sexual, 69, 79, 84, 182n12

afterlife: beating-the-drum ceremony and, 55; care of children in, 113; Catholicism and mourning, 4; children and, 130; Islam and, 132–33; medical care and, 136; mourning and grief, 132–33, 137; Papel religion, 32, 111–13

age groups as social networks and support systems, 48–49, 58, 178n24, 179–80n38

agency: in birth, 73, 85; of children, 89; of infants, 186n12; personal agency vs. structure, 29–30; poverty and, 29–30; pragmatic agency and disease, 134; of women, 191n10

agriculture: division of labor and, 42–45, 57, 178n27; enforced cultivation under colonial rule, 15, 174n30; food production, 174n31; market crops, 43; subsistence agriculture, 10–11, 42–44

albinism, 146

alcohol: breastfeeding and, 79; neglect linked to, 128, 130; pregnancy and consumption of, 72; production and consumption of, 49–50; religious specialists use of, 49–50; violence and, 49–51

Alford, Richard D., 104–5, 190n29–30

Alto do Cruzeiro: breastfeeding in, 86, 185n46; care-seeking behaviors in, 168; on causes of child death, 110; child mortality and neglect thesis, 109–11; conceptualization of children, 4, 7, 90, 140, 168; fosterage in, 90; funeral and

burial customs, 131; last-born children among, 194n33; mourning and grief among, 110–11, 135; naming practices, 90, 187n7, 189–90n27; Papel compared with, 167–68; physical contact with infants and, 103–4; reproductive histories, 194n33; social relationships among, 187n4; values associated with reproduction and motherhood, 86–87. *See also Death without Weeping* (Scheper-Hughes); Scheper-Hughes, Nancy

"animal diseases," 21, 120–22, 127, 153, 192n17

ant-bear disease, 153

Ariès, Philippe, 6

attachment theory, 61–62

Australia, 186n7

Badinter, Elisabeth, 6–7

Baker, Hugh D. R., 142

Balanta, 8, 9, 10–11, 13, 120, 128, 179–80n38, 192n18, 197n14

Ball, Helen L., 6

baloba, 99–100, 111, 112, 119

balobeiru (religious specialists), 33–34; on afterlife, 112; divination consultations, 115; *iran* children and, 152, 156; *katandeira* fostered with, 99–100, 104, 119, 167, 189n21; role in sorcery, 117

Bariba (Benin), 144

beating-the-drum ceremony, 35, 53, 54, 55

Bemba (Central Africa), 187n9

Beng (Ivory Coast), 88–89, 145, 183n26, 187n9

Bijagos, 15

227